The Changing
U.S. Labor Market

The Eisenhower Center
for the Conservation of Human Resources
· Studies in the New Economy ·

The Changing U.S. Labor Market, edited by Eli Ginzberg

Employee Training and U.S. Competitiveness: Lessons for the 1990s, Lauren Benton, Thomas R. Bailey, Thierry Noyelle, and Thomas M. Stanback, Jr.

The New Suburbanization: Challenges to the Central City, Thomas M. Stanback, Jr.

Skills, Wages, and Productivity in the Service Sector, edited by Thierry Noyelle

Does Job Training Work? The Clients Speak Out, Eli Ginzberg, Terry Williams, and Anna Dutka

New York's Financial Markets: The Challenges of Globalization, edited by Thierry Noyelle

Immigrant and Native Workers: Contrasts and Competition, Thomas R. Bailey

Beyond Industrial Dualism: Market and Job Segmentation in the New Economy, Thierry Noyelle

Computerization and the Transformation of Employment: Government, Hospitals, and Universities, Thomas M. Stanback, Jr.

Technology and Employment: Concepts and Clarifications, Eli Ginzberg, Thierry Noyelle, and Thomas M. Stanback, Jr.

The Changing
U.S. Labor Market

EDITED BY
Eli Ginzberg

WESTVIEW PRESS
BOULDER • SAN FRANCISCO • OXFORD

The Eisenhower Center for the Conservation of Human Resources
Studies in the New Economy

Copyright © 1994 by The Eisenhower Center for the Conservation of Human Resources, Columbia University

Published in 1994 in the United States of America by Westview Press, Inc., 5500 Central Avenue, Boulder, Colorado 80301-2877, and in the United Kingdom by Westview Press, 36 Lonsdale Road, Summertown, Oxford OX2 7EW

Library of Congress Cataloging-in-Publication Data
The Changing U.S. labor market / Eli Ginzberg, editor.
     p.   cm. — (The Eisenhower Center for the Conservation of
Human Resources studies in the new economy)
   Includes bibliographical references and index.
   ISBN 0-8133-2163-8 (Cloth)
   1. Labor market—United States.   2. Human capital—United States.
I. Ginzberg, Eli, 1911–   .   II. Series.
HD5724.C485   1994 .
331.12'0973—dc20   94-3994
                                                                     CIP

Printed and bound in the United States of America

The paper used in this publication meets the requirements
of the American National Standard for Permanence of Paper
for Printed Library Materials Z39.48-1984.

10   9   8   7   6   5   4   3   2   1

Contents

Preface

The Eisenhower Center for the Conservation of Human Resources, Columbia University, has been engaged since shortly before the outbreak of World War II in the ongoing study of the nation's changing labor force and labor market.

In more recent decades it has focused much of its research efforts on changes in the nation's demography, in particular blacks, immigrants, and older workers. A second focus of the research staff has been on the transformation of the U.S. economy from manufacturing to business services, particularly within the context of parallel changes in city-suburban locational issues affecting both where people live and where they work.

A third area of concern has been in interaction between the changing urban labor market and the educational system that has the task of preparing children and young people for adulthood and work. Finally, The Eisenhower Center has devoted a great deal of its resources and efforts over the past several decades to evaluating the striking changes that have been taking place in the nation's health care system, including the explosive growth in its health care labor force.

The present volume provides the Eisenhower staff's best judgment of some of the most striking and important changes now under way in the nation's labor market. The volume does not pretend to be comprehensive but is focused on cutting-edge issues, most of which have escaped study in depth.

We are deeply appreciative of the ongoing support of the Ford Foundation, whose three-year grant made it possible for us to explore many new lines of investigation and further enabled us to prepare this volume.

Sylvia Leef and Shoshana Vasheetz oversaw the many details involved in turning authors' drafts into a publishable manuscript; we are greatly in their debt.

Eli Ginzberg, Director
The Eisenhower Center for the
Conservation of Human Resources
Columbia University

1

The Changing World of Work

Eli Ginzberg

This volume, a collaborative undertaking by the senior staff of The Eisenhower Center for the Conservation of Human Resources, Columbia University, is our most recent effort to explore new dimensions of the role of human resources in the American economy, an effort that has inspired our research program since it was first initiated in 1939. As has been true of much of our prior research, the current themes selected for study and evaluation have on the whole escaped close attention, both because the data are hard to come by and because the import of such data as do exist are difficult to assess. But we have long believed that there is more to be learned by focusing on emergent issues rather than those that have long been the center of attention.

The chapters in this volume concentrate on the following aspects of the changing U.S. labor market as the twentieth century nears its end: the implications that follow upon the continuing outmigration of people and jobs from the inner city to the near and more distant suburban locations; the role that the export of advanced business services from the United States plays in the increasing globalization of the world's economy; the demographic trends in the labor force which are transforming the structure and functioning of the U.S. labor market; an assessment of the effect of the steady and increasing flow of new immigrants into the United States on the nation's economy and well-being; the many facets of literacy; the ability of the public educational system in the nation's major cities to adjust to the changing skill requirements of their local changing economies; the labor market lessons to be drawn from the workers in the health care sector; and the reemergence of national employment policy.

Clearly, these issues reflect important new developments in the U.S. labor market about which our knowledge and understanding must be expanded. This opening chapter will provide an overview of the major transformations that have characterized the U.S. labor force and labor market over the past several decades so as to provide a framework for the chapters that follow. Since most Americans spend about two decades preparing for adulthood, followed by about forty years at work, it is essential to assess the changing U.S. labor market from a long-term perspective. Accordingly, we will seek to evaluate at least briefly these major transformations in the U.S. labor market that have occurred since the end of World War II, many of them precipitated by the war itself.

Women

It is hard for young people to appreciate that up until World War II an employed woman who was single was frequently under pressure from her employer, private or public, to stop working once she married. The only women unaffected by such strictures were those at the bottom of the occupational structure, such as black domestics, mill workers, and an occasional independent professional, most of whom were likely to marry late, if at all, after they had established themselves.

Today, women have increased their participation in the labor force to the point where they account for almost half of all employed workers. The majority of married women, including those with young children at home, are in the labor force and they are likely to be employed full time even though a significant minority, circa 12 percent, hold a less-than-full-time position, whether out of preference or necessity. This pronounced trend of women's ongoing attachment to the labor force is characteristic of all advanced nations and reflects, among other factors, the smaller number of children per family, the increase in family dissolution, the reduced importance of physically demanding work, the expanded opportunities for women to pursue careers, and the increased number and proportion of women who have earned higher degrees. On the American scene, the stagnation and in some cases the decline in real weekly earnings for most labor market participants after 1973 put pressure on many to shift to two-worker households if they wished to maintain and improve their standard of living.

With American employers for the most part reluctant to introduce flexibility into the workweek and with managers and executives working on average considerably more than forty hours weekly, many women, especially those with career objectives, put themselves under considerable pressure in seeking to balance their dual role as parent and worker. Although there is growing evidence from such sources as political activists, congressional debates, and survey reports that U.S. employers have been slow to respond to the complaints of time pressure that beset a growing number of employed women, the lack of response characteristic of the past four decades cannot long continue.

Blacks

A second lasting impact of World War II on the U.S. labor market was the substantial loosening of the bonds that had earlier held most blacks captive in the South, largely on marginal Southern farms. The strong demand for workers in the expanding wartime factories created opportunities for blacks that had previously been closed to them. The postwar growth of the economy in the North and Midwest attracted increasing numbers of blacks to urban centers where they had the opportunity to get work, join unions, and earn good wages. The civil rights movement and federal and state antidiscrimination legislation increased the momentum to lower the arbitrary bars that had earlier blocked the employment of many black applicants. In 1970, a quarter of a century after the end of World War II, the proportion of blacks living in the South and only marginally attached to the economy had declined dramatically. Although some encountered serious difficulties in gaining a foothold in the rapidly changing labor markets of the North and West, their economic situation still reflected improvement.

The post-1970 era, however, presented several new hurdles. Many of the better manufacturing jobs were transferred out of the urban areas where the blacks had relocated and the large inflow of white women into the labor market provided many employers with an alternative to hiring more blacks. The most striking increases in good jobs occurred in the service sector, but many of these jobs demanded, at a minimum, an associate college degree—preferably a college degree—and many of the young black men and black women growing up in the recently transplanted families were unable to remain on the educational track and meet these more demanding requirements. Finally, discriminatory hiring barriers, although lowered, had surely not disappeared.

Immigrants

From 1924 until 1965 the United States had both severely restricted the number of immigrants and given preference to Western and Northern Europeans. The new immigration legislation of 1965, when further amended in 1986, created an increase in the number of annual admissions to around 750,000 and simultaneously increased greatly the opportunities of persons from Latin America and Asia to enter the United States permanently. This act also made it possible for large numbers of immigrants long resident in the United States to obtain their citizenship. In addition to the sizable numbers who enter the United States legally, there is a substantial flow of undocumented aliens who cross the border from Mexico for seasonal work or, if not apprehended, remain indefinitely, joining established immigrant communities, primarily in southern California, Arizona, New Mexico, and Texas.

Immigration visas are granted to relatives, to persons possessing scarce skills, and to political refugees. Many of the Asian immigrants are well educated, having completed college or professional school at home. For the most part, these immigrants find it relatively easy to make a satisfactory adjustment once they learn English and have the benefit of the advice, and often the support, of earlier immigrants. A significant proportion of the poorly educated or uneducated immigrants from Mexico, the Caribbean, or Latin America, however, can do no better than obtain minimum-wage jobs in the service sector or in the manufacturing plants still in existence.

Considering the fact that immigrants tend to concentrate in a limited number of coastal cities that are also likely to already have sizable numbers of minorities—blacks, Hispanics, and others—many of whom are themselves still on the periphery of the labor market, the amount of economic conflict among natives, earlier immigrants, and the more recent arrivals, legal and illegal, has been less than might have been expected. The black-Korean competition in Brooklyn two years ago and the mass rioting in Los Angeles and Miami among disparate groups are more the exception than the rule. Most newcomers seek to avoid confrontation and look to their own networks for support and help in their early years in this country.

The Shift from Goods to Service Workers

In the first half of the twentieth century, the strength of the U.S. economy was rooted in the preeminence of its manufacturing companies. It was American production that overwhelmed the enemy in World War II by the output of its shipyards, defense production, munition plants, and, finally, by the successful development of the atomic bomb. But if one looks closely at the data, it is evident that the number and proportion of workers employed in goods production—agriculture, mining, manufacturing, and construction—were steadily losing ground to the sharply rising number employed in the service sector, which today accounts for about 70 percent of all jobs.

The large-scale investments that the federal government and the states made at the end of World War II to expand and improve higher education and the nation's research base was one factor that sped this shift toward services, particularly the advanced service sector, which depends on high educational levels. Another was the availability of large numbers of women workers, many well educated, who could fit readily into the service sector. Still another contributing factor was the leadership role that the United States came to play on the world scene after World War II, which enabled a number of our service industries to assume a dominant role in international banking and finance, air transportation, communications, business support services such as marketing, management consulting, accounting, advertising, and still other fields such as health care.

The dazzling performance of the American job machine between 1982 and 1989, when total U.S. jobs increased by about 20 million, obscured the fact that the number of manufacturing jobs suffered a severe decline in that same period for several reasons: the delayed adjustment of U.S. manufacturing firms from mass to small-batch quality production; the overvaluation of the U.S. dollar, the collapse of U.S. Latin American markets; and, finally, the greater success of European and Asian competitors in responding to changing markets.

In the new manufacturing environment, the modestly educated had little hope of obtaining entrance jobs that led eventually to progress up the skill and income ladder. Moreover, the pressure on manufacturing firms was translated into pressure on trade unions, many of the strongest of which were linked to goods production. As manufacturing weakened, so ...... the jobs of their members ...... nefits.

...... he federal and state ...... tional system and to ...... young people from ...... the GI Bill of 1944 ...... followed by the U.S. ...... onal Defense Educa- ...... eral grant and loan ...... ne investment strat-

...... of Harvard Univer- ...... ese investments had been unduly expanded, a ...... suggests otherwise. With the decline in manufacturing jobs, the gap in earnings has widened between high school graduates and those who obtain a college or higher degree.

In the early 1990s, states and local governments, hard pressed to increase spending on prisons, Medicaid, deteriorating infrastructure, and welfare, shifted more of the costs of a college or professional degree to the students, many of whom are hard pressed to meet these substantially enlarged tuition charges. It is not surprising that only a small number of young people from low-income families apply or are admitted to medical school, where the average graduate accumulates a debt of at least $50,000 by the end of four years. The United States differs from all advanced European nations, where the state assumes all or most of the tuition costs and living expenses of students admitted to institutions of higher learning.

Changes in the Location of Jobs

Americans have long placed a premium on owning their own homes and, once again, the post–World War II era satisfied this desire by providing low-cost mortgages for veterans as well as the right to deduct the expenses of both interest payments on the mortgage and real estate taxes from their income tax liability.

Workers who moved to the suburbs in the late 1940s, 1950s, and even the early 1960s for the most part lived there but continued to commute to their jobs in the city. Clearly, the growth of the residential population beyond the city's limit led to the creation of a large number of new service jobs, from retailing to schoolteaching and dental care. But the major job outflows from the cities came with the substantial completion of the national highway system, and improved local roads. The growing congestion of inner-city areas made them increasingly unsatisfactory as manufacturing sites, and the large inflows of minorities into previously white ethnic neighborhoods led an increasing number of whites to relocate to the suburbs for a number of reasons, including access to better schools for their children.

As the population densities in the suburbs increased substantially, the local economic base became more diversified and in time helped to attract more people and jobs from the city proper. Although many upper-income suburbanites continued to commute to the city because their company headquarters were located there, by the mid to late 1960s many corporations had decided that they could profit by relocating themselves further out. They did so to escape the increased crime and violence, deteriorating schools, and other negatives of the urban environment.

This substantial and continuing outmigration of people and jobs was particularly onerous for poorly educated inner-city youths who could not gain access to the large number of entrance jobs in the suburbs. Their problems were compounded by their lack of qualifications to fill many of the more attractive and higher-paying service jobs that continued to expand within the city. The persistence of segregation based on income and ethnic identity as well as restrictions on housing have combined to segment the metropolitan labor markets to the disadvantage of inner-city, poorly educated minority youth.

The Baby Boomers

At the outbreak of World War II many demographers anticipated that the low birth rate characteristic of the United States would continue well into the future. But starting in 1946 and continuing until 1964, the average age of marriage declined, the marriage rate increased, and the average number of children per fertile woman increased rapidly with the result that the new, very large cohort that came to be called the baby boomers shaped America's major institutions and increased dramatically the demand for housing and schools. By the mid-1960s their sheer number dominated the labor force and will continue to do so until at least the first third of the next century. The oldest of the cohort will become 55 in 2001 and will join the ranks of "older" workers.

Although the steady increase in the number and proportion of married women who became attached to the labor force provided American employers with most of the new workers that they needed to expand their plants and offices in the immediate post–World War II decades, by 1964 a second major new source of supply became available when the oldest of the baby boomers born in 1946 reached 18. Following the reform of the immigration laws in 1965, as was indicated earlier, a third new source of labor became available.

Richard Easterlin has called attention through his research and writings to the interactions that exist between the size of the stream of new workers entering the labor force and their economic prospects. In Easterlin's view, the demographic data foreshadow the economic well-being of different population cohorts, depending on the number of those of working age.[2] Although demography does not of itself determine economic destiny, it plays a significant role, particularly if there are other positive developments, as was the case with the baby boomers.

The substantial expansion of higher education made it possible for a much larger proportion of the baby boomers to complete college and go on to graduate or professional school than was true for any of the earlier generations. For the most part, they were able to obtain well-paying jobs and careers in the steadily expanding professional, technical, and business services. These were the favored members of the baby boom generation.

However, the growth of the U.S. economy began to slow. Further, manufacturing industries, many of which had slipped badly, faltered further under severe foreign competition, making high-paying manufacturing jobs as well as opportunities for promotion increasingly difficult to find. By the end of the 1980s, when most of the baby boomers were at, or close to, their peak earning years, manufacturing jobs suffered a small absolute as well as a large relative decline and were replaced by many relatively low-paying service jobs, with the exception of the better-paying service jobs available to the college educated. The generation into which one is born, as Easterlin has emphasized, significantly influences how well one is likely to do in the labor market. The data suggest that the later baby boomers were not as fortunate as the generation that preceded them.

From School to Work

There are at least three different, if interrelated, perspectives that need to be explored when considering the relation of school to work. These involve the individual young person who must make the transition, the employer who needs to hire and maintain a competent work force, and the relative strength of the general economy in an increasingly competitive world economy.

Many young people, especially those growing up in low-income households, with a parent or parents with limited schooling and exposed to unfavorable neighborhood influences, are likely to become disenchanted and hostile to the school environment relatively early, dropping out when they recognize that they are not holding their own in the classroom and seeing little linkage between school achievement and their later life.

Although some, possibly many, of these disenchanted students might respond to a different learning environment, especially one that was less book focused and that provided them opportunities to work with adults engaged in productive activities, especially if they were able to earn some money while working, such opportunities are relatively rare. The reasons are not obscure: Schools prefer to operate without becoming involved with the employer community, and since most employers are able to obtain the new workers they need from the local labor market, they have little incentive to enter into complex (and often costly) relations with the local school system.

It is true that as a consequence of the much heightened criticisms and concerns with the shortcomings of the U.S. educational system, many employers have reexamined the skills of their work force and have uncovered serious deficiencies. A substantial minority of workers are partially illiterate and larger numbers encounter difficulty in mastering new skills, especially when such skills are more than just a minor addition to what they already know.

The fact that high school dropouts, and even many high school graduates, face serious difficulties in making a successful transition from school to work is not open to question. Nor is the fact that many workers who have held long-term positions successfully face challenges in acquiring new skills if the employer makes radical changes in the ways work is performed. Most observers of the economy believe that the United States would withstand competitive challenges better if its work force had more education, training, and continuing retraining.

But the fact that these shortcomings have been both recognized and discussed and, to some degree, even addressed for more than a decade point to certain conclusions. It is exceedingly difficult to raise the productivity of the U.S. educational system, especially for that part of the population most at risk, for a number of reasons, from lack of commitment to serious shortfalls in facilities and other resources. In the absence of parental and community involvement—always difficult to obtain and maintain—even the best educational systems might not succeed in achieving significant reforms.

When employers do not encounter serious difficulties in recruiting new workers, it follows that they are unlikely to make the complex adjustments required to provide real openings for young people who could most profit from combining school and work. There is little reason to expect any early significant shift in employer behavior that would be of major assistance to high schools that need to provide more occupational activities for their non-bookish students.

But all is not bleak. Fortunately the last years have seen selected school systems, from Philadelphia to Oakland (California), put in place "academies," usually a subsection of a larger high school that has been able to establish linkages to local and regional enterprises, from health to media, and to capture the interest and enthusiasm of at-risk students. The state of California has been sufficiently impressed with the record of the academies to make special state funding available to help them expand.

Although the president and the governors of the fifty states agreed in 1991 on a set of targets for educational reform to be achieved by the year 2000,[3] there is little prospect that the goals that they set will be reached, primarily because parents, students, educators, taxpayers, and employers are not convinced that the current deficiencies are as serious as the reformers insist even if the necessary resources could be obtained, that anyone has knowledge of how to remedy them. The alternative approach would be to encourage the states and localities to make such progress as they can by engaging the parties of primary interest. In the meantime, one must recognize that many young people will not make a successful transition from school to work, at least not on their first try. That makes it all the more important to strengthen all second- and third-chance opportunities by enabling these young people to earn the general equivalency diploma (GED), by making community college careers available to them and by en-

couraging employers to offer them special educational and training opportunities.

The Off-the-Record Economy

With the gross national product (GNP) approaching the $6 trillion annual
level, it should come as no surprise that the nation has a sizable off-the-
record economy, although its scale and scope has not been studied in
depth. Much of it is linked to criminal activity, such as the trade in stolen
goods and in proscribed drugs. The fact that drug dealers have found that
young people, some as young as 12 or 13, can be usefully employed as
lookouts and sellers of drugs has served to draw marginal students out of
school. These youngsters see little point in attending school if they can
earn hundreds of dollars a week in the drug trade. Although the risks of
getting into serious trouble, even of dying, are also high, most young people are risk prone, not risk averse. Many push aside consideration of risk,
seeing in the acquisition of cash their best chance to command the attention and respect of their friends. A sizable number of people who have
been unable to establish and maintain a regular linkage to the world of
work can exist, even prosper for a time, through their engagement with
the off-the-record economy.

There is clearly a mutual relationship between the regular and the off-
the-record economy. The latter could not operate effectively without the
ability to recruit and retain a sizable work force willing to run the risks en-
tailed in this type of work, even with the prospect of going to prison. But
there are a sufficient number of individuals who are on the margins of society, as a result of their dysfunctional experiences and values, to prevent
a shortage in the numbers of persons necessary to keep the off-the-record
economy functioning. Although it is sometimes argued that if the regular
economy had more jobs at reasonable wages for more persons with modest education and skills, the off-the-record economy might find it more
difficult to attract and retain the numbers it needs, there is little evidence
to support what at first appears to be a self-evident proposition. The labor
market and criminal behavior are surely interrelated, but not along a single axis. It remains highly speculative to suppose that if the U.S. labor
market were able to operate at close to full employment that the off-the-
record economy would shrink significantly.

Work and Welfare

One of the innovations of the New Deal was to provide guaranteed payments to mothers of dependent children whose husbands had become disabled or had died. The dominant view in the 1930s and for many decades

thereafter was that keeping the family unit intact was preferred social policy, even if the taxpayer had to foot the bill. But the post–World War II decades witnessed a number of basic changes that complicated the earlier political consensus about Aid to Families with Dependent Children (AFDC). Many married women with young children at home had begun to be more or less regularly employed, many mothers with dependent children had never been married, and a disproportionately large number of all adults on AFDC were black. A disproportionate number of young black women still in high school who were pregnant decided to bear the child and rear it, recognizing that they would be able to qualify for AFDC.

By the late 1980s Congress decided, after many false starts, that it was bad public policy to permit mothers with young children at home to continue a life on welfare rather than to become self-supporting adults. Many legislators were particularly upset by the fact that some families had three successive generations on welfare with the youngest mother in her teens, her own mother in her early thirties, and the grandmother still in her forties. The fact that such intergenerational reliance on long-term welfare support was the exception, not the rule, did not erase the concern that such social pathology existed and that it was supported by public policy. The Family Support Act of 1988 authorized about $1 billion of additional federal funds annually to the states (which were required to provide matching funds) to be used to increase the employability of welfare mothers by mandating that they pursue educational and training opportunities as a condition for remaining on the AFDC rolls. The new legislation addressed two special needs: child care services and the retention of Medicaid eligibility for one year after a welfare mother secured a regular job.

The logic behind the new legislation had much to commend it, but it remains to be seen whether the states match the new federal dollars and whether the federal grant is large enough to underwrite the human capital investments required to make young mothers who are school dropouts job-ready, particularly in the face of a weak labor market.

So long as many young women, not only those in their teens but also those in their twenties, see little prospect of entering into a satisfactory marriage but become mothers, the long-term tensions between work and welfare may be moderated by the new legislative initiatives, but they are unlikely to lead to any large-scale reductions in the AFDC rolls.

Corporate Employment Policies

Acceptance of trade unions came late in the United States. Membership is heavily concentrated in manufacturing, transportation, construction, mining, and selected branches of public employment. As a consequence of the relatively tight labor market that prevailed between 1945 and 1970 and the rapid growth of the GNP, most employers at that time pursued a positive union policy as well as a human resources policy of wage increases and good benefits to encourage competent employees to plan lifetime employment with the corporation.

Since the early 1980s, however, most U.S. corporations have been under severe competitive pressures and have increasingly sought to reduce their labor costs by extracting "give-backs" of wages and benefits, streamlining and rationalizing their plants, and reducing the size of their labor force, including long-term employees and managerial personnel. The commitment to "lifetime" employment for workers who performed effectively has become a thing of the past.

As the economy shifted increasingly from goods production to the output of services, the role of trade unions was substantially undermined since the core of their strength had been in manufacturing. Organized labor lost much of its earlier political power and was weakened in negotiations with employers, many of whom returned to an earlier mode of fighting unionization aggressively and successfully.

With the passage of the Civil Rights Act of 1964 and with later efforts on the part of both the federal and state governments to broaden opportunities for blacks, minorities, and the elderly, the focus of corporate policy shifted increasingly toward issues of affirmative action and accommodation to the new laws, regulations, and public opinion.

Early Retirement

One of the major transformations of the U.S. labor market between 1950 and 1992 has been the striking decline in the number of men who remain at work (part time or full time) after age 65 from about one in two to one in six and the equally striking decline in the proportion of men who withdraw from the labor force between 55 and 64. This trend toward early retirement has occurred simultaneously with a considerable increase in life expectancy. The explanation must be sought both in public policy—the indexing of Social Security benefits in 1972 that greatly increased their real value, the high actuarial value of early retirement benefits until the Social Security amendments of 1983—as well as in private-sector developments, such as the spread of private pensions, the asset appreciation associated with increased home values, and, increasingly, the special inducements offered by many large corporations to encourage employees to accept early retirement.

One can add additional factors that operated to speed the departure of many men in their late fifties or early sixties from the labor force. Many of the early retirees failed to realize that they still had on average an additional twenty or more years of life, a period equal to half the average length of their prior work life. While some would have preferred to shift to a part-time schedule such work was usually difficult if not impossible to locate. Still others who had had physically demanding jobs as manual workers were only too pleased to leave as soon as they qualified for retirement. Waiting in the wings was the large baby boom cohort, younger, better-educated, and eager for expanded opportunities.

The Growing Diversity of the U.S. Labor Force

In the half century since World War II the composition of the U.S. labor force has been strikingly transformed. At the onset of the war white males were in a distinct majority. White women and blacks were largely relegated to peripheral roles as lower-level office staff, mill hands, tenant farmers, or domestic workers. Today, white males are a distinct minority of the labor force of over 120 million, with a corresponding vast increase in the roles of white women, blacks, Hispanics, and Asians, who together outnumber white males and by the year 2000 will have about a 6:4 numerical advantage.

Since the racial-ethnic minorities are heavily concentrated in selected states and in large metropolitan areas, their present and prospective role in these specific labor markets is much greater than the national averages suggest. In New York, Los Angeles, Chicago, Houston, Philadelphia, Dallas, and Detroit—each with over 1 million population—minorities today account for over half of the population. In Philadelphia and San Diego minorities constitute 40 to 50 percent of the population. The contours of tomorrow's largest labor markets are clearly revealed by present population distributions. Diversity is the newest and most important characteristic of the changing U.S. labor market as the United States gets ready to enter the first half of the twenty-first century.

Other factors that have also effected significant transformations in the U.S. labor force and labor market have included the strikingly large additions to the nation's scientific and engineering base, the narrowing and subsequent widening of income disparities, the differentially rapid growth of metropolitan areas along the coastal borders (Pacific, Gulf, and Atlantic), the growth in the contingent work force, and still other developments.

Each of the chapters that follows deals at some length with an important dimension of the changing U.S. labor force and labor market, but the range of each has been determined by the ongoing research program of the Eisenhower Center and the specific areas of interest and specialization of the senior researchers. These factors explain both the subjects that are included as well as those excluded.

The concluding chapter seeks to provide at least some measure of integration among these related themes by focusing on employment policy from a twofold vantage: the policies that governments at all levels have experimented with in recent decades and the directions of possible new initiatives as these have been informed by previous successes and failures.

The dominant view among most academic economists is that the labor market, if left to private-sector bargaining between employers and workers, will provide the highest level of sustainable employment. But the aim of this collaborative volume has been to call the reader's attention to the wide range of societal forces—demographic, cultural, technological, political, racial, and still others—that set the parameters within which the labor market operates and to remind the reader that as these parameters are themselves altered, so are the operations of the labor market, with important consequences for all who are working, looking for work, or preparing for a career.

Notes

1. Richard B. Freeman, *The Overeducated American*, New York: Academic Press, 1976.

2. Richard A. Easterlin, *Birth and Fortune: The Impact of Numbers on Personal Welfare*. 2d ed. Chicago: University of Chicago Press, 1987.

3. U.S. Department of Education, *America 2000: An Educational Strategy*, Washington, D.C.: U.S. Government Printing Office, 1991.

2

Demographic Trends
in the Labor Force

Anna B. Dutka

In the half century since World War II, there have been major changes in the size, age, gender, educational-occupational level, and ethnicity of the American labor force and in the occupational structure of the labor market, changes generated both by the war and by postwar developments. Although the focus of this chapter is on the older worker, the interrelationship of these factors requires attention.

The Changing Size of the Population
and of the Labor Force

The American birthrate had been in decline even before the Great Depression of the 1930s and participation in World War II led to further delays in marriages and family formation. In 1945 the population had increased by only 10 million over the 1930 figure of 133 million fifteen years earlier. In the fifteen years between 1945 and 1960, however, there was an increase of 47 million, and if the time period is extended over the entire baby boom generation born between 1946 and 1964, the increase came to 51 million, a 30 percent increase in the population within a single generation.

This trend was, however, not permanent. The birthrate of 23.7 per thousand in 1960 declined by 1975 by one-third to 14.6 and has stayed around that level to the present. The Census Bureau's middle series projections estimate that, based on current trends, by 2020 the population will increase by 44 million to a total of 294 million or by 17 percent, a much lower absolute and relative rate of increase than occurred between 1960 and 1990.

The sheer size of the baby boom generation, however, ensured that its influence would be profound at every age level. The baby boomers swamped the elementary and secondary schools and later fed the explosive growth in the number who earned higher degrees from 477,000 in 1960 to 1.66 million in 1975.

The large increase in population stimulated the rapid growth of the labor force. Between 1950 and 1960 there was a modest gain from 63 million to 71.5 million but by 1970 the increase in one decade came to over 13 million and by 1980 to over 24 million. Between 1950 and 1990 the size of the labor force had exactly doubled from 63 million to 126 million.

Although the baby boomers accounted for much of this growth, other major factors were the steady increase in the number of immigrants after the revision of the immigration laws in 1965, which fostered family reunification and shifted the locus of immigration from Europe to Latin America and Asia, as well as the very large increase in the labor force participation of women, particularly married women.

The Increase in the Number of Women Workers

There were important differences in gender roles during the period of rapid expansion of the labor force. In both the earlier (1950–1970) as well as in the latter period (1970–1990) the rate of increase in absolute numbers, and still more in relative terms, was much more rapid for women than for men. During the four decades between 1950 and 1990 the number of male workers in the labor force grew by about 50 percent, from 42 million to 64 million. During this same time period the number of female workers tripled from 17.5 million to 53.5 million. In 1950 there were only three women to every seven men in the labor force but by 1990 the ratio was forty-five women to every fifty-five men.

The rapid growth in the number of women in the labor force has been called the most important development in the American labor market that has ever taken place. In the century between 1890 and 1990 the labor force participation rate of white, married women increased from less than 5 percent to more than 60 percent with a marked increase occurring in the 1940s, especially among women in the 45 to 54 age group. (Black women historically have had higher participation rates than white women.)

World War II is usually credited with the dramatic change in the participation rate of married women. In their wartime employment women had frequently exceeded male production norms and this fact, combined with postwar prosperity, led to the complete dismantling of the numerous "marriage bars" to employment that had flourished prior to and during the depression.

After the war there was a relative decrease in the labor force participation of married women in the 25 to 34 year old age group as they began to have families. In 1950, 70 percent of all households were headed by males whose income was the sole support of their families. With the steady increase in female labor force participation in the 1960s and 1970s, however, both the size of the average family and the proportion of male-only supported families decreased dramatically.

The *long-term* effect of wartime female employment on subsequent postwar employment has recently been questioned, with a larger role suggested for the rise in the level of female educational attainment and changes in the general occupational structure that favored women.[1]

Increased Education and Changes in the Occupational Structure

The increase in educational levels and changes in the occupational structure have not only been mutually reinforcing but have had profound effects on the labor force participation of men as well as women. In 1950 blue-collar workers accounted for almost two-thirds of all persons in the labor force, and, as might be expected, the concentration among males (68 percent) was substantially greater than among females (50 percent).

Over the succeeding four decades a major shift occurred. By 1990 three out of four jobs were in the service sector and the white-collar segment of the U.S. labor force had increased by more than half from 37.5 percent to 57.1 percent. In sharp contrast, blue-collar workers as a proportion of all workers declined from 62.5 to 43 percent, or by close to one-third.

During these four decades the number of male white-collar workers increased from 13.6 million to 29.5 million, or by 117 percent. Although these are impressive absolute and relative rates of increase, they were far surpassed by the growth of female white-collar workers whose numbers increased more than fourfold from 8.8 million to 37.8 million. Clearly, the driving force in the shift of the occupational profile of the U.S. labor force to a predominately white-collar pattern was made possible only because of the availability of large numbers of educationally qualified women able and willing to join the labor force when the opportunity offered, as it did in the post–World War II decades.

Surprisingly, the male occupational data reveal that the broadly held belief that male blue-collar jobs have disappeared in recent decades as a result of the stagnation of manufacturing employment since 1970 is unwarranted. After remaining more or less stable for the first two decades (1950–1970) at around 28 to 29 million, the number of blue-collar male workers increased to 35 million by 1990, a respectable gain though considerably lower than the growth in white-collar employment.

Although the absolute number of female blue-collar workers also registered gains in each of the four decades, increasing from 8.7 million in 1950 to 15.7 million in 1990, the far larger increase in the number of female white-collar jobs made for a decline in the relative proportion of females in blue-collar occupations.

Among precision production workers, men outnumber women by a ratio of about 11:1, and in the case of operators and production workers the disparity remains substantial, with 2.5 men for every woman. If these two dominant blue-collar categories are added together, the gender disparity becomes truly striking, with males holding over 21 million jobs and women just over 5 million.

Female employment is concentrated in the top two occupational categories, professionals and managers and technical, sales, and clerical. In the case of men, among all workers 25 years and older in 1990, 46 percent were concentrated in those two top categories but for women this proportion was very much higher, accounting for over 70 percent of all female workers.

Although men outnumber women by about 25 percent in the combined managerial and professional group (15.8 million males and 12.6 million females), in March 1986 the U.S. Department of Labor announced that for the first time in American history women held half of the 14 million jobs in the fifty occupations classified as professional because they are "knowledge based." The survey conducted by the Bureau of Labor Statistics revealed that although women still dominated such traditionally female professions as social work, nursing, and teaching, they also constituted one-third of the lawyers and doctors and their numbers exceeded those of males in such once–male-dominated fields as psychology, statistics, and journalism. Although this dominance does not extend to the top managerial or executive posts, here too women held two of five of such jobs. In the technical, sales, and administration and clerical categories there were 18.4 million women but only 10.5 million men.

The occupational shift of the U.S. economy in the direction of white-collar jobs has been clearly favorable to women, who have provided most of the new recruits for the two rapidly expanding sectors that contain the better-paying jobs. These massive shifts were made possible by the general increase in educational attainment. The predominant proportion of both men (64 percent) and women (50 percent) managers and professionals consisted of persons with four years or more of college.

In the case of the technical, sales, and clerical category, the proportion of men and women with less than a high school diploma was very small (6 percent). Over 60 percent of men and about 80 percent of the women were either high school graduates or had completed between one and three years of college.

The least well educated of both sexes are concentrated in the skilled, semiskilled, and unskilled occupations with the largest numbers having four years of high school or less.

In sum, the American economy has moved decisively from blue-collar work, which has been the area of heaviest concentration for male workers, to white-collar occupations, where women are strongly, even disproportionately, concentrated.

The Aging of the Population: Living Longer and Working Less

In 1900, of the total population of just over 75 million, only slightly more than 2 million were between 65 and 74 and somewhat fewer than 900,000 were 75 or older, making for a total of about 3 million persons in the older age brackets, or no more than 4 percent of the total population.

When Social Security became law in 1935, more than a third of a century later, the number of persons 65 and over represented between 6 and 7 percent of the population, still a small fraction of a much larger population of 125 million. As late as 1950, 70 percent of the total population was younger than 45.

In 1990, with a total population of about 250 million, just about double what it had been at the time of the passage of the Social Security bill, the number of those 65 and older had increased tenfold from less than 3 million at the beginning of the century to over 31 million (or, in percentage terms, from under 4 percent to almost 13 percent of the total). Inspection of the data on the "old-old" reveals that in 1990 there were 3.3 million Americans 85 and above, greater than the total size of the 65 and over cohort in 1900 of slightly under 3 million. In the interim the United States had added over 18.3 million persons to the 65 to 74 age group and another 9.9 million to those between 75 and 84 for a combined total of over 28 million persons between 65 and 84.

It is clear that in both absolute and relative terms there has been a significant increase in the number of Americans 65 and over. The "aging" of the American population during this century has, however, escaped the attention of many, even physicians who should have been alerted to the growing importance of preventive medicine and chronic disease but who until recently paid relatively little attention to the increasingly prominent role that the elderly had come to play in the use of health care services. This unresponsiveness is a reflection of the fact that social policy in a democracy committed to a belief in small government is unlikely to address issues of public education or welfare unless the policy analysts and the media have succeeded in attracting and focusing public attention. For the most part, the growth in the number of persons approaching retirement age was not viewed as a priority item on the nation's agenda because there had been improvements in the scope of Social Security benefits as well as a rapid growth in the savings of individuals. Taken together, these seemed to assure that most, if not all, individuals would be able to cope with retirement without jeopardizing their previous standard of living. In short, little attention was paid to the new reality of the aging of the U.S. population since there was little appreciation of the fact that most Americans who retire in their early sixties have on average between twenty and twenty-five years of life stretching ahead of them, a period about half as long as their total involvement in the adult labor force. It is this phenomenon, which we have called the unrecognized potential, that has largely escaped analysis and action.

The fact that about 13 percent of the total U.S. population was 65 and over in 1990 should alert us, however, to the importance of assessing whether retirement benefits for older workers should be the exclusive or preferred response, either from the vantage of the older person or of the larger society. An answer to this critical challenge requires analysis of the demographic projections for the near-term future (to 2020).

The Census Bureau's middle series projections referred to earlier estimated that by 2020 the total U.S. population will increase by only 17 percent but that a major shift will occur in the age distribution, particularly in the absolute and relative number of older persons currently alive who will be 65 or older in the year 2020. These projections reveal that in 2020 there will be about 31 million persons between 65 and 74, another 14.5 million between 75 and 84, and about 3.3 million 85 and over. The three groups together total about 49 million Americans above the age of 65 in 2020, or one out of every six persons. A century earlier, in 1920, out of the total population of 106 million those 65 and older totaled 5 million, or about one out of every twenty-one persons. In 2020 when those between 45 and 64 are added, the 45 and over group will account for 40 percent of the total population.

Even more challenging than the number of older persons is the quality of their later years. The standard American view of the elderly is one of senescence, impaired mental and physical capacity and declining productivity. Although a relationship between age and disability exists, it is worth emphasizing that this association between aging and reduced productivity should not obscure the more important finding that the increasing incidence of chronic physical illnesses and disabilities increases only modestly among persons between 65 and 75 and that even at 85 the vast majority of Americans are living at home, many fully capable of caring for themselves and only a minority requiring assistance from relatives, friends, or outside agencies. Even among the "old-old" (85 and over), only one out of four or five is in a nursing home.

There is also little hard evidence to support the conventional wisdom that older persons suffer significant retardation in their mental processes and that they are unable to learn as quickly and to retain as well as younger people new knowledge and new ways of doing things. Although people who were not challenged to acquire new knowledge and new competencies and to respond to new environments when younger may well lose some of their innate mental capacity, the opposite is frequently true of those who have faced such challenges. Further, a critical determinant of how people of all ages respond to the new is how they see their present situation in relation to their future values and goals. If persons in their fifties are preparing themselves for withdrawal from work when they reach their early sixties, or even before, there is less incentive for them to keep attuned to change.

In sum, the major part of the population increase by the year 2020 will reflect an increase among those between 65 and 74 years of age who, on the whole, are expected to be in good physical and mental health and many of whom may be interested in continuing to be productively employed either part time or full time. In light of this projection, it would appear desirable to place on the nation's agenda an exploration of policies that reflect the new population structure rather than the old. Since 1935 the focus of public and private interventions has been on providing the elderly with financial resources sufficient to help them maintain their accustomed way of life. Important as this consideration has been—and is—the question raised here is whether the existence of a potential 50 percent increase in the productive years of life should not be included in planning for possible additional adaptations.

Such a reevaluation becomes particularly urgent in light of the changes in the labor force participation rates of older males since the end of World War II. As striking as the increase in the total size of the labor force and the changes in its gender composition between 1950 and 1990 was the sharp decline in the number of males over the age of 55 in the labor force and the differentially more rapid growth of females in that age group. In 1950, 89 percent of all men 55 and over were either working or looking for work, as were almost half of all men 65 and older. By the late 1980s, only 40 percent of the first age group and 17 percent of the older age group were still in the labor force.

As a consequence of the differentially more rapid rate of increase of female workers, the female share in the 55 to 64 year group who remained active in the labor force nearly doubled over the four decades. In the 65 year and older group, the female participation rate of women dipped slightly. The members of this group had been attached to the world of work as early as the 1950s, but since fewer than one in three were in the work force at that time, only a few were still employed or looking for work in 1990. In the succeeding decades the rapid rate of increase in the number of women joining the labor force as permanent or intermittent workers assures their continuing presence in the labor market to age 65 and possibly beyond.

There are other reinforcing factors, all of which point to a greater participation of older women in the labor market in the decades that lie ahead. The most important of these are marital status, educational attainment, and race. In 1987, 70 percent of older women who were divorced worked, in contrast to only 45 percent of those who were married with a husband present. If the upward trend of divorce continues, the odds are that more older women will remain in the work force at least up to age 65.

Higher educational levels have not only facilitated the occupational transformation of the American labor force and radically transformed the economic status of women but have also been found to be inversely related with general morbidity and mortality rates of older workers and thus contributed to their labor market participation rates. The death rate for men ages 55 to 64 with less than a high school education was 50 percent higher than for those with more than twelve years of schooling.

In sum, changes in educational level, occupational structure, marital status, mortality, and morbidity are all potent determinants of labor force participation rates.

The predominant number of men who have reached or approached the age of retirement in the past two decades represented cohorts that contained relatively small numbers of persons who had earned a college degree. The new environment in which older men found themselves in the 1970s and 1980s was not conducive for the most part to their continued employment, a fact that is reflected in their much reduced participation in the labor force. The declining proportion in the labor force of male workers over the age of 55, though greatly influenced by the shift of the economy to white-collar work, also reflected parallel changes in private and public policies that speeded early retirement.

Social Security and Private Pensions

The United States was a latecomer to social insurance because of a traditional antigovernmental bias and idealization of the market as the best mechanism to determine employer-employee relationships. Men were expected to work as long as they were physically capable, an attitude that explains why as late as World War II so large a proportion of men 65 and older were still in the labor force. Europe had taken the lead in providing social insurance about a half century earlier when, for a variety of motives, Chancellor Otto Bismarck of Germany took the initiative to provide for pension payments to workers over the age of 70. Given the limited life expectancy of men at that time, this was not a particularly costly income-transfer program. After World War I, Germany lowered the age of eligibility for a pension to 65 and Britain and France took similar steps to establish a pension system for some part of their industrial work forces based on both employee and employer contributions.

When the Social Security Act was passed in the United States in 1935, the moneys to be paid to the elderly were viewed not as a pension but rather as a benefit that would partially replace the money that they had earned earlier in employment. A secondary objective of the legislation was the freeing up of jobs at a time of severe depression. For both these reasons, Social Security benefits were reduced for each dollar of wage earnings for work performed after age 65 beyond a modest ceiling. Succeeding changes reflected altered perceptions of the needs and entitlements of older workers.

In 1956 Congress lowered the age of eligibility for benefits for women workers from 65 to 62, influenced at least in part by the fact that with husbands on average about three years older than their wives, it made sense to facilitate the retirement of women when their husbands were ready to leave the labor force. In 1961 this choice of early retirement at age 62 was extended to men as well and, in fact, early retirees received an actuarial benefit not enjoyed by those who stopped working at NAR (normal age of retirement).

Probably the single most important modification of the Social Security Act occurred in 1972 when benefits were indexed to the cost of living. The effect of this change is revealed by a comparison between 1959 and the late 1980s of the proportion of the elderly who were trapped in poverty. In the former year more than 35 percent of those over 64 were poor compared with 22 percent of the general population. By 1985, the two rates were 12.6 percent and 14 percent respectively. Not only had the initial situation been reversed, but even greater improvement would have been shown if in-kind benefits for the elderly such as health care, food stamps, subsidized housing, and so on had been included.

As early as 1964, criticisms of the Social Security system were voiced by a number of politicians and analysts as denying "intergenerational equity" on the grounds that the federal government was spending too much on the elderly and too little on the younger generation, but these arguments never gained much attention. Most Americans decided that paying Social Security taxes while they were working in order to receive benefits when they became eligible for Social Security was reasonable, the more so because it was an all-inclusive system to which all workers contributed and from which all would eventually draw benefits. The regressive impact of the flat tax paid by all covered workers was mitigated by the highly progressive payout system with the benefit formula weighted in favor of low earners who also pay less for their Medicare benefits.

Liberalizing amendments to the Social Security Act, however, put the financial underpinnings of the Social Security system under severe strain during the period of slow economic growth that marked the early 1980s. Public and congressional opposition to reduction of benefits stimulated the exploration of other approaches. With guidance from the National Commission on Social Security Reform chaired by Alan Greenspan, Congress passed a number of amendments to the Social Security Act in 1983. To increase the flow of tax revenues into the system and to reduce the incentives to take early retirement, a very gradual increase in the NRA from 65 to 67 over the twenty-three-year span from 2003 to 2026 was mandated. Those reaching 62 in 2000 are the first group to be affected. One-half of all Social Security benefits were also made subject to income tax for those older persons with higher levels of income.

The very lengthy period during which the normal age of retirement will be increased to 67, with the adjustments spread over more than two decades, underscores the caution and restraint demonstrated by Congress in taking any overt action to reduce the benefits that the older population had come to view as inviolable.

Although the experts differ about many technical and policy aspects of Social Security, the vast majority of the American people have become increasingly reliant on old-age survivors and disability insurance (OASDI), under which benefits are related to prior earnings at the same time that they are skewed favorably in the direction of those at the lower end of the wage scale to help assure that in their old age they will have at least the minimum benefits needed to meet their needs.

Congress has, however, been reluctant to respond to considerable pressure from the elderly who want the earnings cap between ages 65 and 70 removed without any decrease in their benefits. The proponents of this change have argued that the federal government should not penalize older persons who wish to continue working by depriving them of their rightful Social Security benefits. Congressional opposition has persisted, however, because of the estimated annual $5 billion loss in federal revenues that would result and by the fact that the savings would largely accrue to highly paid professional and managerial personnel, who are the most likely to continue working beyond age 65. Although it has been pointed out that many older workers continue to work "off the books" and that therefore the elimination of the earnings cap would be "budget-neutral" since taxes would be paid on reported income, congressional resistance to this proposal continues.

During the drafting of the original Social Security legislation, there was some discussion about the desirability of including national health insurance benefits, but the idea was abandoned in the face of violent opposition from the American Medical Association (AMA) and most business interests. The issue reemerged in the late 1940s with President Truman and some liberal Democratic senators taking the lead, but their efforts were unsuccessful because of the lack of solid support from the trade unions as well as the continuing opposition of the AMA and the corporate sector.

By the early 1960s, however, the issue of how to cover the health and hospital costs of retired workers could no longer be ignored. Despite strong opposition, the overwhelming vote that President Johnson had received in the election of 1964 ensured the passage of Medicare legislation in 1965. By 1980, however, the expenditures for Medicare had increased so alarmingly that Congress passed a series of amendments between 1981 and 1985 making the employer the primary payer of health benefits for workers between 65 and 70, with Medicare the secondary payer. The effect of this change is clearly negative for the continued employment of older workers. Employers will hesitate to hire workers in their late fifties or early sixties who might stay on their payroll past 65. In fact, the entangled relations between the employment of older persons and coverage of their health care benefits is even more complicated for the large number of "early" retirees, many of whom lose employer coverage before they are eligible for Medicare.

The age of Medicare eligibility still remains 65 except for persons declared to be permanently disabled, who become eligible at any point after a two-year wait. The relationship between the employment of older persons and their health care benefits has become particularly strained as leading congressional representatives continually explore the prospect of lowering the age of eligibility for Medicare to 60 to help close the serious gap that leaves large numbers of early retirees with little or no health care coverage. The problem of health care coverage also presents a challenge to the large number of workers, elderly and non-elderly alike, who cannot obtain health care insurance from their present or prospective employers because of the risk-management strategies pursued by many private health insurance companies to avoid covering potentially high-cost users. For the intermediate and longer term, the decisions that the United States will make with respect to the reform of its health care financing and delivery system, including Medicare, are certain to have a significant impact on the employment opportunities of older workers.

The federal government as well as some of the states and even some local governments have extended "affirmative action" legislation to penalize discriminatory employment policies directed toward older workers. The federal Age Discrimination in Employment Act (ADEA) of 1967 defines an older worker as anyone age 40 or older, but most legal actions claiming discrimination arising under such legislation center on the "young-old," that is, persons 55 and over. In 1986 forced retirement at any age with a few exceptions was made illegal.

Although the original objective of the Social Security Act of 1935 to provide "security against the hazards and vicissitudes of life" not only for the elderly but for fatherless and other families without a breadwinner may be said to have been met, equitable treatment of single workers was not. Concern for "fatherless families" reflected the view in 1935 that the typical family was headed by a father who was gainfully employed and a mother who was not, so that the loss of the former would lead to poverty. Although the spectacular increase in the number of working women has caused the traditional family to become a minority of all families, this fact has not affected the basic structure of the benefit system.

Although all workers pay the same Social Security tax on the same level of wages, married workers earn retirement as well as death and disability insurance benefits for their entire families while single workers earn benefits only for themselves. Furthermore, since women workers earn on average lower wages and often interrupt their work lives to care for children or elderly parents, they receive lower benefits as workers than do spouses. In addition, the years spent in noncompensated caregiving reduce their earnings record and their consequent benefits.

The identification of the problem is easier than its resolution, however, since it would involve either spending more money or reducing existing benefits, neither of which is politically viable.

The Rise of Private Pensions

Prior to the substantial growth of trade union membership during the New Deal era and the growing importance that organized labor placed on employer benefits, particularly health care coverage and pensions, relatively few corporations had instituted formal pension plans for their nonmanagerial work force. But the early post–World War II decades saw an explosive growth in pension arrangements to the point where about 60 percent of all employed persons in 1990 were enrolled in private or public pension plans, primarily plans that provided defined benefits for retirees.

As noted earlier, Social Security benefits, even when inflation-adjusted, were never intended to serve as a full replacement for preretirement earnings. Private pensions and returns on savings were viewed as the two other principal sources of such replacement. Many retirees do in fact receive private- and/or public-sector pensions, which play a critical role in the maintenance of their postretirement incomes. The growth of private pensions was fostered by the federal government, which established favorable tax conditions for both employers and beneficiaries; by employers desirous of attracting and retaining workers for the long term; by trade union leaders whose members placed a high value on pensions; and by nonunionized firms that saw such benefits as a way of avoiding unionization.

In 1974 the federal Employee Retirement Income Security Act (ERISA) was passed with the intention of both encouraging and regulating private pensions so that workers would have a secure source of income supplemental to Social Security. Another federal initiative provided for individual retirement accounts (IRAs) as a tax-deferred retirement savings vehicle for workers who had no employer-provided pensions. In 1981 IRA eligibility was extended to all workers, although restrictions were later imposed on those above certain income levels. A special incentive was the lower tax paid on funds withdrawn after retirement.

Currently, about 52 million persons are covered by private pensions, about 30 million men and 22 million women, representing about two out of every five workers. In the case of full-time workers, more than half are covered. A significant number of employees are members of more than a single pension plan, having changed jobs in mid-career after they had qualified for a pension with a former employer. Over the past fifteen years or so—from the mid-1970s to the end of the 1980s—the number of private pension plans increased by more than 100 percent, from 340,000 to over 800,000, with correspondingly large gains in annual contributions. During this same period pension payments to beneficiaries increased from $19 to $125 billion.

Types of Private Pension Plans:
Effects on the Retirement Decision

The two major types of private pension plans are the defined benefit plan and the defined contribution plan. The defined benefit plan, as its name suggests, operates on a formula that defines the amount of benefits provided by the employer, usually a flat amount for years of service or a percentage of salary or some combination of both, with special weight frequently given to the highest years of earnings.

The steady decline in the labor force participation rates of older workers is frequently attributed to increases in Social Security benefits, but enrollment in a private defined benefit plan may play an even greater role. In recent years, defined benefit plans have become vehicles to encourage early retirement. In a typical plan, the normal retirement age is usually defined as 65 and if early retirement is the company's objective, supplemental benefits are paid to those leaving earlier who have at least the minimum required years of service. When the benefits received at ages 55 and 65 are discounted to present value, for example, those who retire at age 55 receive larger payouts than the older group. Such non–age-neutral arrangements strongly affect the retirement decisions of older workers once they become aware of the negative effects of delaying their retirement. Olivia Mitchell concludes that such pension buyouts have become common in the past twenty years as firms have replaced older, more expensive workers with younger, less costly ones. She also considers the evidence on "the response to regulation hypothesis"; that is, that employers responded to the legal abolition of mandatory retirement based on age by further sweetening their "early out" incentives to be persuasive.[2]

Defined benefit pension plans, because of the aforementioned features, are usually described as "backloaded" because vested entitlements first accrue slowly at the beginning of the work life, accrue rapidly as the age of early retirement approaches, and then decline after age 65. The dual effects of such an arrangement are the discouragement of mobility at an early age and the encouragement of early retirement (usually at age 55 with 30 years of service).

Whether originally introduced to force the retirement of older workers or not, the existence of the defined benefit plan has that effect, regardless of the ban on mandatory retirement. By having greater benefits at early retirement than at the normal retirement age, the legal requirement that accrual of pension benefits be continued for those working past the normal age of retirement is also circumvented.[3]

The deferred contribution plan, in contrast, is a plan to which both the employee and employer contribute. Each employee has an individual account (usually in the form of a 401[k] plan) and the amount of pension benefits received depend on the size of the combined contributions and on how well the plan was managed. Unlike the defined benefit plan, there are no special arrangements for benefit payouts, which depend simply on the value of the account at the time of the retirement decision. This type of plan favors younger workers, who can accumulate full benefits before retirement by having both employers and employees contribute varying amounts yearly to the pension fund. These contributions as well as the yield on invested funds enable young workers to accumulate full benefits before retirement; older workers are not provided with artificial incentives to take early retirement, as is the case with the defined benefit type of plan. These plans can also be made portable more readily and can enhance job mobility.

According to a recent survey on private pensions by the Bureau of Labor Statistics, 90 percent of employees of state and local government are enrolled in defined contribution plans, 9 percent in defined benefit plans, and 3 percent in both. In the private sector, among small firms with under 100 employees where pension coverage is limited, 31 percent have defined contribution plans, 20 percent defined benefit plans, and the remainder have none. In large firms with over 100 employees, 63 percent are covered by defined benefit plans and 48 percent by defined contribution plans or a combination of both (which brings the total to over 100 percent).

Although deferred benefit plans continue to dominate the private pension scene, the deferred contribution plan became more popular in the late 1980s, when measured by the size of the contributions and the number of participants.

There are other aspects of private pension plans that warrant attention. The first and most important difference between private pensions and Social Security is that most pension plans are not indexed for inflation. That means that in the single decade of 1970 to 1980 about 53 percent of the value of pensions was eroded by the falling value of the dollar. Fortunately, in 1982 the rate of inflation moderated substantially but even in the subsequent period of modest inflation (1981–1991), the value of pension payments declined by 25 percent.

It is interesting to contrast the relative rates of growth of the Social Security system and the pension systems (both private and public) over the past two decades. Between 1970 and the end of the 1980s the total number of Social Security beneficiaries increased from 26 to 39 million and annual payments increased from $32 to $231 billion. Almost all of the increase was accounted for by retired workers and their dependents. There was substantial growth during this period in both the number of beneficiaries and the amount of annual payments.

The growth of the assets in private and public pension plans over the same two decades, however, has been far greater. In 1970 the total assets of all pension funds came to $240 billion, by 1980 to $916 billion, and by 1989 to $2.94 billion, a twelve-fold increase in current dollars during the two decades. Even when translated into constant dollars, the increase is still almost fourfold. The corporate trend to "outsourcing" and contracting out, however, will undoubtedly have a moderating effect on the growth of pensions. Another negative feature is the nonportability of pensions. Pension rights do not accompany the job changer who can receive his or her (vested) pension benefits only at the age specified by the plan.

The Department of Labor surveys show since 1985 a continuing decline in the relative number of workers with private pension coverage. The simplest and most direct explanation for this reversal is the decline in the number of persons employed by large corporations and the fact that small employers are less likely to provide pension coverage of any kind.

Early Retirement: Living Longer, Working Less

Major changes in the patterns of employment for older persons depend in the first instance on the judgments made by management about the relative advantages of continuing to encourage the early withdrawal of employees from the world of work as opposed to alternative approaches aimed at expanding the opportunities of older workers to continue in full- or part-time employment.

From the company's vantage, if a personnel reduction is necessary, it makes sense to encourage older workers to retire. Not only is the threat to the morale of the remaining workers lessened, but since most older employees are likely to be in the higher wage brackets, their earlier retirement would benefit the bottom line. Finally, and not least important, many workers, once convinced that they can maintain their standard of living, will be ready to accept retirement.

The most important of all the actors in the decisionmaking process are the individual older persons whose decisions will be determined in good part by their estimates of their future financial positions. Three in five beneficiaries receive more than half their income from Social Security benefits that are indexed. The second most important source of their cash income—about 26 percent—is interest on prior savings. The residual is divided about equally between private pensions and postretirement earnings.

In addition to cash revenues, a high proportion of all elderly persons own their homes, and most are mortgage free. The value of their home accounts for about two-thirds of the total net worth of the elderly.

In order to gain a deeper understanding of why persons retire as early as 55, it is necessary to look more closely at their cash income and asset position. The life-cycle hypothesis assumes that with retirement both income and assets start to decline, that is, the elderly "disinvest." But Cynthia Taeuber and Barbara Torrey,[4] using 1980 census data, assert that although the elderly do eventually dissave, their income from assets increases until after their eighty-fifth year.

Another indication that most of the elderly are not seriously pressed for cash income can be found in the relatively slow growth of home equity loans or "reverse mortgages," which are able to provide the elderly with additional spending money while they continue to live in their own homes. Many of the elderly are not affluent—in fact almost 7 percent of family householders have a cash income below the poverty level—but with the receipt of in-kind benefits and tapping into supplemental financial resources, they are usually able to maintain their standard of living except for those who confront serious medical conditions that require them to use costly life-sustaining drugs or nursing home care.

The counter-pulls to the financial inducements for early retirement require consideration. Most individuals first enter the adult labor market in their early twenties and retire in their early sixties, spending on average about forty years as productive members of the labor force. Currently, the additional expected years of life of men age 62 is seventeen, of women twenty-one. In short, each retiree will on average have almost twenty years of life left after retirement, about half of the forty-odd-year period spent working. There is both challenge and opportunity in extending the work life of older workers by some part of the 50 percent production potential that is theirs once they retire.

The use of some part of the potential would have both societal and individual payoffs. The former relates to the substantial opportunity for growth of the U.S. economy if a significant proportion of older persons in the 62 to 75 age range who are in good health and in full control of their faculties continue to work. Since this thirteen-year span accounts for about 30 percent of the current productive involvement in the world of work for most American men (and eventually of American women), even if all of the members of the older cohort decided that they wanted to work only part-time past 62, such engagement would still be a substantial addition to the gross national product. The Census Bureau projection that 60 percent of the population increase by the year 2020 will be accounted for by those between 65 and 74 years of age gives special significance to this possibility.

But the potential increase in the output of goods and services is only one way of looking at this opportunity from extended labor force participation. The other is from the perspective of the individual and of the payers of income transfers to the elderly, particularly the federal government and employers through their pension plans. It is also appropriate to raise the issue as to whether most men and women want to be cut off permanently from the world of work and all that that world connotes for their self-esteem, earning capabilities, companionship, and the constructive use of time in order to increase the number of hours that they will have available to spend on the golf links or in other recreational activities, particularly since most will be free from both disease and disability. Even among persons who earlier had only a modest investment in their work and career, it is hard to believe that, if given such an opportunity, they would still decide that a twenty-year retirement period is the most attractive choice.

The editors of a comprehensive study of early retirement in seven countries assess this phenomenon in familiar terms:

> The decrease in the age of exit from gainful work has been one of the most profound structural changes in the past 25 years. It has occurred—albeit to differing degrees—in all Western societies, irrespective of their institutional regimes. In the recent history of these societies, few trends are as consistent and homogeneous as this one. The period spent in gainful work is shrinking, with early exit at the upper end of the extension of schooling and the lower end of the work life contributing to this outcome from both directions. The

period spent in retirement is also expanding in both directions as a result of early exit at the lower end and increasing life expectancy at the upper end. Thus, what has been the "normal life course" is being massively reorganized, and the relations between age groups and generations are being redefined.

Moreover, the trend is (on first sight at least) highly perplexing and even paradoxical. In a period of increasing life expectancy, of increasing concern with the financial viability of the public pension systems, and of increasing admonitions from gerontologists about the fallacy of age stereotypes regarding work performance and productivity, why should there be such a pervasive tendency to leave work earlier and earlier? The paradox defies easy explanations; by posing the question of how life phases and the boundaries between them—especially the all-important boundaries between work and nonwork periods—are socially constructed, it is perhaps the most explicit challenge for life-course theory. It also challenges most current assumptions about the effects of social policy by contrasting the explanatory potential of theories that focus on the state as the key actor and those that focus on actors in the economic sphere.[5]

Notes

1. Claudia Golden, "The Role of World War II in the Rise of Women's Employment," *American Economic Review* 81(4)(September 1991):741–756.

2. Olivia S. Mitchell, "Pensions Reflect Employee and Employer Preferences," in Alicia Munnell, ed., *Retirement and Public Policy, Proceedings of the Second Conference of the National Academy of Social Insurance* (Washington, D.C.: National Academy of Social Insurance, 1991), pp. 197–208.

3. David A. Wise, "Living Longer, Saving Less, Retiring Sooner," in Munnell, *Retirement and Public Policy*, pp. 209–221.

4. Barbara B. Torrey and Cynthia M. Taeuber, "The Importance of Asset Income Among the Elderly," *Review of Income and Wealth*, Series 32, no. 4 (December 1986):443–449.

5. M. Kohli and M. Rein, *Time for Retirement: Comparative Studies of Early Exit from the Labor Force* (Cambridge: Cambridge University Press, 1991), p. 1.

3

Central Cities and Their Suburbs

Thomas M. Stanback, Jr.

This chapter examines the way in which the industrial composition and relative earnings of workers are changing in the central cities and suburbs of fourteen large metropolitan areas.[1] Two general findings emerge from the analysis: (1) that large central cities, though differing significantly among themselves, have undergone major transformations leading to increased specialization in services and a marked upgrading of labor force requirements and (2) that the more rapidly growing suburbs of these large metros have become increasingly mature and complex in their industrial structure with many characterized by rapidly developing agglomerations of economic activity. Thus far, however, the suburbs appear to compete only selectively with central cities for higher-order, well-paying service firms and institutions and are characterized by a much larger proportion of lower-wage activities. A major implication of these divergent developmental patterns within large metropolitan areas is that they are creating increasing problems within central cities, where large numbers of poorly educated and unskilled minorities, especially black males, find a dearth of appropriate job openings.

Population Growth and the Importance of Commuting

Population Growth

In the late 1970s, considerable attention was given to what appeared to be a new trend toward dispersion of people and economic activity within the U.S. economy: Population in nonmetropolitan counties taken as a whole had grown more rapidly during the decade than in metropolitan counties (Table 3.1). What went largely unnoticed, however, was that within metropolitan areas suburban counties had grown at a considerably more rapid rate than had nonmetropolitan counties and, among nonmetropolitan areas, it was in those counties in which there was significant commut-

Table 3.1   Annual Growth Rates of Metropolitan and Nonmetropolitan Population, 1970–1980, 1980–1987

	1970–1980	*1980–1987*
Metropolitan	1.00	1.12
Central city	0.08	0.74
Suburbs	1.74	1.37
Nonmetropolitan counties	1.34	0.58
≥ 15% commute to metro	1.80	1.21
10–14% commute to metro	1.48	0.78
5–9% commute to metro	1.33	0.63
< 5% commute to metro	1.24	0.42
Metropolitan, by population size		
> 5 million	0.33	0.97
1–5 million	1.09	1.23
250,000–1 million	1.38	1.17
< 250,000	1.60	1.03

Source: U.S. Bureau of the Census, *Current Population Reports*, series P-23, no. 159, Population Profile of Employment and Unemployment, 1989 (Washington, DC: GPO, 1989).

ing into the metropolitan areas that growth was most rapid. Since the beginning of the 1980s, the trend toward the increasing importance of metropolitan areas has been reaffirmed: Growth in the nonmetropolitan U.S. population has slowed sharply while growth in metropolitan areas has accelerated.

This tendency for suburbs to grow more rapidly than cities is not, however, a recent development. Wide differentials in growth rates occurred as well during the 1940s, 1950s, and 1960s.[2] Accordingly, the suburban economies of the late 1980s must be seen in light of more than four decades of sustained growth. Older, simplistic views of the suburbs as largely residential extensions of the city must give way to a view of these areas as economies in the process of becoming increasingly complex and mature. Yet we shall observe in the subsequent analysis that suburbs have faced significant constraints in terms of the extent to which they have been able to upgrade the earnings levels of their work forces as compared to those of the cities.

Importance of Commuting

Commuting has increased rapidly in the U.S. economy in recent decades, rising from about 39 million to roughly 68 million between the census years 1960 and 1980.[3]

In a recent study of commuting in the United States, Alan Pisarski noted the following trends for the 1960–1980 period:[4]

1. The most important increases in commuting were in intrasuburban movements with the number of commuters rising from 11 million to over 25 million, resulting in an increase in share of total flows from 28 to 38 percent. Commuting to destinations outside the metropolitan areas (predominantly by suburban residents) also increased (from about 2 to 7 percent of total flows).
2. "Traditional" suburb to central city movements almost doubled, gaining about 6 million workers and increasing the share from 16 to 19 percent of total flows.
3. "Reverse" commuting (city to suburb) rose but remained at about 5 to 6 percent of total flows.
4. Commuter movements within the central city declined sharply in share, from about 46 to 30 percent.

The increasing importance of commuting in cities and suburbs is readily observed in Table 3.2, based on the residence adjustment estimates of the Bureau of Economic Analysis (BEA). These estimates are prepared and published on a county basis and may be consolidated to conform with the city and suburb definitions used in this study. They are estimates of *net* commuter earnings (the earnings of out-commuters minus the earnings of in-commuters). To estimate earnings of workers at place of residence, the BEA uses net commuter earnings to adjust county estimates of total worker earnings at place of work. Where in-commuter earnings exceed out-commuter earnings, the residence adjustment is negative (it is deducted from total earnings at place of work in estimating total resident earnings). Conversely, where out-commuter earnings exceed in-commuter earnings the residence adjustment is positive (it is added to total earnings at place of work in estimating total resident earnings).

In Table 3.2, the residence adjustments are shown as percentages of total worker earnings (place of work) for the years 1969 and 1987 with minus signs shown to indicate *net* in-commuter earnings. An initial finding is that the residence adjustment is negative for every central city in both years and positive for every suburb.

The rather wide range of negative residence adjustment percentages in the cities—from 11 to 60 percent in 1987—should not be regarded as necessarily indicative of differences among cities in the importance of commuting. At least in part they are accounted for by variations in the extent to which central city counties overbound the cities themselves. For example, Cook County, the central city county, overbounds the city of Chicago to a considerable extent. Accordingly, the flow of commuting into the county fails to reveal the full extent of commuting into the city because it does not include the large flow of out-of-city commuters who live within the county. Examination of ratios of city-to-county population (Table 3.3)

Table 3.2 Residence Adjustment as a Percentage of Total Earnings at Place of Work, 1969, 1987

	Central City			Suburbs		
	1969	1987	Change	1969	1987	Change
New York	−23.2	−28.5	−	47.1	30.7	−
Chicago	−9.7	−15.0	−	48.6	43.9	−
Philadelphia	−29.0	−33.2	−	31.6	22.8	−
Los Angeles	−7.4	−11.4	−	32.9	15.4	−
Atlanta	−39.3	−48.3	−	51.9	34.2	−
Boston	−50.2	−52.6	−	16.6	6.7	−
Cincinnati	−19.4	−25.9	−	104.0	70.2	−
Columbus	−6.9	−12.8	−	18.8	39.9	+
Dallas	−10.5	−23.9	−	69.4	118.3	+
Detroit	−16.2	−19.2	−	32.9	20.9	−
Minneapolis	−11.5	−21.7	−	11.5	24.4	+
Pittsburgh	−8.6	−12.3	−	24.9	27.6	+
St. Louis	−52.8	−52.8	=	38.2	15.4	−
Washington	−54.0	−61.5	−	46.5	19.6	−

Note: Residence adjustment is computed by subtracting in-commuter from out-commuter earnings. Negative sign (−) indicates net in-commuter earnings.

Source: Data supplied by the Bureau of Economic Analysis.

Table 3.3 Population of Central Cities and Central City Counties, 1980

	Central City	Central City County	City-to-County Population Ratio
New York	7,072	7,072	1.00
Chicago	3,005	5,256	0.57
Philadelphia	1,688	1,688	1.00
Los Angeles	2,967	7,504	0.40
Atlanta	425	592	0.72
Boston	563	651	0.86
Cincinnati	385	873	0.44
Columbus	565	871	0.65
Dallas	904	1,566	0.58
Detroit	1,203	2,329	0.52
Minneapolis	371	944	0.39
Pittsburgh	424	1,448	0.29
St. Louis	453	453	1.00
Washington	638	638	1.00

Source: U.S. Bureau of the Census, Census of Population, 1980 (Washington, DC: GPO, 1980). Central city data from U.S. Bureau of the Census, Statistical Abstract of the United States, 1984 (Washington, DC: GPO, 1984). Central city county data supplied by the Bureau of Economic Analysis.

indicates a fairly high correspondence between overbounding (i.e., low ratios of city to central county residents) and low negative residence adjustment percentages (Table 3.2). It seems clear that if net inflows of commuters to cities were properly measured they would be substantial in virtually all places.

A second finding from Table 3.2 is that resident adjustment ratios became increasingly negative in virtually all cities from 1969 to 1987, indicating a general trend toward an increasing role played by in-commuters in central city economies.

Paradoxically, the residence adjustment measure also declined in most suburbs (ten of the fourteen), indicating a declining importance of out-commuter earnings as a source of income within these economies. The paradox is explained by the much more rapid growth of the suburbs and the fact that they increasingly are receiving in-commuters from outlying areas. In spite of the larger number of commuters moving into the city daily, this larger net outflow from the suburbs accounts for a smaller percentage of the total earnings of persons working in most of the suburbs.

The Industrial Composition of Employment

To a large extent, the kinds of jobs available to workers in cities and suburbs depend on the industrial mix of these economies—what goods and services they produce. A useful measure of industrial specialization is the location quotient (LQ)—the ratio of the share of employment accounted for by an industry in a given location to the corresponding share of employment of that industry in the U.S. economy as a whole. For example, in 1987 New York City, with 14.68 percent of its total employment in finance, insurance, and real estate (FIRE) compared to 7.95 percent for the U.S. economy, has an LQ of 1.85 and is regarded as heavily specialized. Detroit, with a corresponding LQ of .85, is not. Summary measures for the fourteen central cities and suburbs studied here are presented in Table 3.4.

Among the fourteen central cities, there is considerable variation in the structure of employment. Yet there are three industrial groups in which most central cities are overrepresented when compared to the U.S. economy (i.e., the large majority of LQs are greater than one)—wholesaling, FIRE, and other services—demonstrating their role as specialized producers of services destined for users throughout the region or beyond (Table 3.4).

The low LQs for retailing in virtually all central cities attest to another shared characteristic. Because many in the city's work force are commuters who live elsewhere, the role of the central city's economy as a provider of residentiary services is more limited than in the suburbs and, consequently, a smaller share of the work force is engaged in retail activities.

TABLE 3.4   Distribution (%) of U.S. Employment Among Industry Groups and Summary of Location Quotients, Fourteen Central Cities and Suburbs, 1987

	Percentage U.S.	Location Quotients[a]: Tallies		
		Average[b]	C > S	LQ > 1.0
City				
Construction	5.50	0.69	0	0
Manufacturing	15.51	0.85	4	5
TCU	4.85	1.16	11	9
Wholesale	4.97	1.25	10	12
Retail	16.83	0.86	1	2
FIRE	7.95	1.24	11	11
Other services	26.74	1.15	12	12
Federal, civilian government	2.49	1.17	12	5
State, local government	11.14	0.84	10	3
Other	4.01[c]			
	100.00			
			S > C	LQ > 1.0
Suburbs				
Construction	5.50	1.15	14	13
Manufacturing	15.51	1.08	10	9
TCU	4.85	0.93	3	5
Wholesale	4.97	1.03	4	7
Retail	16.83	1.09	13	13
FIRE	7.95	0.93	3	5
Other services	26.74	1.04	2	8
Federal, civilian government	2.49	0.60	2	3
State, local government	11.14	0.85	4	3
Other	4.01[c]			
	100.00			

[a] Location quotient is the ratio of the share of employment in a given industry group to the corresponding share in U.S. employment.
[b] Modified average: highest and lowest values dropped.
[c] Includes primary industries and military.

Note: Other services include business-related services (SICs 73, 81, 89); repair services (SICs 75, 76); social services (SICs 80, 82, 84, 86); consumer services (SICs 70, 72, 78, 79).

Source: Data supplied by the Bureau of Economic Analysis.

The findings for the suburbs are quite different. In thirteen of the fourteen suburbs, the LQs indicate above-average concentration in two industry groups, construction and retailing. In construction, relatively high employment shares reflect, at least in part, the effect of higher population and employment growth rates—a manifestation of the time-honored "acceleration principle" of economics: The *level* of investment activity (in this case, construction) is a function of the *rate* of growth. In the case of retailing, the converse of what was found for city economies is observed: Suburban economies must provide for the needs not only of the families of residents who live and work in the outlying areas of the metropolis but also of the substantial number who work in the city. In addition, suburbs tend to have larger manufacturing sectors than cities. LQs for nine of the fourteen suburbs are above 1.0; in ten, they are higher than for the corresponding central cities.

The importance of wholesaling varies. In the New York, Chicago, Philadelphia, Atlanta, and Boston suburbs, LQs are relatively high. In the Los Angeles (Orange County), Detroit, Pittsburgh, and St. Louis suburbs, they are roughly at the national norm, and among the remaining they are significantly lower.[5] LQs for the remaining industry groups show considerable variation among the suburbs, although for the most part LQs are below those for their central cities.

Changing Industrial Structure

Changes in the U.S. Economy

An essential first step in understanding changes in city and suburban economies is to examine changes that have occurred in the U.S. economy as a whole, for changes in city and suburb must be evaluated in light of what has been taking place on a broader scale throughout the U.S. economy.

Table 3.5 highlights national changes by presenting the distribution of U.S. employment among major industrial groups in 1969 and 1987. Briefly, we observe that there has been a major shift away from manufacturing and into service employment, with the greatest gains in FIRE and other services. There has also been some decline in the importance of Transportation, Communications and Utilities (TCU) and government as a source of employment and gains in shares accounted for construction, wholesaling, and retailing.

Employment Increases and Decreases in Cities and Suburbs

In making comparisons among metropolitan areas and between central cities and suburbs, we look first at employment growth rates during the two periods and then at rates of job increase and job decrease. Job increases are simply net increases in employment in those industry groups that showed gains; job decreases are net decreases in those industry groups that showed losses. Annualized rates of job increases, job decreases, and net overall employment change for 1969–1979 and 1979–1987 are shown in Table 3.6.

Table 3.5 Percentage Distribution of U.S. Nonfarm Employment, 1969, 1987, and Change in Industry Shares, 1969–1987

	1969	1987	Change
Agriculture service, forest, fishery, other	0.59	0.99	0.40
Mining	0.82	0.77	−0.05
Construction	5.22	5.50	0.28
Manufacturing	24.00	15.51	−8.49
TCU	5.59	4.85	−0.74
Wholesale	4.77	4.97	0.22
Retail	15.64	16.83	1.19
FIRE	5.50	7.95	2.45
Other services	19.07	26.74	7.67
Federal, civilian government	3.41	2.49	−0.92
Military	4.00	2.25	−1.75
State, local government	11.39	11.14	−0.25
	100.00	100.00	

Note: Other services include business-related services (SICs 73, 81, 89); repair services (SICs 75, 76); social services (SICs 80, 82, 84, 86); consumer services (SICs 70, 72, 78, 79).

Source: Data supplied by the Bureau of Economic Analysis.

In general, suburban employment growth rates exceeded comparable rates for central cities by wide margins during both periods. This was not true, however, for Columbus during either period or for Minneapolis and Pittsburgh during the 1980s.

We observe further that several central cities lost employment during one or both periods: New York and Boston (first period only); Philadelphia, Detroit, and St. Louis (both periods); Pittsburgh (second period). Only in the Pittsburgh metropolitan area in the 1980s, however, were there employment losses in the suburbs.

Rates of job increase and job decrease (annualized) provide a sense of the extent of the transformations that were taking place in some of the central cities. Clearly, the 1970s were a period of difficult transformation for a number of the older cities of the U.S. economy, with job decreases well in excess of job increases in New York, Philadelphia, Boston, and St. Louis. The 1980s brought an improved performance for some but not for all. New York, Philadelphia, Boston, and Washington improved, but Detroit, Pittsburgh, and St. Louis appear to be in greater trouble.

In the suburbs, job decrease rates were less than 0.5 percent or negligible in virtually all cases. Only in the Pittsburgh metropolitan area during the 1980s were suburban job decrease rates high relative to the central city.

TABLE 3.6 Annualized Rates of Job Increases (JI), Job Decreases (JD), and Net Change, Fourteen Central Cities and Suburbs, 1969–1979, 1979–1987

	1969–1979			1979–1987		
	JI	JD	Net Change	JI	JD	Net Change
Cities						
New York	0.2	1.4	−1.2	1.9	0.7	1.2
Chicago	1.0	0.6	0.4	1.2	0.9	0.3
Philadelphia	*	1.9	−1.9	0.9	1.1	−0.2
Los Angeles	2.4	*	2.4	2.0	*	2.0
Atlanta	2.3	0.2	2.1	2.2	0.1	2.1
Boston	1.1	1.4	−1.3	2.0	0.5	1.6
Cincinnati	1.3	0.2	1.1	1.7	0.6	1.1
Columbus	3.0	0.4	2.6	2.9	0.2	2.7
Dallas	3.7	0.2	3.6	3.7		3.7
Detroit	0.3	0.9	−0.6	0.3	1.7	−1.4
Minneapolis	2.7	*	2.6	2.4	*	2.4
Pittsburgh	0.9	0.5	0.5	1.3	1.6	−0.2
St. Louis	0.4	1.3	−0.8	*	2.5	−2.5
Washington	1.0	0.6	0.4	1.4	0.6	0.9
Suburbs						
New York	2.3	0.1	2.2	3.0	*	3.0
Chicago	3.9	0.3	3.6	3.7	*	3.7
Philadelphia	2.6	0.5	2.2	3.0	0.3	2.7
Los Angeles	7.1	*	7.1	4.3	*	4.3
Atlanta	5.3	*	5.3	7.3	—	7.3
Boston	2.2	0.1	2.1	3.1	0.1	3.0
Cincinnati	4.1	*	4.1	3.3	—	3.3
Columbus	2.5	0.5	2.1	1.7	0.6	1.2
Dallas	6.0	—	6.0	7.9	—	7.9
Detroit	3.8	0.5	3.4	2.7	*	2.6
Minneapolis	3.4	*	3.4	2.4	*	2.4
Pittsburgh	1.8	0.2	1.6	1.0	1.6	−0.6
St. Louis	2.7	*	2.6	3.4	*	3.4
Washington	4.3	0.4	4.0	4.9	—	4.9

*Rate of JI or JD is less than .1 percent.
Note: For explanation of job increases and job decreases see text.

Source: Data supplied by the Bureau of Economic Analysis.

Distribution of Job Increases and Job Decreases

Table 3.7 summarizes the results of an analysis of job increases and job decreases in individual industry groups. Employment changes were netted out for each industry group in each period and the number of job increases (job decreases) distributed in order to observe the share of job increases (or of job decreases) accounted for by each industry group in each city and suburb. Table 3.7 presents for each industry group a tally of cities and of suburbs with net job increases and with net job decreases. In addi-

TABLE 3.7 Summary of Analysis of Distribution of Job Increases and of Job Decreases Among Industry Groups, Fourteen Cities and Suburbs, 1969–1979, 1980–1987

	Median of Shares JI or JD[a]				Tally; Number of Cities or Suburbs With:			
	1969–1979		1979–1987		1969–1979		1979–1987	
	JI	JD	JI	JD	JI	JD	JI	JD
Cities								
Construction	1.4	9.5	4.0	2.3	6	8	10	4
Manufacturing	7.7	49.1	1.8	69.0	3	11	2	12
TCU	3.4	7.4	3.4	7.4	5	9	6	8
Wholesale	7.4	11.9	4.2	9.2	8	6	5	9
Retail	16.4	16.5	8.7	4.4	8	6	11	3
FIRE	12.4	4.6	14.0	2.1	10	4	13	1
Other services	44.5	—	59.2	20.5	14	0	13	1
Federal, civilian government	3.8	7.1	0.4	1.2	5	9	7	7
State, local government	13.2	—	4.7	7.2	14	0	9	5
Suburbs								
Construction	5.8	31.6	7.4	—	12	2	14	0
Manufacturing	7.7	41.6	4.8	80.6	12	2	9[b]	5
TCU	3.6	—	3.4	43.4	14	0	12	2
Wholesale	8.0	—	6.8	0.3	14	0	13	1
Retail	20.4	—	16.9	—	14	0	14	0
FIRE	10.8	—	10.6	—	14	0	14	0
Other services	31.8	—	48.2	—	14	0	14	0
Federal, civilian government	0.4	13.6	0.9	—	8	6	14	0
State, local government	11.2	—	4.6	8.8	14	0	8	6

[a] Median of even number of observations is average of middle two.
[b] Includes one no change.

Source: Data supplied by the Bureau of Economic Analysis.

tion, it presents the median share of job increases and/or of job decreases for all cities and for all suburbs for each industry group.

Among cities, manufacturing was clearly the principal source of job loss (manufacturing declined in eleven cities during the first period, twelve in the second, with median shares of total job decreases 49.1 percent and 60.0 percent). The job decreases due to declining manufacturing employment reflect the increasing competition from areas with lower labor costs as firms shifted production to the South and overseas.

The other services group was the single largest source of employment expansion in every single city with one exception (St. Louis during the 1980s). The medians of shares of total job increases in other services were 44.5 and 59.2 percent. FIRE was the second most important source of employment gain (job increases in ten cities during the first period and thirteen during the second; medians of shares, 12.4 and 14.0 percent).

Among the suburbs there were job increases in most industry groups during both periods. Although manufacturing employment declined in some places it remained, nevertheless, an important source of employment virtually everywhere.

It is unfortunate that the BEA provides no industry breakdown of employment in the large other services category, which was everywhere the most important source of job increases. It is particularly important to distinguish between business services and other more residentially oriented services. However, a breakdown of the shares of other services job gains and job losses (based on *County Business Patterns* data) in the central cities and suburbs of the New York, Chicago, and Philadelphia metropolitan areas for the 1970–1980 and 1980–1985 periods (not shown) indicated that among the four subcategories of other services—business-related, repair, consumer, and social—business-related and social services were responsible for the major contributions to employment growth in central cities and suburbs in the large other services category, with repair and consumer services accounting for much smaller shares.

Earnings Levels

Earnings measures provide valuable insights into how city and suburban economies are faring. Within a given central city or suburb, relatively high earnings levels in an industry reflect the joint effects of some combination of higher skill levels, greater sheltering of workers through unions and credentialing, greater use of full-time employees, or the employment of fewer young workers, women, or minorities than is found in low-earning industries. An increase in the share of jobs accounted for by industries with high average earnings implies an availability of more jobs for better-qualified workers. Conversely, an increase in the share accounted for by low-earning industries implies a relatively greater availability of jobs for those with lower skills, education, and experience.

Earnings averages are, of course, crude indicators. They tell us nothing about the occupational mix of an industry. Firms in which earnings are relatively low may make heavy use of relatively poorly paid white-collar workers rather than blue-collar workers, and their growth will offer few job opportunities for persons who are qualified only for menial labor.

Nevertheless, earnings levels are a useful indicator and shed considerable light on the way in which changes in cities and suburbs are affecting job opportunities for various groups in the labor force.

Variation in Earnings Among Industries

Table 3.8 presents indexes of the average earnings in several industry groups in the U.S. economy in 1969 and 1987. The earnings are expressed as multiples (i.e., ratios) of the average earnings in all industries combined. We note a wide variation in average earnings per worker among industries for 1987—from 1.44 (144 percent of the national average) for TCU to .58 for retailing. For the most part, the relative levels of the various industries in 1987 do not differ greatly from those of 1969. TCU, construction, manufacturing, wholesaling, and federal government are the five highest in both 1969 and 1987; state and local government, other services, FIRE, and retailing, the lowest. Retailing is by far the lowest in both years.

In some industries indexes rise from 1969 to 1987; in others they fall, perhaps indicating a change in the mix of the industries the groups comprise or changes in employment and hiring practices. For example, the sharp decline in retailing is, doubtless, the result of several factors, including a disproportionate growth in the low-paying food-and-drink subsector of retailing, the increased employment of youth and women, and increases in part-time employment, all of which have characterized retailing as a whole more than any other industrial sector.

Central City–Suburb Comparisons of Industry Earnings

The analysis presented in Table 3.9 is based on industry indexes of average earnings per worker in 1987 for the fourteen central cities and suburbs. For both cities and suburbs, indexes have been computed in the form of ratios of the average earnings per worker in the given industry to average per worker earnings for the *city's total work force*. Accordingly, the index for a given industry in the suburb can be compared directly with the index of the same industry in the central city to determine whether earnings levels are higher or lower.

Table 3.8   Indexes of Average Earnings for U.S. Industry Groups, 1969, 1987

	1969–1979	1979–1987
Construction	8	10
Manufacturing	1	0
TCU	5	2
Wholesale	13	8
Retail	12	7
FIRE	14	13
Other services	14	14
Federal government	0	3
State, local government	5	0

Note: Other services include business-related services (SICs 73, 81, 89); repair services (SICs 75, 76); social services (SICs 80, 82, 84, 86); consumer services (SICs 70, 72, 78, 79).

Source: Data supplied by the Bureau of Economic Analysis.

TABLE 3.9   Comparison of Indexes of City and Suburban Worker Earnings Levels, by Industry Group, Fourteen Metropolitan Areas, 1987

	Average Indexes[a]		Tally[b]		
	City	Suburbs	C > S	=	S > C
Construction	1.21	1.05	12	—	2
Manufacturing	1.29	1.21	8	—	6
TCU[c]	1.37	1.16	12	—	—
Wholesale trade	1.24	1.14	12	—	2
Retail trade	0.55	0.49	11	2	1
FIRE	1.01	0.59	14	—	—
Other services	0.90	0.74	13	—	1
Federal, civilian govt.	1.16	1.04	11	—	3
State, local govt.	0.95	0.85	12	1	1
Total	1.00	0.83	14	—	—

[a] Averages of indexes are modified: Lowest and highest values are excluded.
[b] Where differences are +/− .01, city and suburb scored as equal.
[c] TCU data not available for two suburbs.

Note: In each city or suburb, indexes were computed in the form of ratios of the average earnings per worker in each industry to average per worker earnings for the *city's total work force*. Other services include business-related services (SICs 73, 81, 89); repair services (SICs 75, 76); social services (SICs 80, 82, 84, 86); consumer services (SICs 70, 72, 78, 79).

Source: Data supplied by the Bureau of Economic Analysis.

Average earnings per worker for all industries combined are higher for central cities than for their suburbs in all comparisons (Table 3.9). This does not mean, however, that suburban earnings are low in all industries. In manufacturing, suburban average per worker earnings are higher than comparable earnings in the city in six of the fourteen metropolitan areas. Moreover, earnings in construction, TCU, and wholesaling are well above overall city average earnings levels (though typically below city levels for these industries) in a number of suburbs. Among the remaining industry categories, retailing, FIRE, and state-local government, suburban earnings are for the most part relatively low.

Why Average Earnings in Central Cities Are Higher Than in Suburbs

That city earnings levels are typically higher than suburban levels is hardly surprising because the cost of living is higher in the city, reflecting higher rents, costs inherent in congestion, greater need for public services, and so on. Workers must earn more to live in the city and commuters must earn more to justify the time and costs of traveling daily into and out of the city.

But there are other possible reasons that aggregate and specific industry-level earnings are higher in the central city. One is that the city's economy may be more specialized in the sense of producing an array of more highly value-added goods and services (principally the latter) and in the process must make use of relatively more workers from the higher-paying occupational ranks (i.e., managers, professionals, and technicians). Another is that work arrangements and the labor force drawn upon by the suburban employer may make for lower average earnings. To the extent that the suburban firm makes greater use of part-time labor, average earnings per worker will, ceteris paribus, be lower, as will be the case if the firm is able to draw more readily upon (and use productively) youth or women, who typically command lower wage rates than adult males.

One indication that the differences between central city and suburban earnings are not simply a reflection of cost-of-living differences is to be found in the ratios of central city to suburban earnings computed for individual industries. If the cost of living were the only factor at work, the relationships between central city and suburban earnings and, accordingly, their ratios would be more or less the same among industries. That this is far from the case is evident from inspection of the average indexes of city and suburban earnings in each industry (Table 3.9). The difference in the indexes is particularly large for FIRE. Apparently, the marked difference in city and suburban earnings of this industry reflects a significant difference in mix of activities between suburbs and cities, with suburban firms engaged principally in routine operations associated with serving residents or with back-office activities, whereas central city operations include a heavier mix of high value-added functions.

Evidence of Upgrading in the City and Suburban Economies

In order to shed light on trends in central city earnings levels relative to suburban levels, ratios of average earnings of both central cities and suburbs to the national average in 1969 and 1987 were computed. Among the cities, a majority showed increases in ratios (all industries), whereas among the suburbs, a minority showed increases (Table 3.10).

In most central cities and suburbs, average earnings in manufacturing and wholesaling have risen relative to the U.S. average earnings in these industry groups, suggesting that in the face of sharper competition, firms in these larger metropolitan areas have tended to become engaged in more highly value-added and specialized activities. In TCU and FIRE, most central cities have been upgrading, whereas most suburbs have not (FIRE earnings declined relative to the nation in eleven of the fourteen suburbs). The evidence is less clear in the heterogeneous other services group, although ratios have risen in more cities than suburbs.

These findings must be interpreted in light of two reservations. The first is that in three metropolitan areas the ratios may have been affected by significant increases in the cost of living arising out of rapid growth. In Atlanta, Dallas, and Washington, there were increases in virtually every industry category in *both* central city and suburb, indicating that increases in earnings were strongly influenced by general increases in wage levels as well as by changes at the industry level. The second is that skill transformation need not always be reflected in higher earnings. Greater specialization and higher productivity may in some instances be brought about by rearrangement of work, redefinition of tasks (and retraining), and application of newer technology, without commensurate increases in wages and salaries.

Nevertheless, there is clear evidence here that large central cities have shown a greater tendency toward upgrading relative to the nation than have their suburbs.

The Distribution of City Earnings:
Evidence from the "Journey to Work" Data

The importance of commuters to the city must be seen in terms of the wages and salaries they receive as well as their numbers. The earnings of these workers were relatively high compared with those of residents working in the city in 1980. For example, in New York, they were almost double the wages of resident city workers; in Chicago, 52 percent higher; in Philadelphia, 69 percent higher; and in Boston, 65 percent higher (Table 3.11). In only two of the fourteen cities were in-commuter wages less than 20 percent higher then the average of those residents who worked in the city.

In Table 3.12 average indexes of per worker earnings in 1987 (from Table 3.9) are compared to average nonresident worker shares of city work force employment according to the 1980 Census of Population. We ob-

Table 3.10 Number of Cities and Suburbs in Which Ratios of Average Earnings to U.S. Average Earnings Increased (+), Decreased (−), or Showed No Change (NC), 1969–1987

	Central City			Suburbs		
	+	NC	−	+	NC	−
Construction	10	1	3	8	1	5
Manufacturing	10	2	2	11	2	1
TCU[a]	11	0	3	4	0	8
Wholesale	11	2	1	10	1	3
Retail	7	2	5	6	0	8
FIRE	13	0	1	3	0	11
Other services	8	0	6	5	2	7
Federal government	6	2	6	6	3	5
State, local government	4	3	7	10	1	3
Total	9	2	3	4	3	7

[a] Data not available for TCU in two suburbs.

Note: Other services include business-related services (SICs 73, 81, 89); repair services (SICs 75, 76); social services (SICs 80, 82, 84, 86); consumer services (SICs 70, 72, 78, 79).

Source: Data supplied by the Bureau of Economic Analysis.

TABLE 3.11 Average Earnings of In-Commuters as a Percentage of Average Earnings of Residents Working in Central City, 1980

Central City	Percentage
New York	190
Chicago	152
Philadelphia	169
Los Angeles	147
Atlanta	120
Boston	165
Cincinnati	115
Columbus	126
Dallas	126
Detroit	150
Minneapolis	115
Pittsburgh	126
St. Louis	167
Washington	142

Source: Data supplied by the Bureau of Economic Analysis.

TABLE 3.12 Comparison of Average per Worker Earnings (1987) and Average Nonresident Share of Employment (1979), Fourteen Central Cities

	Average Indexes of Earnings	Average Nonresident Share % of Work Force
Construction	1.21	40.9
Manufacturing	1.29	
TCU	1.37	
Wholesale trade	1.24	27.3[a]
Retail trade	0.55	
FIRE	1.01	
Other services	0.90	
Federal, civilian government	1.16	
State, local government	0.95	
Total	1.00	

[a] Average nonresident share for "trade," which combines retail trade and wholesale trade.

Note: For explanation of average indexes of earnings and data source see Table 3.9.

Source: Averages of nonresident share of city work force employment are based on Census of Population data supplied by Bureau of Economic Analysis.

serve a strong relationship between average per worker earnings and percentage of the city work force accounted for by nonresidents: Nonresident shares of employment are largest in construction, manufacturing, TCU, and federal government, where earnings are highest, and lowest in trade (a combination of retailing and wholesaling in which retailing dominates), state-local government (predominantly local government), and other services, where earnings are lowest (FIRE stands in an intermediate position). Clearly, nonresidents (commuters) are employed in greater numbers where occupational requirements are highest on average, wages and salaries are highest, and the city's unskilled and poorly educated are least able to qualify.

Implications of the Earnings Analysis

These findings add considerably to our picture of the kinds of transformations that are taking place in central cities. As cities have become more narrowly focused in terms of specialization, they have tended to upgrade in terms of average earnings paid, indicating employment of higher proportions of skilled and better-educated workers. Such upgrading has been made possible through increased employment of workers drawn from outside the central city who are, on average, disproportionately well paid relative to resident city workers.

However, as the more rapidly growing suburbs have matured and broadened their economies, different patterns of earnings have emerged. Although earnings levels in a number of suburbs have been upgraded relative to the nation in manufacturing, wholesaling, and state-local government, the suburbs have tended to specialize in low-paying back-office or residentiary financial activities. In the larger, heterogeneous other services category, which has gained everywhere in employment terms, there is evidence that certain of the business services have flourished with earnings levels not greatly below those that obtain in the central city. Social services, consumer services, and retailing have grown apace, but city-suburban earnings differentials remain large in most metropolitan areas.

Agglomeration Economies

Agglomeration Economies and Central City Development

As the U.S. economy has moved rapidly from a goods-oriented to a services-oriented economy, a variety of producer services—finance, wholesaling, insurance, consulting, advertising, engineering, and the like—have risen sharply in importance. The focal point of these activities is the metropolitan economy and within the metropolitan economy the central city itself. It is here that agglomeration economies have played their greatest role and communication and access among firms are maximized.

The changing economic role of large central cities has been accompanied by dramatic physical transformations that have made possible new economies of agglomeration. In describing these transformations in the typical large city of today, Bernard J. Frieden observes major growth and change in five areas:[6]

1. New office complexes. Since 1960, the thirty largest cities have added as much downtown office space as they had accumulated in all the preceding years.
2. New hotels. From 1960 through the early 1980s, the thirty-eight largest metropolitan areas added more than 300 downtown hotels with 110,000 rooms. "In addition to providing lodgings for visitors, many of the new hotels built flashy atriums and dazzling public spaces that enhanced the glitter of downtown."
3. Downtown shopping malls. More than 100 downtown shopping malls have opened since 1970, most of them "distinctly urban" specialty centers (such as Fanueil Hall Market in Boston) or large mixed-use centers (e.g., Walter Tower Place in Chicago).
4. Convention centers. More than 100 cities have built convention centers in the past twenty years. These centers have added significantly to the cities' economic bases, generating many billions annually in local spending.
5. Gentrification. Since the 1970s, there has been a significant increase in interest in city living among young professionals. This so-called

gentrification has brought with it both a restoration of run-down historic neighborhoods and a new demand for upper-income condominiums and cooperatives, which has encouraged expansion of cultural and recreational facilities.

Not mentioned but clearly of major importance has been the increase in highways, intraurban transportation systems, and airport facilities. Even today, forty years after the initiation of the interstate highway system, a number of cities continue to improve access through additions or expansions to major arteries. A number of places, including Atlanta, San Francisco, and Washington, D.C., have put in place or expanded rail systems linking the center city with outlying areas, including in some instances suburban destinations, and most large metropolitan areas have built or expanded airport facilities. All these changes and others have served to increase the attractiveness of the city as a place in which to do business, through improving and expanding the physical infrastructure, enriching amenities, and extending access.

Agglomeration Economies and Suburban Development

Agglomeration economies have long been recognized as important to the central city but their importance is less readily recognized in the case of suburbs. Yet there is considerable evidence that economic growth in the suburbs is increasingly focussed on a restricted number of magnet areas in which locational advantages associated with agglomeration play a key role.

Truman Hartshorn, Peter Muller, and Robert Cervero have called attention to the growing importance of large business and residential agglomerations within the suburbs of a number of major metropolitan areas.[7]

The Hartshorn-Muller and Cervero studies make clear that these large agglomerations have attracted a variety of retailers, business service firms, and corporate offices. The studies also demonstrate that the attractiveness of these centers rests on close linkages to the suburban highway network, which makes it possible to draw upon a large pool of suburban and, to some extent, city workers while offering ready access to the rich suburban market and a variety of business customers.

For firms locating in these "suburban downtown" areas there are important urbanization economies: Each firm profits by the presence of the other. Corporate offices can more readily receive visiting executives, salespeople, and customers because of attractive hotel and restaurant facilities; retail customers gain opportunities to shop a variety of stores; individual stores, in turn, gain from the heavier traffic that large retail agglomerations make possible; and workers of all types are provided opportunities to shop during lunch and after work or to lunch with friends away from the company dining hall. If firms are able to operate at lower costs because of lower rents, taxes, land costs, or wage rates, then the advantages of the suburban locations are, accordingly, increased.

Evidence of Suburban Agglomeration

The analysis that follows seeks to identify major suburban economic agglomerations and to shed light on which among the business and financial services have tended to locate within these suburban centers.

Because only county data are available, much detail is lost. The suburban centers of the Hartshorn-Muller and the Cervero studies cannot be pinpointed. Where they have developed within the central city county but outside the city itself no evidence can be garnered. Yet it is possible to identify those suburban counties that have been most affected.

Two types of evidence are examined. The first is the ratio of employment to population (Table 3.13). Here we look for high ratios indicating substantial agglomeration. We can also look for significant increases in the ratio, especially since 1979, indicating those counties where there have been large employment increases relative to population gains.

We also look at the residence adjustment expressed as a percentage of total earnings of the county's work force (Table 3.13). In evaluating changes in this percentage over time, it is important to keep in mind that the residence adjustment is calculated by subtracting in-commuter earnings from out-commuter earnings. A drop in the residence adjustment percentage indicates that *net* out-commuter earnings have declined relative to all wages and salaries earned in the county workplace, or where the sign has switched from positive to negative, that net out-commuter earnings have given way to net in-commuter earnings. It should be noted, however, that the *value* of the residence adjustment (i.e., net in-commuter earnings) could increase in dollar terms and yet decline as a percentage of work force earnings (if the latter are increasing more rapidly).

Among the counties that were selected as possible (candidate) key or "magnet" counties (Table 3.13), there is considerable variation in the measures. Yet in all there is a significant rise in the employment-to-population ratio between 1979 and 1987 and in all but one, Westchester County, a decline in the relative importance of out-commuter earnings (although in most cases the residence adjustment remained positive in 1987, indicating that, at least in terms of earnings, virtually all counties had some net out-migration, presumably to the central city).

In certain counties, the residence adjustment measures have fallen precipitously. For example, in the Atlanta suburbs the residence adjustment

Table 3.13 Employment/Population Ratios (E/Ps) and Residence Adjustment Percentages, Candidate Magnet Counties and Other Counties, 1969, 1979, 1987

	E/P			Residence Adjustment		
	1969	1979	1987	1969	1979	1987
New York						
Westchester	.42	.49	.59	35	26	28
Nassau	.38	.49	.60	43	35	25
Bergen	.41	.54	.67	31	16	11
Other[a]		.22–.38	.30–.47	57–139	53–198	40–193
Chicago						
Du Page	.31	.44	.58	100	63	29
Other[a]		.33–.49	.32–.49	19–47	22–68	32–81
Philadelphia						
Montgomery	.51	.62	.73	8	0.1	−5
Camden		.42	.50	26	18	12
Other[a]		.34–.47	.38–.53	27–66	32–51	27–54
Boston						
Middlesex	.45	.50	.70	7	0.6	−7
Norfolk	.37	.48	.61	46	25	18
Other[a]		.35–.46	.45–.51	22–68	21–62	25–59
Atlanta						
De Kalb	.35	.48	.64	55	21	2
Cobb	.40	.38	.55	12	71	36
Clayton	.26	.32	.56	89	44	−3
Other[a]		.19–.43	.22–.50	23–218	26–190	37–205
Cincinnati						
Boone	.32	.57	.66	53	7	−3
Other[a]		.23–.38	.29–.39	12–207	34–131	54–114
Columbus						
Union	.45	.43	.55	13	17	−22
Other[a]		.31–.42	.32–.42	4–55	17–70	24–78
Dallas						
All suburb counties[a]		.26–.43	.33–.37	40–112	37–171	60–161
Detroit						
Oakland	.37	.51	.62	35	20	10
Other[a]		.25–.40	.28–.45	16–118	24–159	17–138
Minneapolis						
Ramsey	.58	.68	.72	−21	−20	−22
Other[a]		.32–.42	.37–.44	44–107	49–95	70–84
Pittsburgh						
All suburb counties[a]		.28–.38	.27–.38	19–77	17–39	21–39
St. Louis						
St. Louis	.39	.55	.66	38	18	−4
Other[a]		.26–.42	.26–.44	6–152	9–182	20–166
Washington						
Arlington	.80	.96	1.28	−29	−39	−46
Montgomery	.43	.58	.67	44	23	14
Alexandria city[b]	.53	.79	1.05	23	−0.8	−16
Fairfax	.30	.45	.54	86	55	32
Other[a]		.18–.42	.22–.49	24–211	48–229	26–249

[a] Range.
[b] Independent City.

Note: E/Ps here are ratios of county employment (place of work) to county population. They differ from the E/Ps based on employment of residents. Resident adjustment percentages are calculated relative to total county earnings at place of work. See Table 2.2 for explanation.

Source: Data supplied by the Bureau of Economic Analysis.

percentage of workplace earnings for De Kalb was 55 in 1969, 21 in 1979, and 2 in 1987; in Cobb County, after rising from 12 percent in 1969 to 71 percent in 1979 (indicating increased commuting into Atlanta), it fell to 36 percent in 1987; and in Clayton County the measure fell from 89 percent in 1969 to 44 percent in 1979 and to −3 percent in 1987. In contrast, the residence adjustment percentage rose from 1969 to 1987 in most of the remaining counties in the Atlanta suburbs, and in all counties it stood at a higher level than in De Kalb, Cobb, or Clayton counties in the final year of 1987. Moreover, whereas in 1987 employment-to-population ratios in these three magnet counties stood at .64, .55, and .56 respectively, in the remaining counties they ranged from .22 to .50.

It is interesting that a number of the counties shown in Table 3.13 are sites of suburban counties studied by Hartshorn and Muller or by Cervero. Montgomery and Camden counties in the Philadelphia suburbs and De Kalb and Cobb counties in the Atlanta suburbs are the locations of the King of Prussia, "Silicon Gulch," and Cherry Hill complexes and the Atlanta "suburban downtowns" described by Hartshorn and Muller. Seven of the counties are sites of suburban centers studied by Cervero: Middlesex (Boston): New England Executive Parks and Route 128 corridor; Ramsey (Minneapolis): 3M Parks; Nassau (New York): East Garden City and East Farmingdale; Du Page (Chicago): Naperville/I-88 Tollway; De Kalb (Atlanta): Perimeter Center and North Lake; Montgomery (Washington, D.C.): Rocksprings Park; Fairfax (Washington, D.C.): Tysons Corner.

Because the suburban counties shown in Table 3.13 stand out fairly clearly as areas of significant economic development, it is important to examine the relative size of these counties to assess the full significance of such development. Table 3.14 indicates the 1987 nonfarm employment in each of these counties alongside employment in the central city or central city county, with suburban county employment also shown as a percentage of central county employment.

We observe that employment in most of these rapidly developing counties is relatively large. In St. Louis County, employment is more than twice that of the central city; in Middlesex County it is 47 percent larger. In Montgomery (Pennsylvania), Montgomery (Maryland), Norfolk (Massachusetts), De Kalb and Fairfax (Virginia), and De Kalb (Georgia), employment is more than half that of the central city, and in five of the remaining counties more than one-fifth.

There are, however, two among the identified candidate counties that are quite small: Boone, in the suburbs of Cincinnati, and Union, in the Columbus suburbs. Moreover, there are two metropolitan areas, Dallas and Pittsburgh, in which no counties stood out. In the case of Dallas, rapid suburban economic development does not appear to have as yet extended

Table 3.14 Employment in Central City Counties and Candidate Magnet Counties, 1987

	Employment	Percentage of Central City County
New York (Manhattan)	2,679,977	100.0
Westchester	507,162	18.9
Nassau	784,494	29.3
Bergen	558,580	20.8
Chicago	1,330,029	100.0
Du Page	430,318	32.4
Philadelphia	869,654	100.0
Montgomery	492,299	56.6
Camden	245,482	28.2
Atlanta	685,290	100.0
De Kalb	346,638	50.6
Cobb	224,083	32.7
Clayton	94,144	13.7
Boston	656,311	100.0
Middlesex	962,718	146.7
Norfolk	373,374	56.9
Cincinnati	595,293	100.0
Boone	34,558	5.8
Columbus	625,175	100.0
Union	15,993	2.6
Detroit	1,021,050	100.0
Oakland	648,638	63.5
Minneapolis	856,530	100.0
Ramsey	341,464	39.9
St. Louis	330,240	100.0
St. Louis	662,852	200.7
Washington	740,671	100.0
Arlington	204,175	27.6
Montgomery	460,593	62.2
Alexandria	112,915	15.2
Fairfax	474,983	64.1

Note: Manhattan (New York County) is used here as the city county instead of the five boroughs combined. City of Chicago employment (estimated) is used here instead of Cook County employment. Chicago nonfarm business employment based on a special tabulation provided by BEA; government employment estimated by the author. All other "city" employment is central city county employment, BEA estimates.

Source: Data supplied by the Bureau of Economic Analysis.

to the suburban counties, although this is not to say that within the Dallas County suburbs no such development has occurred. We note that in all suburban counties in the Dallas metropolitan area, employment-to-population ratios are low (.37 or below) and the residence adjustment percentages quite high (60 to 161), indicating heavy commuting into Dallas County. In the case of Pittsburgh, we observe once again that employment-to-population ratios are low in all suburban counties, but residence adjustment percentages are also relatively low. Additional analysis is needed here, but the measures imply that the suburban counties in the Pittsburgh metropolitan area are characterized by relatively high unemployment and relatively low commutation and labor force participation rates.

Comparison of Central City and Magnet Suburban County Distributions of Employment and Levels of Earnings

Although the candidate magnet counties identified in Table 3.13 differ significantly in terms of industrial composition, they have to a great extent shared a common pattern of development. In virtually every county, the basic export sector in 1969 (manufacturing in all counties except the Washington, D.C., suburban counties, where government was the leading industrial category) declined sharply in importance, whereas other services and FIRE increased. In roughly half of the counties, there was an increase in the relative importance of wholesaling and TCU, although in the remaining counties there was little change, with some decreases noted.

Table 3.15 compares central city and the candidate magnet suburban county shares of employment in manufacturing, TCU, wholesaling, retailing, FIRE, other services, and government in 1987. The principal observation is that in manufacturing, wholesaling, and retailing, shares are larger in these suburban counties than in cities in a majority of comparisons. Moreover, shares of other services are quite large, in excess of 25 percent, in all but three counties.

Three counties appear to be unlikely candidates for classification as magnet counties, however, and are not examined further. The first two are the very small counties of Union and Boone in the Columbus and Cincinnati metropolitan areas. Union is heavily specialized in manufacturing and Boone in retailing. The third is Clayton County, site of the Atlanta metropolitan airport, one of the busiest in the nation. In addition to airport facilities and airport-related activities, it is also a retailing center, but its other services sector is relatively underdeveloped.

A critical issue in examining the industrial composition of the remaining counties—those that appear to qualify as magnet counties—is the extent to which business and financial services have located there and

Table 3.15 Shares (%) of City or Suburban County Employment by Industry, Central Cities, and Candidate Magnet Counties, 1987

	Manufacturing	TCU	Wholesale	Retail	FIRE	Other Services	Government
New York	9.6	5.9	6.3	11.0	14.7	34.5	14.4
Westchester	13.2*	4.8	6.3	15.4*	8.2	33.3	10.8
Nassau	10.8*	4.2	7.9*	17.4*	9.6	34.0	10.2
Bergen	18.0*	4.5	12.3*	16.1*	7.2	27.7	8.1
Chicago	17.4	6.7	5.7	13.2	12.4	29.4	11.8
Du Page	12.5	6.1	7.8*	18.2*	8.0	32.4*	8.0
Philadelphia	11.2	5.4	5.3	13.6	9.5	33.8	18.5
Montgomery	18.8*	3.3	5.7*	16.3*	10.1*	30.9	6.5
Camden	14.6*	4.3	7.7*	18.0*	7.6	28.4	13.1
Atlanta	8.6	9.4	9.7	13.8	10.4	29.6	13.8
De Kalb	9.5*	5.8	9.6	17.8*	10.1	28.4	11.7
Cobb	13.8*	4.1	9.5	18.9*	8.9	22.3	12.0
Clayton	6.7	21.1*	5.9	24.1*	4.1	14.6	15.5*
Boston	6.1	5.7	4.2	10.6	14.6	39.4	16.3
Middlesex	20.7*	3.1	6.2*	15.0*	5.5	34.3	9.5
Norfolk	13.7*	4.0	7.6*	17.9*	10.2	30.2	9.2
Cincinnati	20.3	4.9	6.7	16.3	8.0	28.3	10.4
Boone	20.1	13.3*	4.5	22.6*	4.0	21.3	8.5
Columbus	11.0	4.3	5.3	19.3	11.3	27.4	15.7
Union	48.4*	3.0	2.6	11.6	3.2	14.0	11.9
Detroit	22.7	5.8	5.3	15.9	6.8	26.8	13.4
Oakland	17.8	3.1	6.8*	21.5*	9.4*	35.7*	7.6
Minneapolis	15.0	5.7	7.7	16.4	10.3	29.2	11.0
Ramsey	23.4*	4.0	3.8	15.6*	7.8	27.1	13.9*
St. Louis	16.1	7.9	6.5	12.0	8.7	29.1	16.3
St. Louis	17.5*	5.2	6.1	18.2*	8.4	30.1*	8.0
Washington	2.3	3.6	1.2	7.9	6.4	36.8	39.0
Arlington	1.8	10.5*	3.5*	7.9	6.0	32.4	35.1
Montgomery	3.7*	2.4	3.9*	17.5*	9.5*	37.6*	17.2
Alexandria city	2.6*	5.7*	3.7*	16.5*	9.1*	33.9	11.5
Fairfax	4.1	4.5	4.3*	16.9*	10.3*	33.9	16.9

*In these cases, magnet county share exceeds central city share. Because primary industries are not shown, percentages do not add to 100.

Source: Data supplied by the Bureau of Economic Analysis.

whether, under conditions of relatively rapid employment growth in the suburbs, employment in these services threatens the economic vitality of the central city, where, traditionally, such economic activity has been centered.

Table 3.16 disaggregates employment within the large other-services category to reveal the relative size of the business services segment along with that of three other categories, consumer services, social services, and repair services. The business-related services are further broken down into three standard industry classification (SIC) subgroups: SIC 73 (which includes a large variety of business services, principally advertising, credit reporting and collection, services to buildings, temporary-help agencies, computer and data processing services, and research and development); SIC 89 (principally engineering and architectural services and accounting, auditing, and bookkeeping); and SIC 81 (legal services).

We observe that business-related services (combined) play a substantial role in these counties. In Du Page, Montgomery (Pennsylvania), Camden, Middlesex, Oakland, and St. Louis counties, and in the four Washington suburban counties shown, the business-related services account for larger shares of total employment than in the central cities.

Within the business-related group (Table 3.16), the share of employment in legal services (SIC 81) is much larger in the central city than in the magnet counties in most metropolitan areas although this is not the case for either SIC 73 or SIC 89. In each of these latter classifications, central city share is smaller than one or more magnet suburban counties in a majority of the nine metropolitan areas.

Finally, comparison was made between average earnings per worker in the seventeen magnet counties and their central cities for each of the major categories within other services and for FIRE (Table 3.17). County earnings were typically lower than central city earnings except in SIC 73, where average earnings exceeded central city levels in eleven of the seventeen counties and in SIC 89, where average earnings exceeded city levels in seven. In consumer services, legal services, social services, and FIRE, the number of counties in which average earnings exceeded central city levels was quite small.

Closer examination of the measures indicates considerable variation in business service relative earnings levels among magnet counties, both within and among metropolitan areas, suggesting different patterns of city-suburban specialization among the various metropolitan areas. For example, in the three New York suburban counties, average earnings in SIC 73 were well below Manhattan levels, although in two counties SIC 89 earnings were above; in Du Page (Chicago suburb), the opposite was the case.

Table 3.16 Shares (%) of City or Suburban Employment in Other Services and Its Component Industry Groups, Central Cities and Magnet Counties, 1986

		Business-related						Total Other
	Consumer	SIC73	SIC89	SIC81	Total	Repair	Social	Services
New York (Manhattan)	4.0	11.2	2.8	2.7	16.7	0.5	11.6	33.2
Westchester	4.1*	7.2	1.5	0.7	9.3	1.3*	17.8*	32.7
Nassau	4.1*	9.3	2.5	1.2	13.1	1.3*	14.4*	33.4*
Bergen	3.8	8.3	2.2	0.7	11.2	1.5*	9.9	26.8
Chicago	3.4	8.6	2.4	2.3	13.2	1.1	15.0	33.3
Du Page	4.6*	13.0*	1.9	0.4	15.3*	1.9*	13.0	35.8*
Philadelphia	2.4	4.8	2.1	2.0	8.9	0.9	20.8	33.2
Montgomery	3.2*	8.4*	2.3*	0.4	11.1*	1.3*	14.2	30.1
Camden	3.3*	5.5	2.9*	1.3	9.7*	0.8	12.8	28.3
Atlanta	4.8	9.8	2.1	1.3	13.2	1.2	8.9	28.8
De Kalb	3.4	8.0	2.4*	0.5	10.9	1.2	10.9*	27.2
Cobb	4.9*	6.2	2.3*	0.5	9.0	1.1	6.8	22.0
Boston	3.2	7.3	3.5	2.4	13.2	1.0	21.4	39.1
Middlesex	2.2	10.0*	3.0	0.3	13.4*	0.9	15.4	33.6
Norfolk	3.0	7.3	2.6	0.5	10.4	1.3*	14.6	29.9
Detroit	2.8	5.0	1.2	0.8	7.0	1.5	14.6	26.0
Oakland	3.4*	11.0*	3.0*	1.1*	15.1*	1.2	12.1	32.2*
Minneapolis	4.0	8.2	1.9	1.1	11.2	1.1	11.8	28.8
Ramsey	2.7	5.6	1.4	0.8	7.8	1.0	14.7*	26.4
St. Louis	2.8	4.9	1.5	0.8	7.2	0.9	16.3	27.6
St. Louis	2.2	7.2*	2.2*	0.9*	10.2*	1.6*	15.1	29.9*
Washington	2.9	6.9	1.8	3.4	12.2	0.5	20.0	36.0
Arlington	4.6*	12.3*	4.9*	0.5	17.8*	1.1*	7.5	31.3
Montgomery	3.8*	15.3*	3.2*	0.7	19.3*	1.1*	11.9	37.3*
Alexandria	3.5*	10.4*	3.6*	0.9	14.9*	1.5*	11.8	32.6
Fairfax	3.7*	13.7*	5.7*	0.4	19.8*	0.9*	7.5	32.4

*In these cases, magnet county share exceeds central city share. Because primary industries are not shown, percentages do not add to 100.

Note: Cincinnati, Columbus, and Pittsburgh are not shown because the candidate magnet county was small or not identified. Percentages of component industries may not add to other services because administrative and auxiliary employment is not included. For definition of Chicago city see note, Table 3.14. For definitions of SICs 73, 89, and 81, see text.

Source: Estimated from U.S. Bureau of the Census, County Business Patterns, 1986 (Washington, DC: GPO, 1987).

In general, the earnings evidence complements the evidence gleaned from the employment data. Central cities demonstrate a strong comparative advantage in most FIRE activities and in legal services: Employment in these activities is relatively larger and earnings higher. It is here that the special agglomeration economies of the central business district are most pronounced, although a few types of FIRE activities, such as credit agencies and insurance carriers, may operate successfully as a part of the export base of the suburban economy. Moreover, the relatively low earnings levels in FIRE in the suburban counties indicate the predominance of routine consumer banking and real estate services and suggest the presence of back-office activities, whereas lower earnings levels in legal services indicate that law firms are relatively unspecialized with relatively few highly paid personnel.

Among the business services, these well-developed suburban counties are often quite successful in attracting firms that pay, on average, wages and salaries much closer to central city levels than is true for most other industrial classifications. In some activities, such as data processing and research and development, firms find highly favorable conditions for locating. Professional-type business-related services also often do well in these counties, although the data (not shown in Table 3.17) suggest that engineering and architectural firms are more frequently found in the suburbs than are accounting and auditing firms.

The relatively low suburban earnings levels in consumer services shown in Table 3.17 reflect to a considerable extent a difference in mix between central city and county, the central city typically showing relatively more employment in hotels and amusements, the suburbs showing relatively more employment in personal services.

Earnings in the social services are for the most part higher in the central city, but the differences are typically not great. It is interesting that the city-suburban differentials shown for social services in Table 3.17 are, almost without exception, roughly the same as for health services (not shown), the largest category within the social services group. Apparently, the differentials noted for earnings in the social services reflect some combination of (1) the degree of specialization in the services (e.g., central city hospitals are likely to be larger—although there are also large complexes in many of the leading suburban counties) and (2) differences in central city and suburban wage levels.

These findings in no way contradict the earlier finding that suburban economies are on the whole heavily oriented toward residentiary activities and that a larger number of lower-wage jobs are available there. The importance of development of magnet centers is that they increasingly offer competition to the central city economies and that central cities are likely to find the best projects for strength and vitality through increasing

Table 3.17 Average Earnings in Magnet Counties as a Percentage of Average Comparable Earnings in Central City County by Other Services Categories and FIRE, 1986

	Consumer	Business-Related			Repair	Social	FIRE
		SIC73	SIC89	SIC81			
New York (Manhattan)							
Westchester	55.4	69.5	82.6	77.3	93.7	82.6	43.5
Nassau	54.0	64.2	103.6	82.2	97.1	88.6	43.0
Bergen	57.8	75.5	102.3	61.6	98.5	88.6	46.5
Chicago							
Du Page	72.4	115.3	81.2	60.1	110.7	90.9	73.9
Philadelphia							
Montgomery	65.3	102.8	87.0	103.1	NA	86.4	76.7
Camden	69.9	123.2	104.7	98.1	NA	88.1	76.0
Atlanta							
De Kalb	83.2	101.7	100.1	78.8	93.8	96.4	71.0
Cobb	90.6	95.0	105.0	76.2	88.9	94.2	73.6
Boston							
Middlesex	74.0	122.8	85.6	66.0	133.7	89.8	62.9
Norfolk	100.4	96.9	79.1	64.2	120.2	95.7	56.2
Detroit							
Oakland	NA	131.9	111.8	111.3	103.2	107.6	95.2
Minneapolis							
Ramsey	74.5	79.8	102.6	87.6	98.5	93.3	86.6
St. Louis							
St. Louis	58.1	117.0	77.4	81.0	105.0	105.4	87.9
Washington							
Arlington	76.9	112.2	77.6	100.0	125.6	99.4	68.8
Montgomery	71.7	108.5	68.3	91.7	136.0	89.0	86.6
Alexandria	78.3	102.7	63.3	82.4	119.7	104.0	87.1
Fairfax	78.7	115.0	66.8	100.6	152.3	76.1	91.1
Modified average[a]	71.9	102.5	88.3	83.4	110.0	92.8	72.6

[a] In computing modified averages, lowest and highest values are dropped.

Note: For definitions of SICs 73, 89, and 81, see text.

Source: Estimated from U.S. Bureau of the Census, *County Business Patterns, 1986* (Washington, DC: GPO, 1987).

their specialization in the kinds of high value-added service activities for which their agglomeration economies are best suited.

Conclusions

In narrowing the focus of specialization and upgrading those sectors in which they enjoy the greatest comparative advantage, the central cities offer fewer employment opportunities for the poorly educated, especially disadvantaged blacks, and consequently create a growing gap between the more successful and the less successful jobholders resident in the city. A major concern must be the plight of poorly educated, minority youth, most of whom are not in the job market and who have little prospect of gaining entrance into any of the more demanding business service jobs that have come to constitute the expanding sector of the city's economy.

These urban youth cannot readily access the available unskilled jobs in the suburbs because of lack of private or public transportation. There is little prospect of the suburbs providing a significant increase in affordable housing for low-income persons. Hence it is essential for the city's future as well as for the future of these youth that efforts to improve their programs for training and educational preparation be redoubled. The jobs in the central business districts (CBDs) and, to a considerable extent, in the magnet centers as well increasingly require young people who have acquired a high school diploma, preferably a community college degree. High school dropouts and the functionally illiterate cannot handle these jobs.

No city can long prosper if it must support growing numbers of residents who are not qualified for the jobs available. In fact such a city will see more and more of its employers desert. The symbiosis between the city and the new suburbs will be permanently upset unless the city—with the help of the federal and state governments—can assure that all of its potential workers are qualified to get and keep jobs.

Appendix: The Data

The analysis is based largely on employment and earnings data for major industry groups published by the BEA, supplemented in several instances by more detailed *County Business Patterns* (CBP) employment data published by the Bureau of the Census.

All data are county data. The central cities of New York, Philadelphia, St. Louis, and Washington, D.C., are coterminous with a county or counties (the five boroughs of New York City are counties), so for these places use of county data poses no difficulty. In the case of the remaining cities— including two major cities, Chicago and Los Angeles—this procedure is open to criticism because the central city county substantially overbounds the municipal limits of the central city. The city of Chicago accounts for but 57 percent of the population of Cook County, and the city of Los Angeles for only 40 percent of Los Angeles County population. Table 3.3 compares municipal population with central city county population.

Yet all of these central cities do, indeed, dominate their counties. Given that employment data at place of work are available only on a county basis, there is no alternative but to use them, recognizing that central city county employment and population may provide only a rough approximation of the central city itself.

With two exceptions, New York and Los Angeles, the suburbs of the metropolitan areas are simply the combined remaining counties of the Primary Metropolitan Statistical Area (PMSA). In the case of the New York suburbs, the counties of Nassau, Suffolk, and Bergen were added to the PMSA. In the case of Los Angeles, there are no remaining counties, as Los Angeles County alone constitutes the PMSA. Here Orange County, which sends a substantial number of commuters into Los Angeles, was used as a surrogate suburban area.

Notes

1. See Table 3.2 for a list and the appendix for a brief discussion of the use of county data to represent employment and earnings in central cities and suburbs.

2. Cf. T. M. Stanback, Jr., and Richard V. Knight, *Suburbanization and the City* (Montclair, N.J.: Allanheld, Osmun & Co., 1976).

3. Alan E. Pisarski, *Commuting in America* (Washington, D.C.: Eno Foundation for Transportation, 1987), p. 34.

4. Ibid.

5. Not shown in Table 3.4.

6. Bernard J. Frieden, "The Downtown Job Puzzle," *The Public Interest* 97 (Fall 1989):71–73.

7. Truman A. Hartshorn and Peter O. Muller, *Suburban Business Centers: Employment Expectations*, Final Report for Department of Commerce, EDA (Washington, D.C.: Department of Commerce, November 1986); Robert Cervero, *America's Suburban Centers: The Land Use–Transportation Link* (Boston: Unwin Hyman, Ltd., 1989).

4

Services and Globalization: New York City

Thierry Noyelle

Since reaching a peak of nearly 3,620,000 jobs in the mid-summer of 1989, New York's employment has declined sharply from its peak, by almost 300,000 jobs by the fall of 1992. Most students of the local economy appear to agree that the local economy is approaching the end of its decline. Whether or not this prediction proves true and how fast New York will recover from its current condition will likely be a function of several factors, including whether the local and/or national economy slips back into recession or faces another period of structural adjustment or whether a new, large-scale wave of business outmigration hits New York, as happened during the 1970s.

This chapter addresses some of these issues and draws out their implications for economic development policy in New York in the 1990s. The first section looks at selected long-term trends that contributed to reshaping New York City during the 1980s, focusing in particular on its role as a national and international headquarters center, on the transformation of Wall Street, and on competition with its suburbs. The second section discusses whether New York's recent slowdown reflected a mostly cyclical downturn or rather a structural crisis brought about by the onset of selected local, national, or international forces. The third and final section draws upon the findings of the previous two sections to address issues of economic development for the remainder of the 1990s, focusing in particular on taxes, business retention, and infrastructure.

Although I do not underestimate the seriousness of the current crisis— after all, 300,000 jobs is a large number of jobs to lose—I do not espouse the most pessimistic views that surfaced in recent months. As this chapter demonstrates, with 260 of the 1,400 largest publicly held industrial companies, publicly held service companies, and privately held companies headquartered in the city and its suburbs, the area retains by far the largest concentration of such companies in the nation. Furthermore, New York's role as the nation's premier financial center remains largely unchallenged. New York does face a perennial business retention problem, however, which typically hurts the city more during recession than expansion. In addition, New York has been hurt more than other cities by the fact that the 1990–1992 period has been a service-led recession. In short, the current recession clearly is impacting the city more strongly than the 1982–1983 recession; however, we are not dealing with a repeat of the 1969–1976 distinctly local, structural, and economic crises.

Long-Term Trends

New York City, during the 1980s, was affected by a number of key developments that contributed in major ways to its restructuring. Many of these forces will continue to shape importantly the city's transformation in the years ahead. Three such developments include the increasing challenge to New York's role as a national and international headquarters center; external challenges to Wall Street's status as a premier national and international financial and capital market center; and the growing competition between New York and its suburbs. Each of these developments is examined here.

New York as a Headquarters Center

One trend that is emphasized repeatedly by those who worry about the decline of New York as a national and international center of business is the steady outmigration of the headquarters of the largest U.S. industrial corporations from the city under way since the early 1960s. Indeed, 128 of the nation's 500 largest public-held industrial corporations were headquartered in New York in 1965 and the number had declined to 41 by 1990. The importance of this trend is underscored by the fact that headquarters are responsible for generating a substantial amount of the demand for specialized advanced business services, a domain in which New York has excelled. But this seemingly straightforward observation partly misses the point, namely that these very large publicly held corporations may not play, in relative terms, quite as large a role as they once did.

First, although the rate of annual relocations has changed little between the 1960–1970 period and the 1980s (respectively, an average of 3.8 net headquarter losses per annum during the period 1965–1975 and an average of 3.4 yearly net headquarter losses during the period 1979–1990), it is important to explore the changes underlying these losses. As shown in Table 4.1, during the earlier period, more than half (38 losses) of the total number of gross losses (66) were due to outmigration of headquarters to

TABLE 4.1 Changes in the Number of Fortune "Industrial 500" Firms Headquartered in New York City and Its Suburbs

	Firms with Headquarters in New York City, 1965–1975	Firms with Headquarters in New York City, 1979–1990	Firms with Headquarters in New York City Suburbs, 1979–1990
Fortune Industrial 500, 1965 / 1979	128	78	54
Losses, 1965–1975 / 1979–1990	−66	−62	−39
Moved to suburbs / Moved to NYC	−25	−5	−3
Moved out of area	−13	−9	−3
Acquired, bankrupt, privatized, merger	−21	−17	−17
No longer Fortune 500	−7	−20	−16
Shifted to Service 500	0	−11	0
Gains, 1965–1975 / 1979–1990	28	25	34
Moved to New York City / Moved to suburbs	6	7	7
Added to list due to size or reclassification	22	18	27
Shifted from Service 500		0	0
Fortune Industrial 500, 1975 / 1990	90	41	49

Sources: Fortune 500 Directories, various issues.

either New York's suburbs (25 relocations) or other metropolitan areas (13 relocations). In contrast, in the most recent period less than one-quarter (5 + 9 = 14) of the gross losses (62) were the result of outmigration. The major reason for the more recent losses was the disappearance of firms as a result of mergers, acquisitions, privatization, or reclassification of firms to the Service 500 list (33 + 15 = 48).

This last observation is important. Indeed, if we no longer focus exclusively on the headquarters of the Fortune Industrial 500 but include also those of the Fortune Service 500 and the Forbes 400 largest privately held companies, we find that the importance of New York as a national headquarters center changed relatively little during the 1980s, partly because New York attracted several large service corporations and large privately held companies (both Beatrice and RJR-Nabisco, two of the largest leveraged buy-outs [LBOs] of the 1980s repatriated their headquarters to New York in the late 1980s) and partly because a number of the disappearing "industrial" companies were simply companies that changed their status. As shown in Table 4.2, there was a total of 150 Fortune Industrial 500, Fortune Service 500, and Forbes Private 400 headquartered in New York City in 1989–1990 as against 164 in 1983–1984, a relatively small decline. Furthermore, if we add those headquartered in the New York suburbs, the total number of such firms headquartered in the metropolitan area remained virtually unchanged during the 1980s: 260 in 1989–1990 as against 265 in 1983–1984. (See Tables 4.3 and 4.4 for further breakdown of the Service 500 and the Forbes 400.) Put another way, the New York metropolitan area retains, by far, the largest concentration of headquarters of large firms in the nation.

The rationale for adding firms headquartered in the suburbs is their reliance on advanced services offered by firms located in New York downtown and midtown areas. This point was demonstrated for the earlier wave of suburban migration of headquarters in the 1977 study by Eli Ginzberg and his colleagues entitled *The Corporate Headquarters Complex in New York City*.[1] There is little evidence that this suburban headquarters reliance on New York has changed much during the 1980s (more on this to follow).

These observations, of course, are not meant to argue that nothing has changed. As was found in the aforementioned study by Ginzberg and his colleagues as well as in a later study by Thierry Noyelle and Thomas Stanback,[2] New York has become less and less attractive as a headquarters city for nationally oriented companies and more and more specialized as host to those companies that are strongly internationally focused. The buildup in the number of large headquarters in second-tier urban centers

TABLE 4.2   Fortune Industrial 500s, Fortune Service 500s, and Forbes Private 400s Headquartered in New York City and Its Suburbs

	1983–1984		1988–1989	
	NYC	Suburbs	NYC	Suburbs
Fortune Industrial 500	64	52	41	49
Fortune Service 500	56	28	60	29
Forbes Private 400	46	19	49	32
Total	164	99	150	110
Total NYC and Suburbs	265		260	

Sources: Fortune and Forbes Lists, various issues.

such as Atlanta, Washington, Minneapolis, Dallas, and a few others has been conducive to the formation of agglomerations of business services (air transportation, accounting, advertising) in those cities that have strengthened their ability to compete with New York as a national business service center. But at the same time New York was adding headquarters of large service and privately held firms during the 1980s, an indication of the city's versatility and capacity to capitalize on new areas of growth, a fact that is often overlooked. Furthermore, the Fortune Service 500 or Forbes Private 400 rankings account only marginally for the buildup of a sizable base of very large specialized business service firms in New York in recent years in such sectors as accounting, advertising, legal services, management consulting, or public relations, with many of these by now multibillion-dollar firms.

Another dimension of New York's versatility during the 1980s was the arrival of many large and smaller foreign companies that found it appropriate to use New York as a beachhead for their entry into the huge North American market. Although it is clear that foreign firms have come to play an increasingly important role in the city's economy, it is also true that we still know far too little about the size and durability of their presence. Nevertheless, a 1990 survey of offices of foreign companies in New York City by the New York Chamber of Commerce and Industry, Inc., recorded over 1,800 companies from sixty-three countries with locations in New York City and the New York area.[3] Clearly we need to know more about the kind of companies that came to New York (except for foreign banks) and the reasons why they chose to locate in New York.

Undoubtedly, a key issue for the 1990s will be to know whether the headquarters of the same foreign or U.S. publicly held service or privately held companies that have been a boon to the city's economy during the 1980s will remain or whether they will increasingly fall under the same forces that led to the decentralization of a substantial number of headquarters of more traditional, large U.S. industrial companies.

TABLE 4.3   Changes in the Number of Fortune "Service 500" Firms Headquartered in New York City and Its Suburbs

Firms with Headquarters in New York City, 1983–1990		Firms with Headquarters in New York City Suburbs, 1983–1990	
Fortune Service 500, 1983	56	Fortune Service 500, 1983	28
Losses, 1983–1990	−32	Losses, 1983–1990	−19
Moved to suburbs	−4	Moved to NYC	−2
Moved out of area	−4	Moved out of area	−1
Acquired, bankrupt, privatized, merger	−12	Acquired, bankrupt, privatized, merger	−10
No longer Fortune 500	−12	No longer Fortune 500	−5
Shifted to Industrial 500	0	Shifted to Industrial 500	−1
Gains, 1983–1990	36	Gains, 1983–1990	20
Moved to New York City	2	Moved to NYC suburbs	4
Added to list due to size	27	Added to list due to size	7
Shifted from Industrial 500	7	Shifted from Industrial 500	1
Fortune Service 500, 1990	60	Fortune Service 500, 1990	29

Sources: Fortune 500 Directories, various issues.

TABLE 4.4   Changes in the Number of Forbes 400 Firms Headquartered in New York City and Its Suburbs

Headquarters in New York City, 1984–1989		Headquarters in New York City Suburbs, 1984–1989	
Forbes 400, 1984	46	Forbes 400, 1984	19
Losses, 1984–1989	−30	Losses, 1984–1989	−12
Moved to suburbs	−1	Moved to NYC	0
Moved out of area	−1	Moved out of area	0
Acquired, bankrupt, merger	−11	Acquired, bankrupt, merger	−2
Public	−9	Public	−4
No longer Forbes 400	−8	No longer Forbes 400	−6
Gains, 1984–1989	33	Gains, 1984–1989	25
Moved to New York City	2	Moved to suburbs	1
Privatization	8	Privatization	15
Merger, other	23	Merger, other	9
Forbes 400, 1989	49	Forbes 400, 1989	32

Sources: Forbes 400, November 18, 1985, and December 10, 1990.

The Challenges to Wall Street

Another important development that has reshaped New York during the 1980s has been the transformation of Wall Street. Here, too, there is a tendency by some, in my opinion, to overestimate negative developments.

Some point to the relocation of the offices of financial firms away from New York as a sign of weakness. As I will show in the next section, however, with the possible exception of the outmigration of certain financial facilities to Fairfield County, most relocations, when they occurred, have involved lower-skilled back-office employment. For that matter, in the case of the securities firms, as Mitchell Moss and Joanne Brion have shown earlier, there actually has been rather limited relocation outside the city, except for computer centers that are capital intensive rather than labor intensive.[4]

Others point to the decline (partly of their own making through bad loans) of the New York commercial banks—the result of both the decline of wholesale banking, the source of their traditional strength, and interstate banking regulations that have kept New York–based banks out of fast-growing consumer markets—as signs of the city's weakening. As in the case of the headquarters analysis, excessive emphasis on one segment is misleading. Focusing on commercial banking misses the importance of the shift to capital market banking and the resulting rise of new players. This is an area in which New York has shown a good deal of versatility.

Tables 4.5, 4.6, and 4.7 illustrate this point. In 1973, commercial banks held 41 percent of the assets of all financial institutions in the nation; by 1988, that share had declined to 30 percent (Table 4.5). Meanwhile, the share of assets held by "other" financial institutions (mutual funds, pension funds, security firms) had grown from 21 to 35 percent. If we estimate the change in the share of assets held by all financial institutions based in the New York area in order to account for this major shift, and not simply the share held by the commercial banks, we find that New York's share of financial assets has actually changed little between the early 1970s and the late 1980s. Of the group of the nation's 50 largest commercial banks, 50 largest S&Ls, 50 largest life insurance firms, and 200 largest institutional investors (mutual funds, pension funds, private investment funds, and other funds managed by banks), the institutions that were based in the New York metropolitan area captured 38 percent of the nation's financial assets in 1989 against 40.8 percent in 1974 (Tables 4.6 and 4.7 respectively). These two tabulations are not completely comparable, however, because this group of 350 largest financial institutions accounted for a much larger percentage of the assets of the nation's financial institutions in 1989 than in 1974—79 percent as compared to 62 in the earlier year. For the same reason, it is difficult to judge whether the shift in assets from New York to its suburbs between 1974 and 1989 shown in Tables 4.6 and 4.7 represents a true shift or simply an artifact of the tabulations. More broadly, and using different data, I have shown elsewhere that the 1980s were actually a period during which there was increasing concentration of financial activity in New York at the expense of other centers of finance in the country.[5]

As far as competition from abroad is concerned, there is considerable evidence that, at least in the near term, New York may have actually strengthened its position relative to London and Tokyo. The cleansing of

TABLE 4.5   Financial Assets of all Financial Institutions in New York City, 1973 and 1988

	1973		1988	
	$ (billions)	*Percent*	*$ (billions)*	*Percent*
Commercial banks	761.00	41.00	2,922.00	30.00
S&Ls and other deposit institutions	407.00	22.00	1,821.00	19.00
Life and other insurance	315.00	17.00	1,558.00	16.00
Others (mutual, pension funds, etc.)	391.00	21.00	3,359.00	35.00
Total	1,874.00	100.00	9,660.00	100.00

Source: Federal Reserve Bulletin, various issues.

the U.S. financial system, and of New York's by the same token, following the go-go years of the 1980s has been far deeper and more rapid than that of Tokyo, where the regulator is still trying to figure out how to absorb the excesses of the previous decade, particularly in the real estate and stock markets. After years of being shunned by potential Japanese clients and by Japanese security firms in Tokyo, New York's security firms have finally begun to make major headway there, chiefly on the strength of their capacity to innovate, especially in the derivatives markets. Their profits and market share have steadily grown there at a time when the Japanese security firms have been forced to retrench from New York.

In London, the general assessment is that there is still fat to be cut, in terms of the number of firms and employees, following the huge overcapacity buildup that resulted from Big Bang.[6] And, in the opinion of this writer, Europe 1992 is highly unlikely to be the watershed event that it was once forecast to be. It now seems more likely that competing factions in Western Europe will struggle to determine whether the EC should move toward a highly integrated market limited to a selected few or, rather, advance toward a de facto looser system open to a much larger number of countries, with the second scenario increasingly likely.

Meanwhile, in New York, the junk bond market seems to have recovered as more and more former borrowers de-leverage themselves by retiring debt with equity, a development made easier by the fresh inflow of savings from individual consumers reinvesting bank CDs whose rates have deteriorated in the stock market. The RTC (Resolution Trust Corporation) seems to have done much better than anyone had anticipated just a few months ago, having already recovered approximately $195 billion of the $350 billion it had put out so far to clean up the S&L mess. The stock market has by now recovered better than those of London and particularly Tokyo, which still languishes somewhere around 40 percent below its peak. And the security firms are poised to have one of their most profitable years ever, despite the turmoil at Salomon.

TABLE 4.6 Eight Largest Financial Centers Ranked by Total Assets of the Largest Financial Institutions, in $ millions, 1989

	CB 50	S&L 50	Life 50	II 200	Total Assets	Percent Total Assets
Total	1,923,180.5	531,599.4	902,591.9	4,279,787	7,637,159	100.0
% Total assets	25.2	7.0	11.8	56.0	100.0	
1. NY metro area						
NYC	777,288.5	71,921.5	409,873.4	1,644,333	2,903,416	38.0
NYC suburbs	710,722.9	14,102.4	269,154.0	1,293,564	2,287,543	30.0
2. Boston	66,565.6	57,819.1	140,719.0	350,769	615,873	8.1
3. Los Angeles	96,835.8	na	47,591.5	489,005	633,432	8.3
4. Chicago	142,994.4	189,560.7	40,655.6	190,541	563,752	7.4
5. San Francisco	89,830.4	11,549.5	24,885.2	277,210	403,475	5.3
6. Hartford	na	na	153,368.3	166,378	377,999	4.9
7. Pittsburgh	77,127.7	na	na	156,509	309,877	4.1
8. Philadelphia	na	19,513.1	na	154,403	173,916	2.3
Top Eight Cities						72.7

CB 50: Top fifty commercial banks by assets
S&L 50: Top fifty S&Ls by assets
Life 50: Top fifty life insurance firms by assets
II 200: Top two hundred institutional investors (managed funds) by assets

Note: "na" signifies that none of the firms in the ranking were located in this city.

Sources: Fortune Service 500, June 4, 1990; Moody's Bank & Finance Manual, 1990; "Top 300 Money Managers," Institutional Investor, July 1990.

TABLE 4.7 Eight Largest Financial Centers Ranked by Total Assets of the Largest Financial Institutions, in $ millions, 1974

	CB 50	S&L 50	Life 50	II 200	Total Assets	Percent Total Assets
Total	525,419.3	62,171.2	212,560.1	364,446	1,164,597	100.0
% Total assets	45.1	5.3	18.3	31.3	100.0	
1. NY metro area	213,340.3	3,145.9	112,731.9	145,441	474,659	40.8
NYC	213,340.3	1,490.2	73,807.5	123,813	412,451	35.4
NYC suburbs	na	1,655.7	38,924.2	21,628	62,208	5.3
2. San Francisco	86,388.4	5,385.0	na	8,982	100,755	8.7
3. Chicago	46,828.3	3,584.5	2,879.6	35,137	88,429	7.6
4. Boston	8,713.8	na	16,083.3	41,083	65,880	5.7
5. Los Angeles	38,298.5	17,379.0	3,321.3	5,970	64,969	5.6
6. Hartford	na	na	20,860.0	19,693	40,553	3.5
7. Philadelphia	17,783.1	na	4,778.1	9,967	32,528	2.8
8. Minneapolis	14,269.7	3,051.5	1,663.9	10,216	29,201	2.5
Top Eight Cities						77.0

CB 50: Top fifty commercial banks by assets
S&L 50: Top fifty S&Ls by assets
Life 50: Top fifty life insurance firms by assets
II 200: Top two hundred institutional investors (managed funds) by assets

Note: "na" signifies that none of the firms in the ranking were located in this city.

Sources: Fortune Service 500, July 1975; Moody's Bank & Finance Manual, 1975; "Ranking America's Largest Institutional Investors," Institutional Investor, August 1975.

New York Suburbs:
Competition or Complementarity

Perhaps more worrisome for the future is the continuing transformation of the relationship between New York and its suburbs. During the 1980s, while employment increased by about 425,000 jobs in New York City, it rose by nearly 850,000 jobs in a sixteen-county surrounding area of New Jersey, New York, and lower Connecticut.[7] The extent to which suburban employment growth competed head-on with growth in New York City or instead complemented it is a difficult issue to analyze and one that cannot be fully settled here. Nevertheless it is useful to examine some of the evidence.

Recent research by Stephen Leshinski of the Port Authority comparing the contribution of new firm births to business relocations and thus to the expansion of the employment base of New York City and its suburbs sheds light on the nature of local job growth.[8] Between 1976 and 1986, New York City created 464,000 jobs through new firm births, compared to 757,000 in a twelve-county surrounding area of New Jersey and New York. More than three-fourths of the jobs created through new firm births in New York City were in the FIRE and service industrial classifications (one-digit SIC), compared to less than two-thirds in these categories in the suburban counties. When looking at business relocations, Leshinski found that between 1976 and 1986, New York City lost nearly 163,000 jobs as a result of the outmigration of firms, gaining back a mere 37,000 jobs—or less than 25 percent of those lost through outmigration—from firms relocating from outside the city (including 24,000 from firms relocating from outside the region). Of the jobs lost, over 91,000, or 56 percent, were losses due to New York City–based firms relocating to the suburbs.

The implications of these findings, when contrasted with our earlier statistics on nine-year employment growth in the city and its suburbs, are clear. New York City's employment growth is due in a major way to the city's very high propensity to give birth to new firms. This is also true of New York's suburbs, but these also benefit from substantial relocations from the city. In contrast, the city gains little from business relocations. Put another way, these findings stress the fact that New York City's biggest problem is not employment creation, but rather the retention of firms and, for that matter, of mostly small firms.[9]

A major issue to examine in conjunction with these findings is the extent to which employment growth in the suburbs—be it the result of new firm births, the relocation of New York City–based firms, or the expansion of existing local firms—is directly competing with employment growth in the city. To some extent, one could argue that any employment growth in the suburbs competes with growth in New York City. But there is growth and growth. The suburbs may be adding jobs by adding or expanding firms that largely replicate those existing in the city and compete with the city. Yet the suburbs may be adding jobs in areas that the city is abandoning or in firms that provide economically desirable support for more specialized firms in the city and are not growing in areas in which the city is expanding. In the latter case the suburbs are developing a symbiotic, rather than a competing, division of labor vis-à-vis the city. One way to test whether suburban development has been symbiotic rather than competing is to examine the extent to which wage and salary levels in the suburbs have grown closer or farther apart from those paid in the city, particularly in those industries in which wage and salary levels have become high because of employment of skilled specialized personnel. A narrowing of the gap would suggest that, increasingly, the same relatively well-paid jobs as those found in the city are being added in the suburbs; a widening of the gap would suggest a growing difference in the types of jobs added in the city and the suburbs.

Tables 4.8 and 4.9 present evidence permitting a test of these hypotheses. Table 4.8 shows location quotients of employment in detailed sectors for Manhattan and the six largest suburban counties of New York City for both 1978 and 1987. A location quotient is the ratio of two ratios for a given year: employment in a detailed sector in a county divided by total employment in the county divided by the same ratio for the nation. A ratio greater than one indicates that the county is overspecialized in the sector relative to the nation; a ratio less than one indicates that it is underspecialized relative to the nation. A large change (growth or decline) in the location quotient over time is an indication of changing specialization in terms of levels of employment. Table 4.9 shows indexes of earnings levels (wages and salaries) of the six suburban counties relative to Manhattan for the same two years in the same detailed sectors. Earnings levels are computed as average annual earnings per worker in the county in the sector divided by the average annual earnings per worker in Manhattan for the same sector and the same year. An earnings level index higher than one means that workers in the sector are paid better, on average, than in Manhattan; less than one, the opposite. A narrowing of the earnings gap suggests that the employment composition of the suburban county is becoming more similar to that of Manhattan and, likely, becoming more competitive; a widening of the gap suggests that the employment structure is becoming more differentiated and, likely, more complementary. In the following analysis, we focus on detailed sectors of the FIRE and service divisions since it is there that most of the net employment growth has occurred.

A first look at Table 4.8 suggests that employment in each and every one of these counties is becoming increasingly more specialized in de-

TABLE 4.8 Location Quotients, 1987, 1978

	Manhattan		Fairfield		Nassau		Westchester		Bergen		Middlesex		Morris		Two Counties with Highest Specialization in 1987
	1987	1978	1987	1978	1987	1978	1987	1978	1987	1978	1987	1978	1987	1978	
Total	1.00	1.00	1.00	1.00	1.00	1.00	1.00	1.00	1.00	1.00	1.00	1.00	1.00	1.00	
Manufacturing	0.53	0.85	1.30	1.83	0.70	0.93	0.78	1.05	1.03	1.44	1.12	1.81	1.04	1.65	
TCU	0.97	1.35	0.69	0.65	0.82	0.91	1.01	1.00	0.83	0.98	1.52	1.50	1.52	1.15	Middlesex, Morris
Wholesale	1.10	1.37	1.18	0.93	1.31	1.39	1.40	1.48	2.17	1.93	1.77	1.39	1.00	0.81	Bergen, Middlesex
Retail	0.47	0.47	0.86	0.82	0.99	1.07	0.86	0.87	0.88	0.94	0.89	0.82	0.79	0.87	
Retail—E + D	0.44	0.45	0.96	0.93	1.10	1.23	0.96	0.98	1.00	1.07	1.03	0.94	0.86	0.97	Nassau, Middlesex
Eating/drinking (E + D)	0.54	0.50	0.65	0.61	0.77	0.75	0.64	0.64	0.63	0.67	0.61	0.55	0.63	0.66	Nassau, Westchester
FIRE	3.25	2.66	1.02	0.73	1.33	1.15	1.01	0.88	0.84	0.59	0.89	0.53	1.41	1.04	
60 Banking	3.80	3.54	1.20	0.97	1.40	1.28	0.92	0.73	0.70	0.70	0.75	0.54	0.65	0.71	Manhattan, Nassau
61 Credit agency	1.19	0.84	1.24	0.80	1.19	0.89	0.32	0.32	0.52	0.52	0.95	0.54	1.26	0.40	Fairfield, Morris
62 Security	15.04	6.82	1.20	0.45	1.04	0.44	0.81	0.44	1.05	0.46	0.72	0.07	2.05	0.40	Manhattan, Morris
63 Insurance	1.88	2.36	0.60	0.55	1.19	1.39	1.16	0.72	0.42	0.43	0.98	0.88	2.76	2.24	Morris, Manhattan
64 Insurance brokers	1.72	1.49	0.98	0.59	1.88	1.52	1.42	0.97	1.04	0.55	1.00	0.32	1.65	0.52	Nassau, Manhattan
65 Real estate	2.33	2.37	1.02	0.78	1.46	1.16	1.42	1.66	1.04	0.83	0.61	0.51	0.75	0.51	Manhattan, Nassau
Services	1.30	1.08	0.94	0.74	1.18	0.97	1.16	1.03	0.88	0.68	0.79	0.53	0.94	0.70	
70 Hotels	8.65	7.33	6.99	4.14	3.90	2.31	6.09	5.69	5.44	4.08	5.31	4.15	8.71	4.19	Manhattan, Morris
73 Business services	2.17	1.69	1.36	0.75	1.37	1.14	1.25	0.96	1.36	0.89	1.29	0.65	1.63	0.74	Manhattan, Morris
80 Health	0.63	0.54	0.85	0.81	1.21	0.87	1.12	1.01	0.73	0.60	0.74	0.57	0.72	0.80	Nassau, Westchester
81 Legal services	3.15	2.01	1.01	0.77	1.36	0.89	0.77	0.54	0.74	0.51	0.84	0.53	1.10	0.77	Manhattan, Nassau
82 Educational services	1.71	1.38	0.80	0.75	1.61	1.31	1.89	1.57	0.56	0.70	0.35	0.23	0.79	0.99	Westchester, Nassau
86 Membership associations	0.98	1.05	0.66	0.79	0.68	0.68	0.99	1.22	0.56	0.48	0.55	0.71	0.74	0.59	Westchester, Manhattan
89 Miscellaneous services	1.91	1.47	1.05	0.54	1.41	1.03	1.01	0.82	1.09	1.00	0.78	0.35	0.90	0.48	Manhattan, Nassau
Residual (mostly consumer services)	0.81	0.77	0.66	0.62	0.87	0.91	0.96	0.93	0.70	0.53	0.52	0.40	0.55	0.45	Westchester, Nassau

Source: U.S. Department of Commerce, Bureau of Economic Analysis, *County Business Patterns, 1987, 1978* (Washington, DC: GPO).

TABLE 4.9 Industry Earnings Levels of Suburbs Versus Manhattan, 1978, 1987

	Manhattan		Fairfield		Nassau		Westchester		Bergen		Middlesex		Morris	
	1978	1987	1978	1987	1978	1987	1978	1987	1978	1987	1978	1987	1978	1987
Total	1.00	1.00	0.85	0.76	0.74	0.60	0.85	0.67	0.84	0.66	0.82	0.65	0.84	0.72
Manufacturing	1.00	1.00	1.00	1.05	0.91	0.87	1.11	1.01	0.98	0.83	0.92	0.85	1.05	1.09
TCU	1.00	1.00	0.81	0.83	0.82	0.70	0.87	0.88	0.86	0.71	0.91	0.73	0.87	0.93
Wholesale	1.00	1.00	1.86	1.02	0.82	0.79	1.11	0.97	0.89	0.82	0.86	0.81	0.83	0.86
Retail	1.00	1.00	0.81	0.83	0.76	0.77	0.80	0.79	0.78	0.85	0.77	0.75	0.79	0.77
Retail—E + D	1.00	1.00	0.78	0.80	0.72	0.74	0.77	0.75	0.75	0.82	0.74	0.72	0.77	0.74
Eating/Drinking (E + D)	1.00	1.00	0.68	0.71	0.72	0.69	0.73	0.74	0.70	0.69	0.64	0.61	0.67	0.66
FIRE	1.00	1.00	0.76	0.66	0.69	0.45	0.67	0.52	0.66	0.51	0.60	0.49	0.73	0.49
60 Banking	1.00	1.00	0.62	0.59	0.66	0.60	0.65	0.59	0.60	0.50	0.52	0.50	0.62	0.49
61 Credit agency	n.a.	1.00	n.a.	1.09*	n.a.	0.57	n.a.	0.66	n.a.	0.71	n.a.	0.60	n.a.	0.59
62 Security	1.00	1.00	0.90	0.97*	0.94	0.63	0.89	0.88*	0.79	0.74	0.84	n.a.	0.95	0.49
63 Insurance	1.00	1.00	1.16	1.20*	0.82	0.85	0.91	0.88*	0.81	1.08*	0.74	0.82	0.85	0.78
64 Insurance brokers	1.00	1.00	0.88	0.85*	0.75	0.70	0.82	0.85*	0.79	0.78	0.80	0.66	0.68	0.85*
65 Real estate	1.00	1.00	0.85	0.99*	0.81	0.75	0.76	0.87*	0.78	0.81	0.78	0.71	0.85	0.91*
Services	1.00	1.00	0.75	0.85	0.76	0.75	0.71	0.70	0.79	0.82	0.69	0.78	0.70	0.75
70 Hotels	1.00	1.00	0.60	0.61	0.77	0.58	0.67	0.69	0.61	0.62	0.44	0.49	0.58	0.52
73 Business services	1.00	1.00	0.82	0.97*	0.66	0.71	0.69	0.69	0.81	0.79	0.59	0.95*	0.68	0.79
80 Health	1.00	1.00	0.79	0.95*	0.87	0.70	0.80	0.54	0.78	0.93*	0.75	0.78	0.74	0.88*
81 Legal services	1.00	1.00	0.73	0.75	0.67	0.78	0.75	0.70	0.66	0.61	0.73	0.79	0.77	0.78
82 Educational services	1.00	1.00	0.83	1.03*	0.91	0.69	0.83	0.78	0.85	0.97*	0.76	0.73	0.79	0.82
86 Membership associations	1.00	1.00	0.48	0.64	0.56	0.56	0.52	0.54	0.51	0.51	0.72	0.54	0.47	0.51
89 Miscellaneous services	1.00	1.00	0.83	0.99*	0.82	1.06*	0.69	0.92*	0.96	1.06*	0.77	0.89*	0.83	0.90*
Residual (mostly consumer services)	1.00	1.00	0.68	0.67	0.70	0.85*	0.71	1.13*	0.68	0.87*	0.71	0.55	0.62	0.58

*Earnings level for a detailed FIRE or Service sector is 85 percent or more of the Manhattan level.

Source: U.S. Department of Commerce, Bureau of Economic Analysis, *County Business Patterns, 1978, 1987* (Washington, DC: GPO).

tailed sectors of the FIRE and service classifications. The last column in Table 4.8, which lists the two counties that are the most specialized in individual detailed sectors in 1987, suggests that Manhattan and Morris counties are the counties with heaviest concentrations in financial and producer services; Westchester and Nassau, in consumer-oriented services (education, health, retail, eating and drinking, other mostly consumer services). Turning now to Table 4.9, I have marked with an asterisk the counties other than Manhattan in which earnings level for a detailed FIRE or service sector is 85 percent or more of the Manhattan level. Only in Fairfield is there evidence that the county has increasingly grown in competition with Manhattan in the sense of offering, in many detailed sectors, jobs at earnings levels roughly comparable to those of the city. To repeat, this suggests that the local employment base is increasingly mirroring, rather than complementing, that of Manhattan. In Table 4.9, I have also underlined for banking, security, and insurance the suburban countries in which there is evidence of a sizable buildup of jobs during the 1980s (based on the location quotients presented in Table 4.8). These are Fairfield and Nassau in banking; Fairfield, Morris, and Nassau in the security industry; and Morris and Westchester in insurance. Only in Fairfield in the security industry do we observe both an increase in employment *and* an increase in earnings levels relative to Manhattan. In all other cases earnings levels have decreased relative to the city, suggesting that employment growth in those sectors was mostly complementary rather than competitive. The suburban counties were attracting mostly lower-paying jobs rather than the higher-paying jobs found in Manhattan. These jobs are likely to be local service-sector jobs or support-type jobs, including "back-office" jobs.

Whether the mostly symbiotic relationship between city and suburb suggested by the data will turn increasingly competitive remains to be seen. The pattern suggested by the limited transformation in Fairfield in contrast to the other counties may, or may not, be a warning of things to come.

A Structural or a Cyclical Downturn?

Some might quarrel with the picture I have painted so far as being too rosy in light of a relatively sharp downturn. Two years into this recession, however, it is still difficult to discern fully whether New York is dealing principally with a cyclical crisis—as it did during the 1982–1983 recession, albeit sharper—or with a deeper and potentially longer-lasting structural crisis—as it did during the early to mid 1970s. Admittedly, if we are dealing with an incipient structural crisis, such a crisis may find its roots mostly in national or international developments rather than in local developments. Increasingly, my view is that we are dealing with elements of a structural crisis, mostly of a national rather than international or local nature, but, fortunately, one that is unlikely to be as deep as that which affected the New York economy in the early and mid 1970s.

As observed by others, the recent recession was as much a service-led as a manufacturing-led recession. In contrast to previous recessions, the downturn in manufacturing employment has been much smaller; that in services, much larger (see Figure 4.1). To the extent that this has been a service-led recession, New York's disproportionate share of employment in that sector of the economy has meant that the recession has been felt more acutely here than elsewhere. In the 1982–1983 recession, services had partly buffered the impact of the recession on New York.)

The surprising performance of manufacturing over the past two years is due mostly to the fact that manufacturing exports have been one of the few bright lights of the U.S. economy. But this has been of little direct help to New York, which does not manufacture the kinds of high-tech or capital equipment products that have been selling well in overseas markets. Clearly, also, the fact that exports of services have continued to grow nicely during the recession—and we know that New York is a large exporter in this area—has not been sufficient to compensate for declines in other parts of the service economy. This reinforces the view that not only is this recession a service-led recession, but that the explanation must be found mostly either in national or in local developments.

In terms of local developments, as I have suggested earlier, I am unimpressed by the view that Wall Street is about to be challenged in a major way or that the concentration of large service firms and their headquarters that occurred over the past twenty years or so is about to dissipate. This is in part because advanced service firms seem to thrive on the economies resulting from the agglomeration of other businesses and people of the kind that New York is uniquely positioned to offer by virtue of its size. Furthermore, there is little evidence that this underlying dynamic is changing.[10] However, as both the past experience of industrial headquarters moving to the suburbs and the Port Authority's analysis on new firms' migrations suggest, agglomeration economies do not stop at the Hudson River, or at the borders with Westchester or Nassau County, and the possibility of New York suburbs competing increasingly with the city cannot be ruled out. It is here, however, that the city can perhaps do the most to intervene and influence the outcome. This issue is discussed later.

In the near term, however, the biggest potential threat to New York is likely to come from three somewhat distinct domestic structural crises. The first is the crisis in the commercial banking industry, a still disproportionately large sector of the New York City economy. Commercial banking is afflicted by both a financial crisis in the wholesale segment of the in-

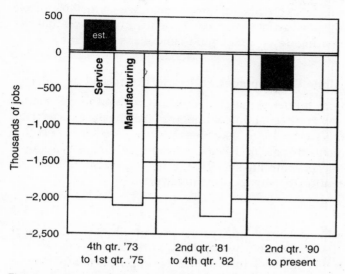

Figure 4.1 Three Recessions Compared: Employment Gains and Losses in Services and Manufacturing *Note:* Government and health are excluded. *Source: Fortune,* June 3, 1991.

dustry and a crisis of overcapacity. In both cases, resolving tensions will likely result in a shrinkage of the industry.

The second is a structural crisis of what might be called the "consumer sector"; that is, those industries that produce mostly for final consumption by individuals. With the maturing of the baby boomers and the aging of their parents, the U.S. economy is being afflicted by large demographic changes of a magnitude not unlike that which affected the economy in the early 1970s when the baby boomers entered the labor market. Consumer needs and, as a result, consumer demand are shifting sharply and rapidly, creating surplus capacity in many areas in which consumer goods and service companies excelled during the 1980s and leaving others underserved in sectors as diverse as general merchandising, restaurant and fast food, or entertainment. This is affecting New York, which traditionally has been a leader and trendsetter in a number of these areas. The aging of the population will likely continue to boost the growth of the medical sector—a strong growth area for New York despite attempts to curb its development. However, the fact that more and more New Yorkers seek to retire far away from the city may dampen future growth.

The third crisis is the fiscal crisis of state and local government, a phenomenon certainly no longer unique to New York City. Growth of the local public sector is likely to remain sluggish for years to come, since little relief can be expected from the federal government, which may be forced to spend much of the long-awaited "peace dividend" (a dividend that has yet to materialize) paring down the gargantuan deficits of the 1980s.

Economic Development Policy for the 1990s

New York's ability to influence national and international economic developments has always been limited and can hardly be expected to change. However, New York can take measures to position itself better vis-à-vis developments that are clearly local in nature. From such a standpoint, three issues seem central to shaping the agenda for the 1990s: local taxes, business retention incentives, and infrastructure.

Local Taxes

In April 1991, New York City's Office of the Comptroller issued a report on the impact of the local tax burden on New York City's economy that created quite a stir.[11] Going back to 1950, the report purported to demonstrate a number of important points. First, since the early 1960s the local tax burden (as measured by the local tax rate on each dollar of gross city product resulting from all local taxes including state income, city income, sales, real estate, and all other existing local taxes) had increased faster in New York City than in the rest of the nation. Second, the increase in the local tax burden gap between New York and the rest of the country tended to grow faster during recessions than expansions. And third, although increases in the local tax burden gap during expansionary periods seem to have limited impact on the growth of private-sector employment in the city, increases of the gap during recessionary periods seem to aggravate the recession in private-sector employment.

The report was attacked on a number of grounds, including its attempt to estimate the impact that the tax increases proposed by the Dinkins administration to close the city's budget gaps in 1991 through 1994 might have on New York City employment, which many argued resulted in an unrealistic and overly pessimistic recessionary scenario. Some also argued that the local tax burden was not the only cost factor that influenced a business decision to shut down or to relocate. It is true, however, that in recessionary environments during which commercial rents often decline, and utility costs may change little, taxes are usually the only other major direct business cost that increases. The report could also be criticized for being somewhat insensitive to the fact that the current local government faces social crises of welfare, homelessness, or AIDS-related health care costs of a magnitude that earlier administrations never had to confront.

Nevertheless, the report did bring out a point that many seemed eager to forget, namely that the more the city is willing to tax its residents and businesses the more it undermines its competitive advantage as a center of business. This is particularly the case since New York can no longer rely on its "uniqueness" to attract talents and high-level workers, as it did during the 1950s or 1960s; it must now compete with fast-growing, relatively cheaper, and, in some respects, equally attractive regional centers of business. Still, accepting the validity of this point about the deleterious effect of disproportionately ever-higher relative local tax rates on the local economy does not begin to address the need for local government to confront an ever more dizzying and growing array of demands. It simply deflects it.

It is here, however, that a second but equally important issue enters the debate: public-sector productivity. The last time the issue received serious consideration was in the late 1970s and early 1980s when a tight fiscal situation and strong controls from the state and the Emergency Financial Control Board (EFCB) made it imperative to address service bottlenecks in different ways than simply raising taxes. The present administration has been very slow to move on this front. This is unfortunate because this is an area in which the city can clearly act to regain better control over its own future. Much more must be done in this important area.

Business Retention

Under the Koch administration, an extensive system of incentives (including real estate tax and utility cost abatements) along with hands-on intervention were put in place in order to retain large firms, especially large service firms considering relocating outside New York. Above and beyond the immediate gains from retaining the jobs of potential relocators, the rationale underlying retention efforts was that these firms create the agglomerations of businesses that serve as the spur for the myriad of small firms started every year in New York simply to respond to the never-ending demands of corporate customers. The other idea behind the policy was to use these incentives to create strong alternative locations for white-collar offices in the outer boroughs some distance from the increasingly congested midtown and downtown Manhattan.

A second element of the city's business retention policy has been a package of incentives geared to retaining small firms, mostly small manufacturing firms partly around the idea of rebuilding certain depressed areas such as Hunts Point in the South Bronx or the Brooklyn Terminal.

As regards the first major component of the city's retention policy, one might ask whether the practice of handing out incentives to large companies on an ad hoc basis is as efficient as an across-the-board lessening of the tax burden might be. As regards the second component of the policy, I suspect that the attention given to the retention of the small manufacturing sector—be it in dollar terms or in terms of engagement of the city's bureaucrats—is seriously out of balance considering the city's almost total neglect of a retention policy for small service firms. The reality, however, is that manufacturing will continue to become more and more marginal to the city's economy while services will continue to grow absolutely and relatively. Furthermore, it is likely that the cost of a retention policy for small service firms to the taxpayer would be far less than a policy focused on small manufacturing firms in light of the far lesser capital intensiveness of service firms. I do not have a blueprint for what such a policy might look like, but in earlier research on the computer service industry in New York I was struck by the fact that much could be done at a relatively low cost by the city to assist expanding small local service firms by cutting through administrative red tape, assisting their negotiations with real estate brokers, negotiating with NYNEX and other utilities on behalf of those firms, and so on.[12] The dynamics of growth, expansion, and relocation of new service firms in New York City is a poorly understood topic but one on which a good part of New York's future depends. The research by the Port Authority on this issue has opened up important issues. The city must pick up from there and move forward to address the needs of this long neglected but growing sector of the economy.

The Infrastructure

In the 1970s, under the burden of the economic crisis, the city and key local public authorities cut off any substantial capital investment for nearly a decade. In retrospect, this was a costly mistake. Beginning in the early 1980s, the city launched major investment programs to rebuild the bus and subway systems. New investment programs were also launched to start rebuilding the region's suburban commuter railroad system. Much more is needed, including a major program of repair of the region's roads and bridges. The city, the state of New York, and the region (primarily via the Port Authority) must resist any temptation to reduce capital investment now, as happened during the 1970s. In the short term, any new investment will boost employment in the construction sector; in the long term, the quality of the infrastructure is a strategic asset to the well-being of the city and the region.

In the context of an economy that has become increasingly specialized in the advanced services and has turned more and more toward international markets, two sets of infrastructure may deserve special attention: air transportation and telecommunications.

The city and the region have been hurt by the decline of locally headquartered airlines that failed to adapt to the new world of deregulation (Eastern, Pan Am, TWA). But the regional market is too important for major domestic and foreign airlines to abandon it, unless the city and the Port Authority fail to respond to the opportunity. Above and beyond the industry's current recession, air transportation is a business that is poised to grow significantly during the 1990s. The potential for both JFK and Newark airports to expand their role as hubs to the European, Latin American, and Asian markets remains considerable. Especially, as the United States is forced to open more and more of its domestic market to foreign airlines, there will be a growing need for some of those airlines to develop mini- or even full-blown hub-and-spoke operations in the United States. The two airports are logical places to host such hubs.

New York also has a major competitive advantage as a custom clearing site for air freight. In both cases—freight and passenger air transportation—the city and the region must do all they can to preserve and strengthen those advantages.

The Port Authority has entered upon major construction programs at both JFK and LaGuardia. It would be reasonable to examine how these programs could be both expanded and accelerated so that New York would be better positioned to pick up business when the next surge of activity begins.

When deregulation in the telecommunications industry was set in motion in the late 1970s and early 1980s, there was fear that competition might lead to a sharp reduction of profits and in turn a reduction in investment. For various reasons, this has not been the case. Indeed, attempts by newcomers to seize market share away from the Bell Operating Companies (BOCs) and AT&T on the basis of both quality of service and price competition have unleashed a process of large new investment that has greatly benefited New York City. By almost every measure, New York City is *the* telecommunications mecca of the late twentieth century, with no other city anywhere in the world yet able to match both the density and diversity of network services available here. There is no indication that this trend is about to change, but the city must keep watching to make sure that its telecommunications network remains in the lead in the twenty-first century.

Conclusion

The United States is facing elements of a structural, mostly domestic, crisis that may slow the recovery of New York City for months to come. In addition, New York must watch out for continued competition from other population centers, especially from its own suburbs. However, the U.S. economy is not confronting a crisis of international competitiveness similar to that of the 1970s, either in manufacturing or in the services. Neither is New York City confronted with local structural dysfunctions of a scope similar to those it had to address in the 1970s. In sum, once the recovery sets in, New York City's economy should do reasonably well during the 1990s, particularly if it addresses squarely and manages efficiently the issues that it can influence.

Notes

1. Eli Ginzberg, Matthew Drennan, Robert Cohen, *The Corporate Headquarters Complex in New York City*, New York: Columbia University, Conservation of Human Resources, 1977.

2. Thierry Noyelle and Thomas M. Stanback, Jr., *The Economic Transformation of American Cities*, Totowa, N.J.: Rowman and Allanheld, 1983.

3. New York Chamber of Commerce and Industry, Inc., *Foreign Company Offices in New York City*, New York: Chamber of Commerce and Industry, November 1990.

4. Mitchell Moss and Joanne Brion, *Back Offices and Data Processing Facilities in New York State*, New York: New York University, Urban Research Center, June 1988).

5. Thierry Noyelle, "New York's Competitiveness," chapter 5 in Thierry Noyelle, ed., *New York's Financial Markets*, Boulder, Colo.: Westview Press, 1989.

6. See, for example, "Five Years Since Big Bang," *Economist*, October 26, 1991, pp. 23–26.

7. These estimates are for the period 1979–1988 and are based on data prepared by the Bureau of Economic Analysis not shown here.

8. Stephen Leshinski, "Regional Business Startups," May 10, 1990, "Regional Employment Relocations," October 12, 1990, New York: Port Authority of New York and New Jersey.

9. This point was starkly illustrated in a survey of New York–based computer services and data processing firms that two colleagues and I conducted in 1988. See Thierry Noyelle, Penny Peace, and Leo Kahane, "Computer Services and Data Processing in New York City," New York: Columbia University, Eisenhower Center, March 1989.

10. See Thierry Noyelle and Penny Peace, "Information Services: New York's New Export Base," New York: Columbia University, Eisenhower Center, November 1998.

11. "Report by the Chief Economist Comptroller's Budget Office on the Impact of the Local Tax Burden on New York City's Economy," New York City: Office of the Comptroller, April 1991.

12. Thierry Noyelle, Penny Peace, and Leo Kahane, "Computer Services and Data Processing in New York City," New York: Columbia University, Eisenhower Center, March 1989.

5

Literacy and Work

Lauren Benton

Warnings about the perils of waning U.S. competitiveness are by now a permanent feature of the American political landscape. One claim that is subscribed to widely is that inadequate and inappropriate training for U.S. workers presents a key obstacle to enhanced competitiveness. This position appeals to those who would favor more government intervention to prevent declining competitiveness because it suggests, among other measures, a need to invest quickly and heavily in both public education and new forms of job training—even, perhaps, requiring firms to contribute more to both. At the same time, the view is favored by those who want to vindicate U.S. corporate strategies and shift the blame for industrial decline elsewhere. Proponents avoid the appearance of being overly critical of American workers by pointing to structural changes in the work force that presumably lead to declining skill levels, particularly the increasing participation of "untraditional workers" (women, minorities, and migrants).[1] They also blame schooling, both for the supposed "mismatch" between workers' competencies and skills actually required in the workplace (see Bailey in this volume) and for presumed high rates of illiteracy among adult workers.[2]

I will argue in this chapter that it is possible to accept the notion that strong pressures exist to change the nature of jobs and the structure of firms without also concluding that worker preparedness, and low literacy levels in particular, are responsible for American firms' slow response to new competitive conditions. It is undeniable that firms are being forced by trends such as intensified international competition and market fragmentation to move away from classic patterns of Fordist production and toward more flexible systems of organization. Workers in the post-Fordist economy will increasingly be required to do more than routinized tasks. Firms will also rely increasingly on their workers' abilities to contribute to design changes, fix production problems, and participate in a more fluid flow of information among more loosely structured departments.[3] There are various barriers preventing some firms from moving quickly in these directions. Although the skill mix and capacity for retraining of workers may sometimes brake change, their importance is dwarfed by that of other factors, most notably politics inside firms and wider institutional structures that may not support such a transformation.[4]

This view does not imply that critical assessments of education and of adult worker training are unwarranted. Indeed, any analysis of adult literacy problems (I leave aside the wider examination of schooling in this chapter) must begin with the observation that most adult instruction in literacy and basic skills is plainly ineffective. The problems, though, stem not from learner deficiencies but from a combination of other factors: the persistence of flawed ideas about the goals of adult learning and the support such ideas hold out for failed techniques of training; the unwillingness to move away from hierarchical structures inside the firm that impede new types of training; and the institutional context surrounding firms that tends still to support approaches to training appropriate to Fordist production. These factors are clearly related. Changing how we think about work and literacy will not by itself improve worker training, but doing so is essential to assessing the problem accurately and responding to it with new strategies of restructuring inside firms and with more effective public policies.

I expand on these themes in the next section. Subsequent sections analyze the influence of three strains in thinking about the literacy problem, focusing particularly on the implications of these approaches for responding to post-Fordist pressures to restructure work. This analysis draws on a burgeoning literature on the history of literacy as well as on recent research on literacy workplace programs and studies of industrial restructuring. Finally, I will return to the question of how larger institutional structures require change to provide better support for innovative strategies that may promote both firm competitiveness and enhanced literacy for workers.

Literacy and Work: The Problem

There is so much bad and vague writing about literacy that one is tempted to ignore it all and begin with a clean slate in analyzing the relationship between literacy and the restructuring of work in the post-Fordist workplace. Yet, much recent work on literacy does address the relationship implicitly, and we must start with its analysis. A new orthodoxy about literacy has recently emerged that redefines it as a context-driven competency rather than a simple "skill" that can be taught effectively in a standard way. This trend is often dated from work on literacy by UNESCO beginning in the late-1950s that redefined literacy in "functional" terms. The idea emerged then that it was not useful to gauge people's abilities against any standard measure (nor, indeed, do proxy measures make this possible) but that what really mattered was people's abilities to function in particular contexts—at work, at home, in community life, or in all three settings.[5] With this reorientation, literacy as a social issue focuses not on those who are bereft of any reading and writing ability but on those who have some ability but who cannot perform adequately or participate fully in social life as a consequence.

In the United States, much of the early and influential writing on functional literacy referred to the experiences of soldiers in the armed forces. The army's chief concern was not with true illiterates, who were simply not accepted, but with low-level literates and how they should be treated. One key piece of research sponsored by the military separated the concept of functional literacy from functional competency. It found that performance on the job could not in fact be predicted by reference to soldiers' performance on literacy tests when entering the army, even for jobs that demanded more reading, writing, and arithmetic (Sticht, 1975). The finding was also important because it supported other evidence that people learn best how to function in a particular context, including learning the literacy skills needed, through experience and learning *in* context. This position has now become a central pedagogical tenet of the new orthodoxy. It challenged "a view of literacy as a context-neutral, content-free, skill-specific competence that can be imparted ... with almost scientific precision" that served as the "technological paradigm" for literacy instruction in much of the postwar period (de Castell and Luke, 1986:88). This redefinition has now been operationalized in a series of group and national literacy assessments in the United States and Canada that have sought to measure respondents' abilities to do the literacy tasks required of them to "function" in adult roles they might be expected to assume—as consumers, informed voters, and, of course, workers.[6]

These views on literacy are surprisingly uncontroversial. It is striking how quickly and with how little resistance this recasting of the literacy concept has moved into the mainstream. Ideas about how this redefinition affects an understanding of the relation of literacy and work have followed quickly. For example, a 1988 publication of the federal government makes a strong, unqualified argument for workplace literacy training that is context specific and describes a series of steps firms need to follow to assess literacy problems and implement job-related literacy training.[7]

The new orthodoxy in thinking about literacy presents a number of rather clear prescriptions for instruction, including the idea that literacy training must be context specific, that literacy must be viewed as a set of interlocking functional competencies, that literacy and basic skills instruction should be blended, and that learners need to be free of stigma in pursuing training.[8] If these views are indeed becoming widely accepted, then we must ask why they have had so little influence on what most programs do. The little that we know about literacy and basic skills programs suggests that most programs continue to remove learners from contexts that they value, to reproduce traditional school environments that many learners find intimidating or stigma producing, and to retain learners for too few hours to do much good even for the most motivated and accepting students.[9]

Parallel to this problem is a question about why, in light of compelling evidence that radical changes are needed in American firms to restore and retain competitiveness, firm structures, including the role of training, continue to reflect in many places older organizing principles of Fordism. Clearly developing alongside the new ideas about functional literacy has been a revised concept of work that responds to the conditions and pressures of the post-Fordist economy. Work in the restructured setting should, the argument goes, offer greater autonomy to workers and an opportunity for firms to benefit from worker creativity and increased responsibility. The shift represents the abandonment of the idea of work as routinized, as a product of an inexorable trend toward deskilling, and as essentially alienating in its effects on workers. Business leaders have by now embraced such ideas with surprising enthusiasm. However, just as older ideas about literacy die hard, ideas about work that belong to the epoch of Fordism linger conspicuously. One sees their effect in the persistence of hierarchical structures that make other piecemeal changes largely ineffective. Many U.S. firms have tried to avoid restructuring work altogether by pursuing forms of modified Fordism. Some have retreated to markets that are still relatively standardized and in which economies of scale and increased mechanization can keep them competitive, at least in the short run. Other firms continue to try to effect deskilling through automation, particularly for some levels of the work force, or to refine recruiting strategies in order to reduce the burden on training.[10] Thus ad hoc training inside the firm, complemented by the same bland training in basic skills (if this is offered at all), must not look so bad to many employers.

Economists have argued persuasively that this approach will not be enough. Short-term strategies ultimately expose firms to the same pressures to move toward more flexible systems that can manage quick response. Communications within such systems are at a premium. Workers not only need to send and receive messages to others about design problems and production flow, but they need an understanding of the way the pieces of the system function together so that they may both perceive problems and transmit information in appropriate ways.[11] In a rapidly changing workplace, workers will also have to engage in fairly frequent retraining as a condition of their employment; since jobs themselves will be structured to change, skills related to learning new sets of skills will also be both required and rewarded. As firms increasingly make the way they process information an integral part of the projection to the market of what they do, it will become more difficult, too, to separate professional or vocational knowledge from simple communications skills on the one hand and from proprietary technology (such as software) or styles of doing business (as in firms with elaborately developed procedures for customer service) on the other.

Rather than blaming learners and workers for the failure of literacy programs and the slowness of firms to revamp training, we need to explore other explanations for this disjuncture between theory and practice. One possibility is that older ways of thinking about literacy and basic skills instruction persist and influence how programs are structured and how they relate to work settings. The case for extending or enhancing literacy has been made in the past century in the United States (and sometimes much earlier) with reference to three themes: literacy as a path toward enlightenment; literacy as an avenue toward economic advancement, both for groups and for nations; and literacy as a vehicle for empowerment. These themes continue to inform much public discussion about literacy today. Not only does each theme pose problems as a framework for understanding the new demands for training in the workplace, but there is much in the record to suggest that the rhetoric has never been firmly grounded in historical reality and instead has consistently represented elements of an ideology about literacy's benefits. A further problem is that this older rhetoric continues to influence even views of literacy that purport to break with the past. The new orthodoxy about literacy as a context-driven competency in fact perpetuates some of the older ideas and is not yet an adequate framework for understanding (or substantially improving) literacy training for adult workers in the new economy. The rhetoric about literacy also influences institutional practices in important ways. Fashioning an appropriate public policy, as well as formulating specific recommendations for managers, educators, and learners involved in literacy instruction, depends on our understanding of these connections.

Literacy in Historical Perspective:
Literacy as Enlightenment

Harvey Graff (1977; 1987) has argued persuasively that much of what now passes for popular wisdom about literacy as a social issue reflects the continuities of a "literacy myth," a set of ideas about the benefits of literacy to both groups and individuals that constitutes part of the ideology of liberalism. The discussion that follows draws in places from Graff's work, but its focus is different. It is, to begin with, somewhat narrower. I will return throughout this analysis to the significance of persistent ways of thinking about literacy for an understanding of workplace training. I attempt, too, to separate various elements of the composite "literacy myth" and discuss the implications of these ideas separately. The emphasis here is different, too. Whereas Graff makes the point repeatedly that the history of literacy must be viewed not through the distorted lens of a concern with literacy as a social issue—a perspective that he sees as quite damaging to an assessment of literacy as a social phenomenon—I am interested precisely in these distortions. My focus is less on clarifying the historical record itself than on revealing the ideas lodged in historical experience that inform thinking about literacy now and thus shape debates about current policy and practice.

The strain in thinking about literacy that is perhaps the most striking and consistent is the notion that literacy presents an avenue toward enlightenment. This belief was tied directly to the expansion of literacy in the newly Protestant countries of northern Europe, where literacy and schooling were seen as fundamental to the practice of a faith predicated on the direct appreciation of the word of God. Protestantism was not, however, necessary to this representation of literacy, and there are indeed historical cases in which it worked against the extension of literacy. The idea of individual enlightenment through learning is clearly broader and permeated thinking about schooling and its influence.[12] Both literacy and schooling were viewed as means for communicating a message about morality that was seen as central to both individual redemption and the maintenance of social order.

Education reformers in North America continued this tradition.[13] The emphasis on religious understanding gave way more quickly here to a more diffuse notion of the instruction of morality as being inextricably tied to literacy learning (see Graff, 1977; de Castell and Luke, 1986). Indeed, there was genuine fear that literacy, if unconnected to moral messages, would be harmful. Attempts to control carefully the contents of early public library collections, even to the point of excluding fiction altogether because of its frivolous and corrupting influence, stand as evidence of the strength of these views.[14]

Historians underscore the degree to which this belief in the benefits of literacy to individual development and morality represented an ideology about literacy rather than a reflection of the actual impact of literacy learning. Rather than leading consistently to a widening of learners' horizons, literacy has often functioned historically as a means of guarding specialized information and controlling social behavior. The "contexts" in which reading and writing flourished not only restricted entry but also sought to constrain members' thought and actions; guilds, professional associations, religious groups, and other organizations thus promoted literacy at the same time that they sought to define its purposes narrowly. For example, literacy in colonial New England was advanced by Puritans, but Lockridge (1974) has argued that the emphasis on education served essentially conservative goals that restricted rather than liberated individuals. In the nineteenth century, we find reformers espousing the need to teach literacy and basic education to prison inmates, since criminality and immorality were openly associated with illiteracy. In fact, though prison authorities diligently kept records of educational levels and rates of literacy among inmates, they were never able to demonstrate a correspondence between criminality and illiteracy or between improving literacy rates and declining crime.[15]

The rhetoric about literacy as an avenue toward enlightenment continues to pervade literacy campaigns today. The media coverage that accompanied the Literacy Plus campaign in the United States typically presented narratives about individuals whose lives had been transformed through literacy. Before learning to read, they were described as intellectually and culturally impoverished. Many of the profiles emphasized the degree to which illiterates' lives were marked by a perpetual need to lie about themselves, even to close friends and relatives—a subtle but effective representation of moral failure as a side effect of illiteracy. This portrayal continues, with the participation of many scholars and educators. In a typical article, one educator portrays illiterates as "outsiders" who are "cut off throughout life from a basic understanding of civilization" and deprived of a life of literacy, which is simply "more fun" (Delattre, 1983:52). Energetic promoters of educational reform are thus cast in the curious role of describing the lives of people in need of literacy instruction as being without meaning:

> [Illiterates] live in a truncated present tense. The future seems hopeless. The past remains unknown. The amputated present tense, encapsulated by the T.V. moment, seems to constitute the end and the beginning of cognition.[16]

This perspective has been curiously strengthened, too, by some scholars' borrowing of concepts from cognitive psychology and psycholinguistics in writing about the development and spread of literacy. In this view, the development of literacy through history is mirrored in the development of the individual. The characteristics of literate societies (or, more precisely, societies where writing systems were known to some) are contrasted to the features of societies without writing systems. And the development of writing is linked with the societies' capacity to transmit information effectively across time, to represent and communicate abstract thoughts, to codify and administer sets of "decontextualized" rules, and to perform a range of other vital "modern" functions. The narrative is one of human progress and achievement and of an inevitable superseding of the "traditional." Ong and Goody have been the main purveyors of this perspective and although they have at times revised and even recanted some of their earlier views, these continue to inform a generation of scholars writing about literacy and its effects (see Walters, 1990; Goody, 1987). Ong (1982) has described people who remain attached to oral modes of expression and related forms of thought as "residually oral." Others practice a "secondary orality" because they have learned to think like literate people but still continue to switch back to thinking more like "residually oral" people—perhaps like "nonliterate Russian peasants."[17] It may be quaint to see that evolutionary constructs that have been energetically banned from cultural anthropology for decades continue to flourish in other fields, but the serious implications for educational practice rob this schema of some of its humor.[18]

Ong goes further to suggest that each individual recapitulates this historical development; that is, in moving from illiteracy to literacy, individuals presumably also develop the capacities for higher-order thinking that literacy makes possible. This perspective has had considerable influence on educators, some of whom seem to rely on Ong as their most important source of information on human cognition. One composition specialist summarizes his views as follows:

> The thinking of preliterate and nonliterate people is concrete, syncretic, diffuse, perceptual, affective, situation-bound, additive, and digressive, concerned with everyday events, actions and happenings rather than with abstract ideas. The thinking of literate people tends to be more abstract, discrete, definite, and articulated, consisting of generalizations, deductions, and inferences. Without writing, according to some scholars, the mind cannot participate in the kinds of analytical, sequential thinking necessary to develop even a single magazine article. Writing may be artificial, but it is also an artifice and an art that *seems to be essential for the development of consciousness.* (D'Angelo, 1983:104; emphasis added)

This view goes much further than that of nineteenth-century moralists in asserting the power of redemption that literacy holds for individuals. In comfortably adopting an evolutionary framework, it recapitulates the biased view of early social theories that "traditional" cultures (and now illiterates) are childlike predecessors to their more sophisticated "modern" cultures (literates). Not surprisingly, a cogent critique of this perspective has emerged on at least two fronts. One critique questions the portrayal of oral societies as fundamentally less well equipped to communicate effectively and to handle such tasks as transmission of information through generations or the representation of abstract thought. A recent anthropological study by Akinnaso shows, for example, that formal schooling is not limited to literate societies and identifies examples of institutional learning of an established body of knowledge (abstract, durational) without the benefit of writing. Akinnaso further points out that some learners also fail in nonliterate schools, and this is "not because of cognitive deficiencies or some specific incapacities" but because of discontinuities between formal schooling and everyday life that are especially exacerbated (as they are in schooling in literate societies) "when the school system is based on cultural and linguistic practices that are markedly different from those of the learners" (Akinnaso, 1992:101).

Another critique, even more pertinent to our focus, is that the ontological and evolutionary perspective draws the boundary between literate and illiterate much too sharply. Illiterate and poorly literate individuals may in fact "read" their environments with considerable sophistication. Different sorts of literacy exist—even "teleliteracy," as a recent spate of books and articles suggests—if one defines literacy broadly as a capacity for understanding and interpreting coded systems. More broadly, as other critics point out, there is in fact little evidence that the developmental processes of societies and individuals are fundamentally similar, and there is much danger in assuming this to be the case. Scribner and Cole argue on the basis of their empirical research on literacy acquisition that it is important to distinguish between cognitive capacities and cognitive skills (Scribner and Cole, 1973; Cole and Scribner, 1974). The former may be understood to be universal, whereas the latter are variable and depend on culture, context, and a range of other factors. Thus, as Akinnaso summarizes, "although literacy facilitates the acquisition of certain cognitive skills and operations, it does not, in itself, engender novel cognitive capacities" (Akinnaso, 1992:72).

Exposing the false assumptions of the "enlightenment" perspective teaches us where to look for false promises of literacy campaigns now. The idea that literacy instruction "opens new worlds" to learners may be supported by individual cases, but it is not well substantiated as a general fact. The vast majority of literacy trainees stay with programs for too little time to experience a significant improvement—even of one grade level—in their reading skills (Mikulecky, 1989; Dickhoff, 1988). Literacy program directors often report, too, that most learners are not seeking self-change but rather have practical, often limited, goals in mind when they begin training. In one community-based organization in Washington, D.C., for example, learning is centered around such practical, immediate goals rather than around educators' ideas about what literacy should make possible. The director reports that his program "will do things like teach [students] how to vote without reading the ballot or how to pass the driver's test by memorizing answers rather than being able to read the test. These are the things that keep them coming back to learn."[19]

A quite different set of program goals and institutional arrangements seems to be supported by the literacy-as-enlightenment perspective. One approach is the reliance on volunteers as instructors. The rhetoric of transformation used in volunteer literacy campaigns does seem to attract volunteers—in fact, the campaigns are better at recruiting volunteer instructors than learners—since volunteers seem to be drawn to the paternalistic vision of helping illiterates struggle for social maturity.[20] Such campaigns tend to receive backing from government agencies, too, in part because they are relatively cheap but also in part, no doubt, because the rhetoric of personal rather than social transformation is seen as politically safe. Yet the actual accomplishments of volunteer literacy campaigns movements are questionable. Critics point toward evidence of low completion rates and of an inability to reach learners who are most in need.[21] Still, despite an unproven track record, volunteer programs continue to get considerable attention from the press and much official backing. In some states and regions, they are the main providers of literacy training.[22]

Another institutional arrangement that also fits well with the idea of literacy as an agent of personal transformation is the use of traditional classroom settings. If one operates on the premise that illiterate or poorly literate people are themselves deficient, then the medium in which they were first offered instruction cannot be blamed or receives at least less blame. And if learning literacy skills is about self-betterment (and not about, say, responding to new demands of jobs or of the household), then what better environment to set learning in but the school, where conveying mere skills can be coupled with the opening of the literate worlds of traditional subject matters, ranging from literature to mathematics to theology. Yet so many literacy practitioners report that many learners have a deep aversion not to learning but to *school*. One official at a union-management program run by GM and the United Auto Workers (UAW) commented that this was particularly true of older workers who may have already failed in school settings. He described the experience of returning to the classroom as one that they found "extremely painful."

Finally, it is important to see that the literacy-as-enlightenment approach makes assumptions not just about learners' styles and goals of learning but also about what literacy is in a general sense. In this view, literacy produces order and conformity. Once admitted as "insiders," it is assumed that people will see the world in essentially similar ways. For nineteenth-century reformers, the vision was a religious and moral worldview that the literate would come to share. For twentieth-century educators steeped in popular psychology, the vision is one of relentless self-improvement now made possible through the window of abstract thought processes that only literates possess. Yet, it seems abundantly clear that whereas literacy can be about these visions of enlightenment, it can also be stupefying and limiting. In a role it has played historically, it can be a tool for teaching people how to follow instructions more efficiently and to internalize sets of imposed rules faster.

What implications does this critique have for an understanding of literacy at work? If, in the post-Fordist, flexible workplace, a premium is being placed on workers' abilities to analyze systems and processes, to think abstractly, and to transfer abilities from one set of tasks to another, and if these capacities are clearly associated with literacy, then promoting the latter seems a sure way of shaping a competitive work force. The conclusions are clearly different if one views the ties between these phenomena as conditional. If critics of the ontological view are correct, then some workers have the capacity already, regardless of their literacy skills, to participate in a restructured workplace that gives them more discretion and control. And if literacy instruction is used to promote a limited vision of self-transformation that excludes other goals, the result may be uncritical acceptance of structures at work that will work against the goal of wide participation in continual innovation.

It is worth noting, too, that the idea that literacy functions primarily to enhance personal development represents a version of a context-specific notion of literacy. The context in this instance is the message about morality and/or self-improvement that is seen as inseparable from the learning of literacy. Paradoxically, its context-based nature has had something to do with the robustness of the idea of literacy as a path to enlightenment. The postwar notion that literacy could and should be taught independently from context—as a generic skill—produced instructional materials that were so general in subject as to be excruciatingly boring.[23] Purveyors of enlightenment at least delivered some drama with their training—the threat of hell or, at least, poor social standing—and probably drew some support from those who found the blandness of the new approach to literacy repellant or just unworthy as a cause. We can conclude that advocating context-based literacy training does not, in itself, guarantee a departure from some of the misguided and ineffective approaches of the past, a point to which I will return later.

Literacy as a Means of Empowerment

The view of literacy as being essentially about the empowerment of particular groups seems to stand in direct opposition to the idea that literacy is a tool for enlightenment. To begin with, this view promises to reveal all the conflicts that the "enlightenment" perspective ignores or helps to conceal. By encouraging learners to identify individual rather than group goals, the argument runs, we in effect conspire to prevent significant social change, particularly changes in the balance of power among classes. Further, this view takes "context-based" ideas about literacy a step further. As Freire in particular has pointed out, it matters deeply not only what messages constitute the context for literacy instruction but also who controls programs, who designs instruction, and who identifies goals for learners (e.g., Freire, 1971). Put differently, how, when, and where one reads, and for whom, are at least as important as what one reads or even if one reads at all.

This perspective, too, has a particular historical narrative that supports it. To begin with, it is largely true that literacy has tended to be the prerogative of the powerful. Literacy rates in Europe through the nineteenth century were much higher for men, for city dwellers, and for members of the upper classes. In the United States, rates for men and women were more nearly equal, but there were striking and persistent inequalities in literacy rates between whites and nonwhites and between native whites and immigrant whites. In North America in general, family wealth and social status were closely correlated with literacy.[24] Despite the rise of mass schooling, this correspondence persists. The recent national assessment of literacy skills in Canada shows that literacy rates correlate strongly with income, that economically depressed regions show lower overall performance than more advanced regions, and that French speakers, a cultural and religious minority, also score lower on average. In the United States, literacy skills are also distributed in a pattern consistent with the distribution of economic opportunity. A 1985 Department of Education study of young adults found that blacks and Hispanics both scored lower than whites and that unemployment, too, could be linked with lower levels of literacy.[25] The closeness of this relationship between literacy and social status and/or wealth has supported the theory that literacy training has failed because it was meant to fail: Illiterates serve an economic and social function as perpetual flunkies and dupes, they are prevented from ever attaining the skills or social identities needed to move up, and, most disturbingly, they are deprived of the abilities to recognize this situation for what it is.

It should be noted that historically subscribers to this view have not all come from the political left. Indeed, representatives of upper-class and business interests for a time opposed the expansion of basic schooling precisely out of a fear that literacy would lead to worker unrest. More broadly, literacy if unconnected from moral teaching was thought to be subversive of the social order. Though this view subsided in the late nineteenth century and the reverse position—support of public schooling as a means of exercising greater control over working-class minds and spirits—substantially replaced it in the twentieth century, it is not difficult to find its impact lingering.

Literacy probably cannot be understood as a social phenomenon, and possibly cannot be effectively taught, without reference to the structures of power that encompass learners, educators, and those who stand behind the campaigns and programs. The fundamental weakness of this perspective, however, lies in key assumptions associated with it. First, as Freire himself clearly recognizes, the fact that literacy may be used to sustain or extend hegemony does not mean that empowerment follows reliably from its attainment. Second, although power relations certainly affect how literacy is used, what it stands for, and who can have it, the underlying conflicts are not simple and consistent, nor is their relationship to literacy so straightforward. To simplify one's analysis of power is perhaps as distorting as having no insight into the importance of power at all.

Again, one can read the historical record differently in support of the first part of this critique. Various groups that sought empowerment in the United States through extending education and literacy found that the relationship between these achievements and political or economic advancement was weak. For example, the percentage of black children in school more than tripled between 1870 and 1900, and the percentage of illiterates among blacks declined during the same period from 80 percent to 44.5 percent. These advances occurred, though, at a time when employment opportunities for educated blacks were stagnant and, in some cases, becoming more restricted and when politically blacks faced mounting opposition in the form of discriminatory legislation—including legal changes to establish segregated schooling as the norm (Tyack, 1974). Indeed, one must wonder after reviewing this and other experiences whether literacy attainment may not be one of the least certain ways to obtain political influence. Forms of political organizing ranging from protest movements to systems of voting patronage have been far more important in promoting group interests and contributing to establishing and maintaining participation in the political process. Yet these other forms rely very little, it seems, on literacy or even educational levels for their success.

Even if there are few cases in the historical record that substantiate a belief in the reality of the tie between literacy and empowerment, what possible negative influence on educational practice could such a view generate? Would not it be reasonable to assume that the most transformative image of literacy would be the most appropriate for a workplace seeking to incorporate not only the manual but also the mental contributions of its workers? To the extent that the newly competitive flexible firms in fact rely on innovation at all levels of the work force, and on a breaking down of the traditional Fordist hierarchy in the production process, empower-

ment seems an appropriate result to wish to achieve through improved
education.

Some difficulties do suggest themselves. To begin with, the rhetoric of
empowerment may fit all too well with the framework that opposes management and worker interests at every turn. Certainly the fear of unleash-
ing workers' critical capacities contributed historically to employers' re-
luctance to expand training beyond narrowly defined and easily
controlled areas. This fit with the broader Fordist goal, explicated by
Braverman and others, of systematically separating workers from broad
knowledge about their jobs and how they fit with the rest of the production process. Although those who would seek empowerment through increased literacy surely did not invent this or related ideas, it is curious that
their views fit the framework so neatly. Learning, in this perspective, is in
fact potentially dangerous to management because a sharpening of critical
and analytical skills would necessarily reveal to workers the unbalanced,
and truly conflictive, nature of their relationship. Curiously, "empowerment" comes close to "enlightenment" as a goal for those who would become literate: The way to attain either is by transforming one's vision of
reality through learning a particular *message,* not, in fact, through the attainment of new capacities.

Problematic institutional arrangements may also be related to the idea
that learning must intensify the felt opposition between workers and
management. One problem is that employer-sponsored education programs, including literacy instruction, have tended to remain conceptually
and physically separated from other forms of employee training. A complex institutional matrix supports this arrangement. Management and
unions in Fordist firms negotiate painstakingly about job categories and
pay scales in a way that sustains rigidity and protects "senior" workers,
and this system focuses the attention of unions—when they do focus on
training—on the types of training needed for particular jobs. Programs
designated as more broadly "educational," including most literacy programs, in contrast, tend to get very little union input. It is common for
firms to try to meet perceived educational needs of their workers by either
working with local community colleges to create traditionally structured
programs or by contracting with private or nonprofit groups to offer relatively standardized basic instruction. Particularly the latter types of programs tend to be run with little or no input from worker representatives.[26]
Even when educators try hard to be sensitive to learner goals, they are
rarely given the opportunity to understand the workplace and workers'
roles in production. Indeed, a large number of programs, particularly
those with a remedial content, tend to follow standard formats and content; although no figures are available, one must suspect that completion

and advancement rates are as poor for such programs as they are in similar programs not connected to job sites.

In contrast, a handful of cases in which unions have participated strongly in literacy and basic skills programs have demonstrated the impact that this involvement can have. The largest union-management education program for workers is in the American auto industry. The United Auto Workers and Ford agreed in 1982 to establish jointly run education programs available to all workers, and the other two big auto makers made similar agreements soon after. The programs are richly funded since they draw off a "tax" based on the total number of employee hours worked. A look at the largest of the three programs, that run by the UAW and GM, gives some insight into both the promise and the problems of such efforts. One thrust of the UAW-GM program has been to provide an opportunity for displaced workers to seek retraining. Interested displaced workers are tested and, if necessary, placed in remedial programs to prepare them for more advanced training. But the program also serves other employees and responds in part to the retraining and basic skills needs in plants where job classifications are becoming broader and requiring workers to do a different mix, and sometimes greater variety, of tasks. Workers affected by such changes tend to be skilled tradesmen who are between 40 and 45 years of age and have been out of school for some time.

The UAW-GM program has relied on contracts with outside providers to fill the needs of both sets of workers and of others who may pursue training for other reasons. But the joint management-labor staff has found that traditional school settings present serious problems. Workers do not feel comfortable in school settings and often do not complete programs, and many workers who are in the greatest need of basic training stay away from programs that are labeled as "remedial" because of the stigma attached to such instruction. Not surprisingly, administrators have started to look for alternatives. A current plan is to set up pilot projects at several plants that will offer literacy instruction that is work related and centered around the performance of tasks on the job. It is hoped that union backing at the plant level will make recruitment easier since one of the worries of participating employees is that admitting that they have literacy problems will adversely affect their chances for promotion.

Union participation has led to a more radical restructuring of basic skills training in a program run by the Ontario Federation of Labor. Entirely under union direction, the Basic Education for Skills Training (BEST) program offers instruction in about 100 small groups set up at work sites and partially funded by employers. The groups are run by volunteers from the workplace, who are trained to emphasize the skills that workers already possess rather than stress their deficiencies. Learners supply educational materials and are encouraged to bring in anything with which they are having trouble. Program organizers have found that as a result instruction is often directly related to work tasks and problems. By making instruction more accessible and more responsive to learners' interests, the BEST scheme has addressed both the recruitment and retention problems encountered by the UAW-GM program staff. Long-term institutional support for BEST remains uncertain, however. Some combination of flexibility and experimentation with secure funding of the type provided by the UAW agreements with the auto industry would appear to be ideal.

Worker participation in the design of programs is perhaps a minimum requirement for their success. One can imagine effective forms of restructuring training that would go still farther. Certainly one of the lessons from analysis of successful examples of flexible production is that remaking the Fordist order involves not just a reorganization of job tasks but a restructuring of hierarchy within the firm. Boundaries between supervisory and worker positions, for example, often become blurred as foremen mix with shopfloor workers to solve technical problems and as both levels are more active in feeding information to marketing personnel and higher management. Further, the important role of smaller firms in regions where larger Fordist firms have been broken up or dissolved has meant that groups of new entrepreneurs, sometimes drawn from the ranks of skilled workers, have themselves been seeking training in order to be better able to handle firm relations with customers, banks, suppliers, and government agencies.

Internal restructuring tends by itself then to remove the stigma of "remedial" training since it requires workers and managers at a variety of levels to sharpen basic skills. The restructuring also logically favors types of training that are closely related to work contexts and, in particular, that are built into the structure of work itself, so that learning takes place through cooperative group efforts on the job. Off-site programs with standardized formats and content appear to be poor alternatives to the possibility of creating formal learning groups that graft onto existing informal learning structures that are already in place.

More broadly, the significant implication of many case studies of flexible production is that the new work strategies are based upon a newly forged trust between workers and management. It is this trust that allows the two sides to abandon certain bargaining positions that impeded the reorganization of production without fearing the consequences (Sabel, 1992). The extent to which such trust can emerge and persist will determine whether job training will be able to redefine itself as something created rather than imposed. New work structures that build on trust do not make the "empowerment" perspective meaningless; power will continue to be a part of workplace politics, and training programs will continue to reflect its distribution. But interpreting literacy learning consistently in terms of the opposition of interests of workers and management is clearly a mistake when alliances inside firms conform to a range of patterns and begin to recast traditional conflicts.

Literacy as a Path Toward Economic Development

The assertion of links between literacy rates and economic advancement is hardly new. In a broad sense, literacy has been seen as one of the preconditions for capitalist growth. This view was particularly prominent among modernization theorists, as they imagined various scenarios by which the developing countries would come increasingly and gradually to resemble the economically advanced countries.[27] More narrowly, literacy acquisition has been thought of within the national sphere as a means for securing entry into the job market. This view represents a kind of modernization theory writ small: Particular groups become fully incorporated in the capitalist economy only when they have adopted the social characteristics required for entry.

A brief look at the historical record reveals that the relationship between literacy and economic advancement, or literacy and employment, is much more tenuous. The Industrial Revolution in England was clearly not dependent, even in a weak sense, on the spread of literacy. In fact, growth was greatest in a period of stagnating literacy rates.[28] Further, there is strong evidence that the short-term impact of industrialization was in fact to inhibit literacy growth. In both France and Britain, industrial towns showed declining literacy rates as the rigors of factory labor disrupted schooling and the boom in population outstripped institutional capacities to provide it. In the United States, the rise of factories appears to have caused skill requirements to decline.[29] Although educational requirements rose for commercial activities supporting industrial growth, jobs in manufacturing themselves rarely required even basic literacy and thus did little to encourage its spread.

In the later Fordist period, too, there is little evidence that literacy per se represented a basic requirement for job entry. Indeed, the vocational movement in education in the United States both responded to and helped to shape a market in which basic literacy was needed, if at all, as a prerequisite for studying specific sets of skills closely associated with particular occupations. Technical knowledge was in fact conceived of as different from scientific or liberal knowledge because it relied fundamentally on visual and manual skills rather than on symbolic notation (Stevens, 1990). Much current comment on the importance of literacy for labor market entry fits this established tradition of vocationalism. That is, literacy is conceived as something that must come before skill attainment. It is remedial instruction, separated in the curriculum from the teaching of job skills.

This perspective differs, then, from the "enlightenment" and "empowerment" views in one important respect. It represents literacy not as context specific, or rooted in a particular message of personal or social transformation, but as a generic skill, detached from specific content. The view may represent an overcorrection. One problem is pedagogical: The view assumes that knowledge and abilities cannot be widely applied unless they are taught in the broadest possible context. But this capacity may develop differently, through analogy-building after decoding in a specific setting is mastered. The second problem has to do with the biases disguised by the perspective's emphasis on literacy as a technical tool. Viewing literacy as a threshold for employment *seems* to be rationally rather than ideologically based, yet it agrees with and supports the evolutionary vision of illiterates as being less than fully "modern." They lack not a moral fineness that makes them fully human but a technical capacity that makes them fully functional. For that matter, it is easier in this perspective to castigate people with low levels of literacy because the learning of a discretely defined generic skill should be within their grasp; they are offered the standard instruction, and if they do not learn from it, then the failure to learn must lie with them.

These unresolved difficulties are clearly seen in the functioning of literacy and training programs all over the country. Literacy in most places is still taught as a remedial skill and separated from job-related (or otherwise practical) applications. In a few cities and states where reformers have attempted to change this relationship by teaching basic skills in job-related contexts or by teaching job skills while imparting general strategies rather than specific techniques, they have met with considerable institutional rigidity and even active resistance.[30] The vocational educators, as their critics charge, have a strong interest in preserving a definition of what they do as something separate from what other educators do. Indeed, the system of funding, from the federal level down, reinforces this quality, as I discuss later.

Just as there is little evidence that this imagined "basic" literacy was essential for employment in the heyday of Fordism, there is little to suggest that it would be appropriate or sufficient for employment in the wake of Fordism's restructuring. Flexible production implies a need for a more complex mix of capacities and a certain difficulty in separating literacy skills from other competencies. Although skill requirements of jobs may be greater, however, literacy levels would not by themselves function as a powerful determinant of growth or employment. As various case studies have shown, flexible production works best in settings where the restructuring of production inside firms is supported by a network of relationships linking firms in the same and related sectors and tying industry participants in webs of social relationships outside of work.[31] The importance of this complex matrix of communications in determining the dynamism of particular industries and regions suggests a significant change in the way we think about literacy and work. The "context" of literacy use that is important is not defined just by what people do on the job. More important is the *social context* of literacy that encompasses both work relationships (rather than work tasks) and networks of communication that overlap with those at work. Much more so than mere literacy rates, whether or not workers and managers are able to participate fully in creating a vibrant web of communications will determine opportunities for dynamic growth.

Reinventing the Problem

Traditional ways of thinking about literacy support institutional responses of questionable effectiveness. They also mirror ways of thinking about work that are more appropriate to Fordist productive organization than to many work settings today. I now turn to the question of how both sets of ideas may be revised and to the trends in literacy training that this revision would support.

The work on functional literacy and literacy as a context-specific set of abilities has certainly helped to move debates slowly away from the three themes we have identified. Yet, given the persistence of the three approaches I have discussed (and given the shortcomings of most policies and programs), one wonders whether the approach has gone far enough.

Consider one of the key ideas associated with the idea of functional literacy. It has by now been convincingly argued that people learn literacy skills better when these are related to a context that is meaningful to them. This point constitutes, indeed, one of the strongest arguments for integrating job skills instruction with literacy training rather than having one follow the other in a way that derails many students. The idea of learning in context also stands in opposition to the "enlightenment" and "empowerment" perspectives. Place literacy training in the context of what learners truly want to know, the argument goes, and they will learn; conceal literacy training in the context of a message that you think they *should* know, and they will learn less well, if at all.

Yet, recommending grounding literacy training in specific contexts seems still to suggest that literacy is essentially about receiving a certain kind of message. Functioning in limited contexts is surely not the goal of literacy, and it does not truly reflect its possibilities. Taking literacy instruction away from the moralists and putting it into practical contexts is only a step forward if we recognize and somehow incorporate the idea that literacy does not *confine* learners in particular contexts. If this is the goal, then we are merely in the presence of a new form of vocationalism, one that is still tailored to Fordist forms of production. The enabling promise of literacy is to enhance participation in the transformation of social environments, to include, presumably, job sites badly in need of criticism and reform from within. The most meaningful context for literacy is not encompassed in fixed job categories (or in particular professions) but in volatile social relations. It may be impossible to devise effective pedagogical strategies for flexible production workers without recognizing this fact.

Put differently, context-based programs cannot be effective if the context of work is poorly understood or wrongly represented. The distortions of interpretation occur on a number of levels. To begin with, we know surprisingly little about what actually gets read on most jobs and under what circumstances. Deeper analyses of how people communicate with one another (not just whether they do so orally or in writing, but what sorts of conventions they use to communicate, such as work stories or personal histories) or of how circulating printed materials relate to how people actually do their jobs are lacking for the vast majority of workplaces. The studies we do have suggest that a quick assessment that would look at written materials on the job and devise strategies for learning how to read them, or read them better, would be missing the mark. For example, Orr (1991) found in a study of photocopier repair technicians that the workers relied extensively on oral narratives supplied by other workers about repair problems. In part as a result, what they did while repairing machines was quite different from what training manuals instructed. The latter were relied on very little. Reviewing this and other cases, Baba (1991) concludes that skills already held by workers often are overlooked by management because they reside not in individuals but in a knowledge base generated through informal group interactions. Thus managers or their representatives who would assess skill levels through individual testing or review of printed materials would arrive at a distorted view. Significantly, they would also be overlooking an important way in which skill is an asset of the firm because it is inseparable from sets of social relations within the firm.

On a second level, work settings and how knowledge is used in them cannot be assessed without reference to the conflicts that organize people's perceptions and efforts at work. Ethnographies of industrial work, for example, tell us that workers often conceive of their jobs in ways that are entirely different from formal descriptions of the same jobs. They base their understanding in large part on perceptions of social ties and conflicts at work, and they may alter their behavior according to their assessment of how it will affect their membership in particular work groups. For example, Buraway (1978) found in his ethnography of a machine shop that workers made strenuous efforts to meet production targets for various jobs because of a shopfloor culture that socially rewarded those who could "make out" consistently. Again, an assessment of worker skills that missed this very skillful maneuvering on the part of workers or that ignored the extent to which it enabled exchanges of information relevant to those skills would undervalue and misrepresent the relevant "context" of the workplace.

Understanding the context for literacy instruction would thus require much more than learning the vocabulary of a particular setting or of assessing the reading levels required for particular jobs. Some program planners have tried to approach this problem by asking learners what it is they wish to achieve through training and by involving them in its design. Such learner-centered approaches mark an important improvement, but it is likely that many learners themselves cannot describe accurately the patterns through which on-the-job communications and learning take place.

Just as educators need to address these pedagogical questions about how context-based instruction is to work, firms must also overcome obstacles to restructuring work in ways that will allow such training to be effective. The message of a good deal of writing about innovative firms and fast-growth regions is that out of the chaos of restructuring in the late 1970s and early 1980s came more chaos. That is, firms that were able *not* to replace old, failed strategies with new, equally rigid routines fared best. In a sense, they gave up trying to predict what was going to happen and shifted toward a strategy of attempting to create and lead markets through product and process innovation. Many headquarters were gutted and sections eliminated, and more scope for action was necessarily taken by subsidiaries, branches, and field units. This process is still under way. Although many firms have been able to survive without such radical restructuring, business is well aware of the pressures that are upon them to move in these directions. Yet the legacy of Fordism cannot be expected to disappear overnight. Managers often tend to view literacy and basic skills instruction very positively but see it as a kind of lubricant to the system of work rather than something more fundamental.

Consider one example. A textile firm outside Athens, Georgia, offers workers a variety of courses of instruction to raise literacy levels as part of a response to the purchase of new electronic equipment that requires workers to key in numbers and words periodically as they work. The new machinery is also generating a need for new kinds of skilled workers to troubleshoot technical problems, and the basic skills instruction is seen as a way of bringing line workers up to skill levels they would need to complete the technical training course. These educational needs are not being responded to with changes on the factory floor. The emphasis, if anything, is on altering production roles as little as possible and hoping that workers will pick up enough from unconnected literacy and basic skills courses to work more efficiently. Literacy skills are not viewed as being related to a capacity for recognizing how to do their jobs differently, or better, or by finding fault with the current system of organization.[32]

An option for firms that would seem to address both training needs and competitive goals is to restructure work radically so that learning is built into jobs. Teamwork, rotation of tasks, encouraging hands-on work by supervisory staff (and breaking down the distinction between line workers and supervisors more generally)—these are a few beginning strategies that may allow training, and even basic skills learning, to be incorporated into workers' daily experiences. But these strategies will not amount to much without more fundamental restructuring of hierarchy—a reconstruction of "trust" that allows older ways of organizing work to be truly abandoned before new and necessarily ad hoc arrangements have been worked out (Sabel, 1992). Simply to introduce new ministructures of cooperation would be parallel to the pedagogical error of teaching the old remedial curriculum with a new vocabulary. Actually, a profound transformation of work relations would make the latter transparently unworkable, since the "context" in which workers utilize skills, in such cases, could not be fully replicated in the classroom even through painstaking efforts; workers and management would still be inventing it.

Getting to this point may involve not only reorganizing production work but also reconceptualizing the relation of training to other firm functions. Human resources and personnel offices often run worker training programs, and these offices are usually quite remote from knowledge about the production process. This certainly is true when production processes are changing quickly. Shopfloor supervisors may abandon the goal of training specific workers for specific tasks long before training departments are willing to do so; in fact, building in learning on jobs too effectively would threaten the very existence of separate training managers. Trainers themselves thus seem in need of retraining through the restructuring of their own jobs.

It should not be difficult to see the differences between adopting new concepts of work and literacy and continuing to be guided by older ways of envisioning their meaning and relation. Even well-funded and well-intentioned programs that adhere to older paradigms will continue to separate learners from work environments, place them in alienating classrooms, and have them follow, rather passively, a generic course of instruction that seems to them remote—beyond their influence or control and of questionable application to their own experience. Yet, at the same time, we should be careful to point out that merely recasting the concepts of work and literacy is not enough. The context in which we want learners to function better needs itself to be better understood and changed. Further, complex and long-standing institutional arrangements must respond to and support this redefinition. This larger context is as important as the immediate context of instruction.

The Challenge to Institutions

I do not have the opportunity here to analyze the organization of literacy and basic skills training in any detail, and, in any case, this has been done elsewhere. But I need at least to identify the key problems that present themselves for reform in the United States.

In contrast to some Western European countries, the United States has no strong tradition of federal leadership in education matters. Although the Department of Education has made a formal commitment to support literacy training, federal funds for this purpose remain very limited. By one estimate $1 to $2 billion are distributed through a range of federal programs, leaving the burden for most spending on the states (Chisman, 1989). A more serious problem seems to be that the funding that does exist is administered in such a way that it places formidable constraints on the actions of states and localities. State officials admit that they are often bewildered about which programs or agencies to go to for support of literacy initiatives. The fragmented funding system distributes adult literacy training funds among the Job Training Partnership Act (JTPA), Adult Basic Education (ABE), and a handful of other, smaller programs, an approach that is then replicated at the state level. The confusion has spawned a number of efforts, including one at the national level, to create clearinghouse organizations for information on literacy programs, but this strategy hardly addresses the fundamental problems of a fragmented funding structure and inadequate spending.[33]

Since states find themselves administering a fragmented series of programs, it is not surprising that the minibureaucracies attached to these often oppose change that might signal their obsolescence. A logical accompaniment to these turf battles is a resistance throughout the education establishment to measures of accountability. We know next to nothing about which kinds of programs actually train people better—which programs retain learners longer, graduate them at higher rates, or place them in appropriate jobs. The existing system rewards programs for maintaining levels of enrollment and not on the basis of other criteria such as completion rates, student performance, or postgraduation placement.[34]

More broadly, alliances among the institutions of the state, labor, and business must be strengthened at the local, regional, and sectoral levels. A few states such as Mississippi and Michigan have already moved toward plans to coordinate training programs and centralize the placement of learners. One way of improving the contribution of business to this effort is by inviting sectoral or regional associations to work with educators in planning context-specific instruction for their industries. Unions, as I argued in an earlier section, are essential participants in such efforts. Finally, the federal role must be substantially altered to provide for more scope locally to determine how best to organize such training.

In all these efforts, U.S. policymakers need at least to examine the lessons of regional development efforts in Western Europe. Training there has figured as part of a series of supports extended to networkers of businesses in so-called industrial districts. A key feature of successful support programs is that they have in fact relied on tripartite alliances at the local and regional levels, both to generate information from the ground up (rather than relying on bureaucrats or educators to discern what is needed) about the sorts of training that are most pressing and that can be provided for the least well by firms acting on their own. Such approaches have also been effective in mitigating recruitment problems; worker and business associations help to spread the word about the availability of training, and their participation in planning the training helps reduce suspicions on the part of business owners and workers that government-backed programs will be unresponsive to their needs. Significantly, many of these efforts have blurred the distinctions between "basic training" for workers and "advanced training" for management; many small business owners are as much in need of basic skills training as their employees, and many are eager, too, to master the technical skills used on the shopfloor so that they can understand and reorganize production more effectively.[35]

It is unclear to what extent such strategies would be appropriate to the United States. Improving literacy levels of adult workers is part of a broader problem of adjusting to post-Fordist conditions. As a policy issue, it should not be separated as an "educational" issue from other problems such as the need for credit and managerial support for new small firms forming in restructured industries, the dissemination of technology in loosely configured sectors, and cooperation among groups of smaller firms to compete internationally. Whether training and literacy problems get addressed effectively will depend in part on whether we see the emergence of unorthodox alliances to address such problems. Sectoral or regional associations starting to respond to particular restructuring problems may be able to devise more effective training strategies in a reactive and ad hoc fashion than education planners would ever be able to do. For policymakers, this may be a frustrating message. Like the other problems of the new economy, this one has no quick fix and no standard fix either. There is much, of course, that can be done by outside agents who are willing to dedicate themselves to improving communications among the various players and who will demonstrate a willingness to understand work contexts in all their complexity. Discarding antiquated frameworks for conceptualizing the relationship between learning and work is a significant start, for it at least opens us to the possibility of new solutions.

Notes

1. Although the demographic trends are undeniable, the fears that they will lead to a less skilled work force appear to be exaggerated. The view implies, certainly, a contradictory assessment of those already in the work force. On the one hand, they are assumed to be more skilled and adaptable than new entrants; on the other hand, when they are displaced, they are seen as poorly prepared for retraining. In the absence of detailed studies of how various groups actually fare in training, blaming poor performance on newer entrants to the labor force makes unwarranted and possibly biased assumptions about the abilities of workers who are not white native males. The view also romantically contrasts the labor force today with a "traditional" work force that never existed in pure form, even in the heyday of Fordism.

2. The media have consistently cited the grossly exaggerated figure that two-thirds of adult Americans are functionally illiterate. The figure was originally based on an extrapolation of results of a 1975 survey (the APL survey) that required respondents to perform a range of literacy-related tasks. Though rejected by experts and subsequently disproved by more sophisticated, and larger, studies using a similar approach, the figure continues to be used in the public discussions of the ties between American workers' education and flagging U.S. competitiveness.

3. The best analysis of forces leading to firm restructuring and a break with Fordist strategies remains Piore and Sabel, 1984. The amount of detailed research actually done on the changing requirements of jobs as a result of these trends is disturbingly thin. Nevertheless, the coherence of the perspective that bundles the effects of restructuring, together with scattered case studies that seem to confirm the trends in job style and content (e.g., Bailey, 1989; Benton et al., 1991; and Scribner and Sachs, 1990), stand against very little evidence that jobs or management attitudes are static.

4. See Benton (1990) for an analysis of political barriers to flexible production in one case.

5. For further discussion of the development of thinking about functional literacy, see Benton and Noyelle (1992) and especially De Castell, Luke, and MacLennan (1986).

6. A more detailed summary of the U.S. and Canadian assessments is in Benton and Noyelle (1992). See also Kirsch and Jungeblut, 1986; and Kirsch, Jungeblut, and Campbell, 1992.

7. The handbook is *The Bottom Line: Basic Skills in the Workplace*, published jointly by the Departments of Education and Labor in 1988.

8. *The Bottom Line* (see note 7) gives a good summary of the practical applications to literacy training of contextual approaches.

9. Mikulecky (1989) points out the dearth of information on student completion and performance in literacy programs. In a small but significant study, he found that no program surveyed retained students for long enough on average to make a significant impact on their reading abilities. An estimated 100 contact hours are needed to raise a learner's grade-level reading ability by only one year; most students in literacy programs spend far less time in instruction before leaving.

10. The textile industry is an example of a sector in which many firms have tried to maintain Fordist production styles by retrenchment in more standardized markets, a strategy that appears to offer short-lived success given the way even these markets are fragmenting. In retailing, one finds changed recruitment strategies and automation being used to confront perceived training problems. For discussion of these examples, see Benton et al., 1991.

11. Reich envisions production workers being recast as "symbolic analysts" who have knowledge of the interconnections of all the parts of the production process and the competency to pass coded messages about problems. Still, he emphasizes not on-the-job experience and instruction as key to these abilities, but rather "a solid grounding in mathematics, basic science, and reading and communications skills" (Reich, 1991: 248). In a later section I discuss the origins of this questionable division of basic skills from workplace competencies. I should also note that most of my analysis refers to restructuring in manufacturing firms, but many of the same observations apply to the services. On the implications of restructuring for worker training in banking, financial services, and retailing, see Benton et al., 1991.

12. In some countries, most notably Sweden, a surge in literacy between 1660 and 1720 was linked closely to church activism (Johansson, 1981). In other cases, the influence was less marked and perhaps less important than other factors. For a broad discussion of the role of the Protestant church, see Kaestle, 1991. Graff (1977) gives a good discussion of the moralizing of many literacy proponents in Canada in the nineteenth century.

13. The influence is compounded by the perspective of many education historians who also view education as essentially a liberating force in American culture. Kaestle (1991:4) observes that this is a view held by Cremin, who is arguably the most influential historian of U.S. education.

14. Curtis' discussion of a controversial gift of a collection of works of fiction to a Canadian library in the 1840s helps to make this point: "Debate raged on literally for months as members tried unsuccessfully to sell the collection and refused to contemplate simply destroying it. At issue were the serious consequences upon the character of the individual—and hence upon social order in general—which the consumption of particular kinds of books might have. Reading and the cultural basis of civilization were seen to be inextricably linked" (Curtis, 1990: 621).

15. Analysis by Graff of Ontario records show that ethnicity, occupational class, and gender were far more important than illiteracy in determining interactions with the judicial system. Illiterates did tend to be overrepresented, not among those arrested but among those convicted, a finding that Graff argues explains more about judicial biases against social groups with lower literacy rates than about the moral standing of illiterate defendants (Graff, 1977).

16. From Kozol (1985:35). Kozol argues that those who represent illiterates' lives as better than this are merely playing into the hands of insincere reformers who wish to feel comfortable about high illiteracy rates. This may sometimes be the case. But it strikes me that to portray people as having limited capacities for cognition as a way of shocking others into a realization of their plight is questionable as a political strategy.

17. The remark about Russian peasants is from D'Angelo (1983:104), a scholar of rhetoric and composition who takes Ong's ideas at face value and applies them to thinking about writing instruction. Poor writers are cognitively backward, in his view.

18. I exaggerate somewhat. Goody (e.g., 1987), though more careful in examining the complexity of oral cultures and traditions, has helped to spread evolutionary ideas about literacy in anthropology.

19. Interview with Michael Fox, director of Plan, Inc., in winter 1990.

20. For example, a national adult literacy campaign in Britain begun in 1975 with the help of the BBC attracted thousands of learners but considerably more volunteers.

21. See, again, Mikulecky, 1989. The campaign in Britain described in note 20 was most successful in recruiting learners who were white males, a group that did not have the highest illiteracy rates.

22. The recent national assessment of literacy in Canada, for example, shows the lowest rates in the eastern maritime provinces, Nova Scotia and Newfoundland. The only literacy programs of any size are those run by volunteer organizations. In contrast, British Columbia, which has one of the highest rates of literacy, funds an extensive network of literacy and basic skills classes through community colleges. Other western provinces have found ways to siphon public funds to community organizations. See Benton and Noyelle, 1992.

23. De Castell and Luke (1986) make this point. However, they see the technocratic view of literacy as supplanting previous moralistic approaches, whereas I view the them as continuing to exist side by side.

24. See Kaestle (1991) and Graff (1987). As Graff is careful to qualify, literacy was not a cause of the disadvantaged status of certain groups but was undoubtedly a symptom.

25. For summaries of the results of the U.S. and Canadian studies, see Benton and Noyelle, 1992.

26. Many of the programs are also run away from the job site, which impedes access for some workers and removes the programs from worker or union influence. Some educators, though, argue that off-site training is essential to allowing workers to study without fearing that their attendance or performance will influence their standing at work. No studies have been done of the effects of off-site training, to my knowledge.

27. See Anderson, 1965; and McClelland, 1966.

28. Stone, 1969; Schoffield, 1973; see also Kaestle, 1991, for a summary of findings on this relationship.

29. See Furet and Ozouf (1976) on France and Sanderson (1972) on England. On the Massachusetts case in the United States, see Field, 1980.

30. Karl Haigler, creator of a new literacy campaign in Mississippi, is especially critical of the turf battles created by the fragmented bureaucracy and their impediments to innovation. He likes to cite the example of a course created with private-sector help called "Math for Plumbers" that was to help trainees with basic skills in math while also teaching plumbing skills. Vocational education officials objected to mixing basic skills training in a vocational course, and the effort was stopped. Interview with Karl Haigler, winter 1990.

31. There has now been extensive research on the social relationships supporting dynamic growth in various "industrial districts" in Western Europe. See Pyke and Sengenberger, 1992.

32. For more detailed discussion of this case, see Benton et al., 1991.

33. As one critic points out, the strategy also does not address the problem that nearly all existing literacy programs are failing. "What do these networks literally do? They network nothingness. ... They 'keep in touch'—or so they claim. With what? With one another's failure" (Kozol, 1985: 50).

34. Frustration with this system of funding according to full-time enrollment (FTE) rates led one state, Mississippi, to implement new evaluation systems. Mississippi's program is under the direction of Karl Haigler, a former director of federal adult education, who in an interview identified the problem of accountability as perhaps the most serious one facing state and federal administrators, who simply do not know which programs are valuable to maintain and which should be ended.

35. Local provision of various types of training both for small entrepreneurs and for workers has played an important role in the vibrant industrial districts of central Italy (see Capechi, 1989; Piore and Sabel, 1984). It is significant that other regions are trying to provide access to a wider range of short-course training, ranging from technical instruction to bookkeeping and marketing, and that they are targeting small entrepreneurs in particular. In the Valencian region in Spain, technical centers have been set up to serve the numerous geographically concentrated manufacturing sectors, with precisely the Italian model in mind. See Benton, 1992.

References

Akinnaso, F. Niyi. 1992. "Schooling, language, and knowledge in literate and non-literate societies," *Comparative Studies in Society and History* 34(1):68–109.

Anderson, C. A. 1965. "Literacy and schooling on the development threshold," pp. 347–362 in C. A. Anderson and M. J. Bowman (eds.), *Education and Economic Development*. Chicago: University of Chicago Press.

Baba, Marietta. 1991. "The skill requirements of work activity: An ethnographic perspective," *Anthropology of Work Review* 12(3):2–11.

Benton, Lauren. 1990. *Invisible factories: The informal economy and industrial development in Spain*. Albany, N.Y.: SUNY Press.

_____. 1992. "The emergence of industrial districts in Spain: Industrial restructuring and diverging regional responses," pp. 48–86 in F. Pyke and W.

Sengenberger (eds.), *Industrial districts and local economic regeneration*. Geneva: International Institute for Labour Studies.

Benton, Lauren, Thomas Bailey, Thierry Noyelle, and Thomas M. Stanback, Jr. 1991. *Employee training and U.S. competitiveness: Lessons for the 1990s*. Boulder: Westview Press.

Benton, Lauren, and Thierry Noyelle. 1992. *Adult illiteracy and economic performance*. Paris: Organization for Economic Cooperation and Development.

Buraway, Michael. 1978. *Manufacturing consent*. Cambridge: Cambridge University Press.

Capecchi, Vitorio. 1989. "The informal economy and the development of flexible specialization in Emilia Romagna," pp. 189–215 in Alejandro Portes, Manuel Castells, and Lauren Benton (eds.), *The informal economy*. Baltimore, Md.: Johns Hopkins University Press.

Chisman, Forrest. 1989. *Jump start: The federal role in adult literacy*. Washington, D.C.: Southport Institute for Policy Analysis.

Cole, M., and S. Scribner. 1974. *Culture and thought*. New York: Wiley.

Curtis, Bruce. 1990. "Some recent work on the history of literacy in Canada," *History of Education Quarterly* 30(4):613–624.

D'Angelo, Frank. 1983. "Literacy and cognition: A developmental perspective," pp. 97–114 in Richard W. Bailey and Robin Melanie Fosheim (eds.), *Literacy for life: The demand for reading and writing*. New York: Modern Language Association.

de Castell, Suzanne, and Allan Luke. 1986. "Models of literacy in North American schools: Social and historical conditions and consequences," pp. 87–109 in Suzanne de Castell, Allan Luke, and Kieran Egan (eds.), *Literacy, society and schooling*. Cambridge: Cambridge University Press.

de Castell, Suzanne, Allan Luke, and David Machennan. 1986. "On defining literacy," pp. 3–14 in Suzanne de Castell, *Society and Schooling*. Cambridge: Cambridge University Press.

Delattre, Edwin J. 1983. "The insiders," pp. 52–59 in Richard W. Bailey and Robin Melanie Fosheim (eds.), *Literacy for life: The demand for reading and writing*. New York: Modern Language Association.

Dichkoff, George. 1988. "An appraisal of adult literacy programs: Reading between the lines," *Journal of Reading* (April):624–630.

Field, Alexander. 1980. "Industrialization and skill intensity: The case of Massachusetts," *Journal of Human Resources* 15(2):149–175.

Freire, Paolo. 1971. *Pedagogy of the oppressed*. New York: Herder and Herder.

Furet, Franqis, and Jacques Ozouf. 1976. "Literacy and industrialization: The case of the Départment du Nord in France," *Journal of European Economic History* 5:5–44.

Goody, Jack. 1987. *The interface between the written and the oral*. Cambridge: Cambridge University Press.

Graff, Harvey. 1977. "Pauperism, misery, and vice: Illiteracy and criminality in the nineteenth century," *Journal of Social History* 11:245–268.

———. 1987. *The legacies of literacy: Continuities and contradictions in Western culture and society*. Bloomington: Indiana University Press.

Johansson, Egil. 1981. "The history of literacy in Sweden," pp. 152–153 in Harvey Graff (ed.), *Literacy and social development in the West: A reader*. Cambridge: Cambridge University Press.

Kaestle, Carl F. 1991. "Studying the history of literacy," pp. 3–32 in C. F. Kaestle et al. (eds.), *Literacy in the United States*. New Haven and London: Yale University Press.

Kirsch, Irwin, and Ann Jungeblut. 1986. *Literacy: Profiles of America's young adults, National Assessment of Educational Progress*. Princeton: Educational Testing Services.

Kirsch, Irwin, Ann Jungeblut, and Anne Campbell. 1992. *Beyond the school doors, the literacy needs of job seekers served by the U.S. Department of Labor*. Washington, D.C.: U.S. Department of Labor.

Kozol, Jonathan. 1985. *Illiterate America*. New York: Plume.

Lockridge, Kenneth. 1974. *Literacy in colonial New England: An enquiry into the social context of literacy in the early modern west*. New York: W. W. Norton.

McClelland, D. C. 1966. "Does education accelerate economic growth?" *Economic Development and Cultural Change* 14:257–278.

Mikulecky, Larry. 1989. "Second chance basic skills education," paper prepared for the U.S. Department of Labor, Commission of Workforce Quality and Labor Market Efficiency.

Ong, Walter. 1982. *Orality and literacy*. New York: Methuen.

Orr, Julian. 1991. "Contested Knowledge," *Anthropology of Work Review* 12(3):12–15.

Piore, Michael J. and Charles F. Sabel. 1984. *The second industrial design: Possibilities for prosperity*. New York: Basic Books.

Pyke, F., and W. Sengenberger, eds. 1992. *Industrial districts and local economic regeneration*. Geneva: International Institute for Labour Studies.

Reich, Robert. 1991. *The work of nations*. New York: Alfred Knopf.

Sabel, Charles. 1992. "Studied trust: Building new forms of cooperation in a volatile economy," pp. 215–250 in F. Pyke and W. Sengenberger (eds.), *Industrial districts and local economic regeneration*. Geneva: International Institute for Labour Studies.

Sanderson, Michael. 1972. "Literacy and social mobility in the industrial revolution in England," *Past and Present* 56:75–104.

Schoffield, Roger S. 1973. "Dimensions of illiteracy, 1750–1850," *Explorations in Economic History* 10:437–454.

Scribner, S., and M. Cole. 1973. "Cognitive consequences of formal and informal education," *Science* 182:553–559.

Scribner, S., and P. Sachs. 1990. *A study of on-the-job training*. Technical paper no. 13, National Center on Education and Employment. New York: Columbia University.

Stevens, Edward W., Jr. 1990. "Technology, literacy, and early industrial expansion in the United States," *History of Education Quarterly* 30(4):523–544.

Sticht, Thomas G. 1975. *Reading for work: A functional literacy anthology*. Alexandria, Va.: Human Resources Research Organization.

Stone, Lawrence. 1969. "Literacy and education in England, 1640–1900," *Past and Present* 42:102–126.

Tyack, David B. 1974. *The one best system: A history of American urban education.* Cambridge: Harvard University Press.

U.S. Department of Labor and U.S. Department of Education. 1988. *The bottom line: Basic skills in the workplace.* Washington, D.C.: U.S. Government Printing Office.

Walters, Keith. 1990. "Language, Logic, and Literacy," pp. 173–188 in eds. A. Lunsford, H. Moglen, and J. Slevin. *The Right to Literacy.* New York: Modern Language Association.

6

The New Immigrants

Roger Waldinger and Thomas Bailey

New York City's brush with fiscal insolvency in the mid-1970s signaled the end for the U.S. urban-industrial economies. Its revival in the 1980s heralded the emergence of the nation's largest cities as world service centers. For the smokestack cities of the industrial heartland there is unfortunately no replacement for their run-of-the-mill production activities, steadily eroding under the twin impact of computerization and foreign competition. But in the largest urban agglomerations—Chicago, Los Angeles, Philadelphia, and especially New York—the advent of a postindustrial economy triggered a new phase of growth. The key activities of the new economy—information processing, the coordination of large organizations, and the management of volatile financial markets—are overwhelmingly urban based. And their dynamism has yanked these largest cities out of the economic torpor into which they had sunk.

Growth makes news from the urban front not as grim as in urban crisis days of yore. But notwithstanding the new urban vitality, there is little question that the cities remain deeply troubled—perhaps more so than before. The paradox of urban plenty is that comparatively few of the city's residents have been able to enjoy the fruits of growth. The number of poor people living in central cities has not fallen but has risen, and dramatically so. The economic turnaround has not arrested social dislocation in the poorest urban communities. On the contrary, the severe social problems first identified twenty-five years ago appear both exacerbated and more concentrated. Though differing on social policy responses, both right and left agree that a sizable segment of the poor has been lopped off into an "urban underclass"—persistently poor and with no connection to legitimate ways of making a living.[1]

Demography is the subtext to the contemporary tale of urban woe. "Back to the city" has been the catchword of the new urban professionals—today's huddled masses, piled up in neighborhoods in and around the downtown business centers. But the influx of these much maligned gentry has never matched up to the attention it received in the press. The tide of people flowing cityward remains what it has been for the past forty years: America's big cities attract mainly nonwhites. First came blacks, displaced from the technological backwaters of the agrarian South. Then came a wave of immigrants from the labor-surplus areas of the developing world. Today's urban newcomers are arriving in numbers that rival the great migrations of a century ago.[2]

Thus the city of services is also a "majority minority" city. But how does this population base fit into the urban economy of today?

The received academic wisdom is that there is no fit at all. This is a story about the passing of the city of production and its consequences for the urban poor. The industrial city grew because it possessed labor and what it demanded of its labor was willing hands and strong muscles—not diplomas or technical expertise. But in the city of information processing and the transaction of high-level business deals, these qualities count no more. In the equation between the city's economic function and its population base, the unlettered, no matter how willing, have irrevocably lost out. The decline of the industrial city has left minorities high and dry.[3]

There is also a dissenting interpretation, now sufficiently repeated, to be a conventional wisdom of its own. This rival story of the postindustrial city is a tale of occupational polarization amidst industrial transformation. Modern urban development generates growth of high-level professional and managerial jobs and a proliferation of low-skilled, low-income "service" jobs. In the polarized metropolis, minorities are far from useless: They are the new drawers of water and hewers of work. In this version, it is not the poor who depend on the rich for their beneficence and for a trickle-down of jobs and income. Rather, the rich need the poor—to provide low-cost services, to maintain the city's underbelly, and to prop up what remains of the depressed manufacturing sector.[4]

The argument of this chapter is that both stories—however intuitively appealing they may be separately or together—have it all wrong.[5] Neither metaphor of polarization or dislocation captures the impact of the postindustrial urban transformation. Both stories miss out on the new sources of opportunity and also obscure the barriers that keep groups from exploiting chances to get ahead. Both stories treat the people they are describing as an undifferentiated, passive mass. Neither considers the possibility that African-Americans and immigrants can call on strengths within their own communities to meet the challenges presented by the evolving urban economy. And each story skips over history, forgetting how disparate the past experiences of African-Americans and new immigrants are and how those differences in experience condition expectations and behavior.

Our interpretation of the new urban reality will be developed in a single, sustained argument in the pages that follow. In briefest compass, the argument reads like this: The conventional perspectives lack a supply-side approach. The loss of white city residents is seen as the source of urban disaster. But in fact, the outflow of whites is what gives newcomers their chance. During economic downturns, whites have fled the city at rates that outpace the rate of decline. And when the economy has re-heated, the outward seepage of whites has slowed down but has never stopped. Proportionately, whites have thus been in constant decline. This shift in ethnic proportions of a population is what we call "compositional change." That change generates opportunities for other groups up and down the hierarchy of jobs—but particularly where employer requirements are not too high.[6]

Compositional change, resulting from the outflow of whites, in turn creates what we shall call "replacement demand." In a race-conscious society like ours, workers are ordered by ethnic and racial characteristics in a hiring queue. All things being equal, white persons of European ancestry rank at the top. But when the top group is no longer available—or can be recruited only in greatly diminished numbers—then employers hire workers whom they previously would have rejected.[7]

As we shall show in the remainder of this chapter, replacement demand is a powerful source of urban labor market change—and one that conventional interpretations have ignored to their peril. But if there are opportunities to be exploited, to whom and under what circumstances do these spoils go?

These are questions that the conventional stories cannot begin to answer. At a conceptual level, the stories mistake the category "minority" for something more than an invention of official statistics.[8] African-Americans and third world immigrants may constitute an acceptable aggregate for counting who's who and how many are who. But the underlying social reality is one of sharp group boundaries and distinctions: African-Americans and third world immigrants occupy very different places in the urban economy.[9]

Once one moves beyond the all-purpose concept of "minority," the contradictions between the prevailing stories of urban change come fully into view. To account for rising levels of unemployment and poverty among African-Americans one points to the decline of low-level jobs. But the supposed proliferation of these very same jobs is used to explain why *immigrants*, many with educational levels well below those of blacks, continue to arrive in large numbers in the "postindustrial" city. Clearly, the two cannot both be true.

Though the distinction between African-Americans and immigrants is forgotten in the discussion of the changing urban economies, it conveniently appears in arguments that make the case for the declining significance of discrimination against blacks. If new immigrants, who are unlike

whites in recognizable cultural or physical traits, have higher employment rates and faster earnings growth than African-Americans, does this
not show that blacks, and *not* the broader society, are to blame for their
economic problems?[10] But this assumes that blacks and immigrants are
alike simply because they are somehow different from whites. The reality,
however, is that the labor market differences between new immigrants
and African-Americans are both real and profound.

Why should that be? Here again, the prevailing stories have too simplistic a view—as if individual workers were simply sorted into jobs or industries in accordance with the skills that they somehow acquired. In fact
there is no mechanism that puts some individuals here and others there.
Immigrants and African-Americans are not simply collections of persons
that differ in individual characteristics. They are groups with collective resources such as access to social networks based on family and ethnic ties
that can be used to get jobs, information, labor supplies, and capital. And
as groups they also have shared experiences that shape their economic
orientations, predisposing them toward some lines of work, diverting
them from others. Sorting in the labor market involves the mobilization of
these group resources, in directions influenced by underlying job orientations, and their deployment in struggles to break down discriminatory
barriers and to capture the best pieces of the pie.

African-Americans and third world immigrants are sharply disparate
in the discriminatory barriers that they face, in job orientations, in group
resources, and in the ability to mobilize those resources competitively. For
these reasons, they have responded to the opportunities and constraints
of the postindustrial urban transition in very unlike ways. The key points
are these: African-Americans and third world immigrants actively shape
their own fates by creating distinctive ethnic economic niches. But history
affects where those niches are to be carved out. A crucial fact is that African-Americans are the migrants of a generation ago. The earlier pattern of
rejections and successes shapes the searches of today, closing off options
that immigrants, with their very different experiences and orientations,
might pursue. Moreover, both immigrants and African-Americans have
limited discretion as to where viable niches can be found. Social and institutional barriers to good jobs are often stoutly defended. These discriminatory efforts are more likely to be directed at African-Americans than at
immigrants, and African-Americans are also more vulnerable to strategies
of economic exclusion. Finally, niche creation by African-Americans and
immigrants involves a mutually exclusive carving up of the pie: In carving out a place in the ethnic division of labor, the two groups effectively
open or foreclose opportunities for one another.

Thus ethnic employment concentrations or niches are a result of differences in the barriers that immigrant and native-born minorities face, in

the group resources that they can mobilize, and in the job orientations that influence the opportunities they pursue. At the same time, niches can be traps that confine groups to backwaters of the urban economy or launching pads that can be used to gain access to mainstream employment.

New York City is the prism through which we develop this argument in full. New York is a critical case for any explanation of urban change and its impact, as the city is America's first postindustrial place. It is first in the sense of arriving at postindustrialism before its urban rivals and first in the sense of having moved further toward the advanced service economy than any other principal urban center.

New York also exemplifies the new melting pot—heated at full boil. New York is not only a "minority majority" city. It is also the mecca for the newest immigrants, just as it has been throughout the history of the United States. Nowhere else does one find quite so complex an ethnic mosaic. Consequently no other city provides as good a platform for studying how ethnic group resources and strategies can interact with structural changes to shape ethnic group fates.

This chapter is organized into three parts. In the next two parts we return to the conventional stories about urban economic change, showing the intellectual development of these perspectives and providing a more detailed critique. In the last part, we elaborate on the stylized alternative presented just above and then illustrate this new perspective with examples from our case study research.

A Skills Mismatch?

The mismatch thesis occupies the place of honor in the literature on urban poverty. The city was once a place where low-skilled newcomers could get a job and slowly start the climb up the occupational ladder. The advent of the postindustrial economy, argue mismatch proponents, undermined this historic role of city as staging ground of upward mobility.

The mismatch hypothesis first emerged as part of the structural unemployment controversy of the late 1950s and early 1960s. Analysts concerned by a then-sluggish economy and fearful of an impending technological revolution fingered skill inadequacies as the source of employment dislocation. Whether the effects of the 1964 tax cut disproved the structural unemployment thesis, as some Keynesians argued, or not, the low unemployment rate of the late 1960s eclipsed the controversy as well as the fears of technological displacement. At the same time the public policy agenda sharply shifted, with worries about the fate of blue-collar workers eclipsed by the preoccupation with race. In this context, the mismatch discussion took a new twist and now focused on the problems of black workers. More than two decades after this reformulation, the basics of the mismatch argument have remained unchanged.

This revised mismatch explanation was essentially a story about black men and how they have been harmed by the decline of manufacturing. As Frank Levy notes in his recent volume on income inequality in the 1980 Census Monograph series:

> Between 1950 and 1960 New York ... had sustained its population through high birthrates and signficant in-migration from rural areas. Many of the in-migrants were black, and over the decade the proportion of blacks in the city's population rose from 10 to 15 percent. The in-migrants were coming in search of higher incomes, and in these early postwar years the cities could accommodate them. Cities had both cheap housing, and most important, manufacturing jobs. ... Because of these jobs, cities could still serve as a place for rural migrants to get a start.[11]

But what was true in the late 1950s rapidly changed. As manufacturing declined, the central cities—and in particular, the older urban centers—lost their absorptive capacities. Whereas manufacturing jobs had long permitted "immigrants access into the mainstream economy (albeit to the bottom rungs of the socioeconomic ladder),"[12] the growth of employment in services changed all that. The new economy typically generated two types of jobs—high-level managerial or professional occupations requiring college degrees or more and low-skilled positions in highly feminized fields. Both developments did little to widen the chances for black males. On the contrary, as Levy argues, "for poorly educated black men from rural areas, things were getting worse."[13] One generation after these mass migrations there are even more unskilled minority men chasing after fewer jobs. As William Wilson, another mismatch proponent argues, "much of what has gone awry in the inner city is due in part to the sheer increase in the number of young people, especially young minorities."[14]

Those young people are in so much trouble because they are failed by urban public schools. Here the criticism of urban education joins the crescendoing chorus of complaints about American education. But proponents of the mismatch hypothesis go beyond the argument that American schools are graduating students who lack the skills needed to fill sophisticated new jobs. The problems of minority students are far more severe: "A great many black students, and a growing number of Hispanic students, are trapped in schools where more than half drop out, where the average achievement level of those who remain is so low that there is little serious pre-collegiate instruction, where pre-collegiate courses and counselors are much less available, and which only prepare students for the least competitive colleges."[15]

Thus, on the supply side there are two problems: too many minorities and stagnant or slowly rising educational levels. But as we approach the year 2000, these woes take on a particularly aggravated form since the unfolding economic landscape will offer far fewer low-skilled opportunities than ever before. In the words of the scenario spinners at the Hudson Institute, "very few new jobs will be created for those who cannot read, follow directions, and use mathematics."[16] Fast-track growth is predicted for those jobs that require much higher education than current jobs. Though the bulk of employment will still remain in medium- to low-skilled jobs like cooks, secretaries, and cashiers, "workers will be expected to read and understand directions, add and subtract, and be able to speak and think clearly."[17]

Put demand and supply-side trends together and the recipe is for an "impending U.S. jobs 'disaster.'"[18] With the entire work force straining to keep up with enhanced job requirements, those minority workers who start out behind are unlikely to make up the gap. The Hudson Institute offers the following dim forecast:

> Given the historic patterns of behavior by employers, it is ... reasonable to expect that they will bid up the wages of the relatively smaller numbers of white labor force entrants, seek to substitute capital for labor in many service occupations, and/or move job sites to the faster growing, more youthful parts of the country, or perhaps the world. Blacks, and particularly black men, are those most likely to be put at risk if such strategies dominate.[19]

That the mismatch hypothesis has survived a quarter century of intellectual twists and turns is testimony to its intuitive appeal as well as the impact of repetition and the prestige of its proponents. But the mismatch hypothesis offers a particular, if not to say curious, interpretation of minority employment problems. And a close look at those particularities highlight its deficiences.

First, the mismatch hypothesis has a definite political twist. The culprits are no longer discriminating whites, but rather the loss of central city manufacturing jobs and the failures of the educational system. To be sure, mismatch proponents do not deny that discrimination persists, though its main effect results from the continuing legacy of bad deeds done in the past. And the significance of discrimination, like that of race, is on the decline. Twenty-five years ago the Kerner Commission could still argue that "racial discrimination is undoubtedly the second major reason why the Negro has been unable to escape from poverty."[20] Though the contemporary literature is rarely so explicit in its causal ordering, the fact that one reads the literature on the mismatch with barely a mention of discrimination speaks volumes.

But if discrimination has lost its force, what explains the peculiar industrial and occupational distribution of blacks? Blacks, in a theme that we shall sound throughout this chapter, are not dispersed throughout the economy but rather are concentrated in a handful of sectors. The puzzle, from the skills mismatch point of view, is that the black economic niches do not happen to coincide with the principal clusters of low-skilled jobs. Take the case of construction. Here are positions for which one trains on the job, as in the past; educational levels are very low, relative to the urban average; and these are jobs that men are particularly likely to seek. But construction is an industry from which blacks continue to be largely excluded and it is just a special case of skilled blue-collar work. Here is a domain, relatively low educational levels notwithstanding, in which blacks have much less than a fair share. Bad as the racial practices of construction employers and unions are, they actually offer an open door to blacks when compared to skilled blue-collar jobs in manufacturing. When one moves outside the goods production sector, the asymmetry between black concentrations and low skill clusters remains.

Although mismatch proponents have no doubt about what the source of the problem is, they are not so consistent about the population at risk. In the early formulations, the mismatch was essentially a story about black migrants from the South. But the hidden history of the mismatch controversy is that black migrants were not the most seriously troubled. Indeed, a number of studies using the 1970s Census showed that even controlling for age and education, black migrants from the South living in northern cities had higher incomes, lower incidence of poverty, lower unemployment, and less frequent reliance on welfare than northern-born blacks.[21]

Two decades after the end of the great black migration north, there is no longer any talk about the specific disabilities of black newcomers. But there is a cohort of new urban arrivals, this time immigrants from overseas. Although the immigrant phenomenon is intuitively difficult to assimilate into the mismatch framework, the attempt is made nonetheless. Thus, the population mismatched with the urban economy is now an undifferentiated aggregate of everyone not classified by the government as white.

This approach simply will not do: The mismatch hypothesis is fundamentally at odds with the immigrant phenomenon itself. If indeed urban employers are hiring none but the highly educated, then why have the leading postindustrial centers also emerged as the principal settlements of the new immigrant population? The key problem, first highlighted by the comparisons among northern and southern-born blacks, is that labor market outcomes vary in ways that are not explicable in terms of differences in schooling and educational skills. In the cities with which we are concerned, the employment of immigrant Hispanics has grown while the employment of native blacks has declined. And yet, it is the immigrants—not the blacks—whose educational levels are out of sync with that of the rest of the labor force. In Chicago, for example, the Mexican-born population increased by 83,000 between 1970 and 1980, despite Chicago's loss of 115,000 manufacturing jobs over the decade. In fact, the newcomers had low educational levels—just over six years, on average.[22] By contrast, schooling among native blacks compared closely with that of native whites, yet the employment situation of the former suffered sharp erosion.

A closer look at the employment patterns of immigrants raises even more questions about the basic mismatch assumption. Immigrants were far more dependent on manufacturing than were blacks in 1970—a time when the central city goods production base was still intact. If the decline of manufacturing is to blame for the employment problems of blacks, then why has the economic base of immigrants not blown apart? And since no one argues that educational requirements are a barrier to black employment in manufacturing, why were immigrants and not blacks able to make substantial gains in factory jobs?

This line of questioning leads to another observation: that manufacturing was not particularly important for the economic fate of blacks. Blacks were already underrepresented in New York's manufacturing sector as of 1970 and in the years since then they have shifted even further away from goods production jobs. In fact, by 1980, the chief black employment concentrations were in sectors that would expand in the succeeding years. Whatever the factors impeding employment, those blacks already employed should have been well positioned to have experienced the changes of the 1980s. That black economic opportunities have *not* substantially widened suggests that there is more to the game than being in the right industrial place at the right time.

As we noted earlier, there are really two sides to the mismatch equation: the supposedly fast-changing requirements of jobs and the sluggishly moving schooling levels of blacks. Of course, everyone "knows" that more and more education is needed for urban jobs; hence mismatch proponents have not lingered overly long on establishing this fact. But what everyone knows turns out to not quite be the case. Though we do not disagree that educational requirements are rising, people with modest levels of schooling still fill a surprising number of jobs. In 1987, persons with twelve years or less of schooling held just over one half of all New York City jobs.

If mismatch proponents move quickly over the question of changing educational requirements, they never stop to examine their assumption about the schooling levels among blacks. This issue speaks to both the empirical and theoretical basis of the mismatch hypothesis. We will return to the empirical matter in a moment. The theoretical question is how to explain the lag in black educational attainment. Poor school performance is of course one possibility. But that argument leads directly to the issue of inequality between urban and suburban school systems, the consequences of continued educational segregation. But why are black children confined to inferior inner-city schools? The answer is that the housing market, as the very latest research shows, is not just segregated, but "hyper-segregated," with white communities remaining as closed to blacks as before. Hypersegregation in housing markets is certainly a curious contrast to the supposedly diminishing significance of race at work—one imagines that racial prejudice must be turned off the second one crosses the office or factory door and turned back on the second one walks back out.[23]

Of course the educational problems of blacks may not be due to the actions of misbehaving whites. Perhaps there is something about the characteristics of blacks themselves, or of their communities, that impedes them from realizing that employers want workers with more schooling and then responding in the appropriate way. This reasoning flows logically from the mismatch argument but violates its overall conceptual thrust. The point of the mismatch is to locate the causes of black economic distress in the root changes of the postindustrial society. And thus neither possible explanation of blacks' educational problems—residential segregation or some unspecified characteristic of blacks—is consistent with the basic mismatch claim.

What about the empirical side? Here arguments in favor of a skills mismatch engage in a bit of slight of hand. Anyone familiar with the educational history of blacks will find irony in the argument that economic problems have been aggravated because schooling performance has gotten worse. The historical record, entirely obscured in contemporary debates, is one of tremendous progress against extraordinary obstacles: prohibitions against teaching reading and writing during slavery; not just separate, but woefully underfunded schools in the postbellum south; and the highly segregated, overcrowded systems that greeted the migrants when they came up north. Bad as urban schools may be today, the educational environment of black schoolchildren never had any "good old days."

The crucial issue is the pace and extent of *change*. Have black-white disparities in educational attainment narrowed or increased? More important, have blacks kept up with the educational requirements of urban employers—whose work force, as we have noted, is hardly lily white?

These questions about change are not raised by mismatch proponents at all. We do know, from studies using national data, that educational gaps between blacks and whites have narrowed considerably. The long-term increase in enrollment rates has been greater for blacks than for whites. By 1980 blacks at most ages were just as likely to be enrolled as whites, and the racial gap in attainment among those in their twenties was very small. Relative to older cohorts, young blacks have an educational profile that much more closely mirrors that of similarly aged whites.

The same story can be told for the cities with which we are concerned. In New York, in 1970, only 14 percent of the city's 16 and older black residents had some college education, but that number had risen to 30 percent by 1987. The trends are similar for narrower age ranges. The share of all 20- to 24-year-old black male residents in the city with some college education rose from 16 percent in 1970 to 32 percent in 1980. The college-attendance rate for black women in this age group increased even faster during the decade. Similarly, in 1970 only about 40 percent of all black New Yorkers 25 years of age and older had graduated from high school, but in 1980 fully 58 percent had high school diplomas.[24]

Thus, the skills mismatch rests on a series of "facts" that everybody knows but which on closer examination turn out not to be the case. Blacks never made it to manufacturing in such numbers that manufacturing's later decline would be a disaster. And the schooling story is far more complicated than the simplistic mismatch contentions, with plenty of evidence that blacks are less behind with respect to schooling than they were ten, not to speak of twenty years ago.

A Dual City?

If the mismatch is off target in its story about blacks, it has nothing to say about the new immigrants who have flocked to the largest postindustrial cities. The puzzle is why the new immigrants have converged on the largest urban centers at precisely the time when so many of the traditional routes of immigrant economic mobility have presumably been blocked.

The best known answer to this question is that the growth of services has polarized the cities of high finance. The shift to services does indeed breed new jobs requiring high levels of education, as the mismatch hypothesis asserts. But critics of the American economy contend that the growth of services also involves a process of economic restructuring. The idea of restructuring means that service growth at the top simultaneously generates jobs for chambermaids and waiters, investment bankers and lawyers, while positions in between these extremes are being slowly but steadily reduced. Restructuring also results in a deployment of new labor force groups. Immigrants from overseas have come to fill the expanded bottom-level jobs.

The coming of the hourglass economy thus creates the demand for immigrant labor. But the relationship between cities and immigrants works both ways: The arrival of the immigrants is a main reason why the past fifteen years have seen a new "urban renaissance." The influx of foreign-born workers has given the comatose manufacturing sector a new lease on life. Immigrants, so the story goes, have been a more pliable labor force, so factory employers have not been obliged to keep wages at parity with national norms. In contrast to nationals, immigrant labor can also be deployed in more flexible ways, thereby giving urban manufacturers the scope to customize production and place greater reliance on subcontracting. As yet another plus, urban manufacturers can also draw on a large, vulnerable population of illegal immigrants. Their presence has given new meaning to the word exploitation, thus making the new immigrant sweatshop "a significant U.S. central city employment growth sector in the past decade."[25]

Immigration has also propelled the service economy along. Saskia Sassen-Koob, who has researched New York, argues that immigrants can be seen as "contributing to the *operation* (of the advanced service firm) itself ... (e.g., by working on the night shift as a janitor in an office, or as a night-time elevator operator in a residential unit).[26] Immigrants are also a permissive factor in the continued expansion of the labor supply for newly created professional and managerial jobs. As Harrison and Bluestone argue, "The provision of ... services to the office workers becomes *the* major economic activity for the rest of the city." In their view, "the high cost of living in cities containing corporate headquarters requires that professional households include more than one wage earner in order to sustain a middle-class life style. This, in turn, forces this new aristocracy to consume more and more of the services that workers in an earlier generation would have produced for themselves."[27] By furnishing the "large cohort of restaurant workers, laundry workers, dog walkers, residential construction workers, and the like,"[28] immigrants lower the costs of keeping a high-skilled labor force in place. Thus were it not for the foreign-born, the advanced service sectors in New York or Los Angeles would have to pay their highly skilled workers even more and thus lose out in the broader competitive game.

The contrast between restructuring and mismatch hypotheses shows that the virtues of one are the vices of the other. The restructuring hypothesis offers a plausible explanation of the immigrant arrival in the postindustrial city. But it entirely begs the question of why all the new low-level jobs went to immigrants and not to blacks. Indeed the issue of the economic problems of blacks does not even merit mention. Amazingly enough, at a time when the specter of displaced, unemployed blacks looms so large in the mismatch hypothesis, the restructuring hypothesis has returned blacks to their old place as "invisible men."

Clearly any adequate account of the urban postindustrial change has to explain the new ethnic division of labor. But the restructuring hypothesis is not just weak on this count alone; it also falls short on strictly factual grounds.

Consider the key contention about the changing *structure* of jobs and skills. Evidence that polarization is under way comes from Bureau of Labor Statistics projections of the absolute *number* of new jobs to be created between now and the turn of the century. Much has been made of the large number of jobs in low-skilled occupations that are expected to be added to the economy by the turn of the century. Of the ten occupations that will require the largest number of new workers, one, primary school teaching, necessitates a baccalaureate degree. Most registered nurses (RNs) are licensed with an associate degree. All of the others—janitors, cashiers, truck drivers, and the like—involve skills that can be picked up on the job with little, if any, schoolroom knowledge. But this pattern is largely an artifact of the occupational classification system itself. Low-skilled jobs tend to be less differentiated than higher-skilled jobs; thus there are relatively few detailed occupational categories containing many workers at the lower end of the job hierarchy. When one regroups the occupations into broad categories (executive, administrative, managerial, professional, and so forth), the broad occupational groups with above-average education are those that grew at above-average rates between 1976 and 1988 and those that are projected to grow fastest between 1988 and 2000.[29] Thus whereas the projections suggest that by the turn of the century there will continue to be workers in occupations that generally have low educational levels, the data also suggest that there will be a steady decline of such jobs. The figures just presented cover the U.S. economy as a whole. But what about the major urban centers? Occupational polarization is clearly not the right way to characterize the job trajectory in New York. Though the number of jobs eroded during the bad days of the 1970s, some occupations did grow. The number of professionals increased by 16.5 percent, managers were up 27 percent, and service workers gained an additional 5.8 percent. All of the blue-collar occupations shrank. The growing tilt toward services explains part of this story, but only part. Within every sector—whether manufacturing or transport, retail or business services—the mix of occupations underwent considerable change. Overall, the trend was toward occupational upgrading, not polarization. The proportion of workers employed in all blue-collar occupations (craft, operative, laborer, and service) substantially declined in every sector except professional service.[30]

Although changes in occupational classifications prevent a direct comparison to the data from the 1970s, available data do suggest that the same pattern holds true for the 1980s. For example, in New York City, professional and managerial jobs grew by almost 24 percent between 1983 and 1986 whereas operator jobs continued to decline.[31]

Thus despite tales of the growth in the number of janitors and fast food workers, data on occupational change and projected occupational growth for the country as a whole and for New York fail to provide any support for the notion that there is a relative proliferation of low-skilled jobs. Given this trend, how can the arrival of new immigrants be explained?

Not only does the argument about polarizing urban economies move us no further in answering this question; the contentions about immigrant dependence on services lead us further off the track. Surprisingly, the traditional immigrant-absorbing industries have continued as the shock absorbers for the latest immigrant inflow. Manufacturing remains overwhelmingly the chief immigrant employer in the major urban concentrations of the foreign-born. And it has also been the industry where immigrants have made their largest job gains. The contrast with polarization claims is even more glaring when one looks at the service side. There is indeed one service sector in which immigrants are greatly overrepresented—that old immigrant standby, personal services. Those sectors composing the "new" urban economy—finance, insurance, real estate, business services, professional services—rank below the average in their reliance on immigrant labor. And there is no evidence to suggest that these industries have significantly changed in this regard.

Thus the polarization hypothesis has the story about changing urban economies wrong. It also missteps in treating the other side of the equation—immigrants. Though much is made of the exploitability of a large, illegal immigrant labor pool, this point cannot be pushed too far. The illegal immigration numbers game has now been played out: We know that the guesstimates from the early days widely inflated the size of the undocumented population. The number of illegal immigrants—about 3.5 million as of the late 1980s—is greatly overshadowed by the number of new immigrant legal residents and citizens. Similarly, the view that illegal immigrants constitute a group that is more vulnerable to exploitation than their legal counterparts can no longer be sustained. A decade and a half of research on illegal aliens has shown that their economic, demographic, and human capital characteristics differ little from those of legal immigrants of similar ethnic backgrounds. According to a recent U.S. Department of Labor report, "in many instances, illegal status does not lead to significantly lower earnings, nor does it appear to impede mobility substantially."[32]

Absent the masses of exploitable illegal immigrants, support for the contention about burgeoning sweatshops also collapses. Official statistics show that immigrants are overrepresented in certain key industries. Chinese in New York's apparel industry, for example, are overrepresented by a factor of almost seven, and Dominicans by a factor almost five. And the new immigrants also participate in the labor force at rates that equal, if not exceed, the level for native whites. Thus, the idea that there is a massive shadow labor force toiling in underground factories simply has no support.[33]

The Ethnic Division of Labor Transformed

If the prevailing accounts of the impact of the postindustrial urban economy do not hold up, what alternative might there be? The answer is an explanation that can provide a single consistent story for blacks *and* for immigrants. To do so, we begin with a model of how jobs are allocated among ethnic groups.

The simplest model assumes that in a race-conscious society like ours, entire groups of people are ranked in terms of desirability for preferred jobs. Whites stand at the top of this ranking, and other nonwhite groups follow, with their positions determined in part by skill, in part by employers' preferences. Under these conditions, job growth at the top of the hierarchy principally benefits whites; as they ascend the totem pole and fill up these new positions, jobs lower down the ladder will open up for everyone else. Conversely, should the overall economy, or even particular sectors, turn down, whites' average position might be depressed. But whites would still hold on to their jobs on the first-in, last-out principle, pushing non-whites further down or possibly even off the hiring queue.

Thus far we are treading familiar ground, and there is little here to which proponents of mismatch or polarization theses would object. Now let us keep the aggregate size of the economy stable and vary a different condition: the relative size of the preferred group, that is to say, whites. If their proportion in the labor market declines, then there are relatively more jobs for everyone else. Moreover, a relative decline in the number of whites is good for those whites who remain. Since there are now fewer competitors among the preferred group for the more desirable jobs, many persons among the thinned ranks of white workers can push on up toward the top. Thus a vacancy chain is created: Whites who have moved on to greener pastures must be replaced by nonwhite workers who had previously been confined to depressed and undesirable jobs. And as these positions are vacated, additional slots are opened up for those who must start at the very bottom.

This model, with its assumption that the needs for replacement labor will be directly proportional to the shifting supply of whites, needs further correction. American industry has always been distinguished by its reliance on migrants to fill low-level jobs. Industries in the "secondary sector," like clothing or restaurants, have traditionally been havens of employment for immigrants and their children. But that same dependence breeds a chronic dependence on outside sources of new recruits. As the children of earlier migrants enter into the labor market, fewer of them feed into the secondary sector. This process of cycling through industries and sectors breeds an additional demand for replacement labor—beyond that generated by compositional changes alone.

These propositions move us beyond either mismatch or polarization hypotheses because they identify the sources of opportunity within an otherwise unfavorable economic environment. During the same time when urban economies shifted from goods to services, their demography changed at an even more rapid pace. Whites, who make up the preferred group, have been a steadily diminishing component of the population base. In cases of economic decline, as in New York in the 1970s, the white outflow has greatly exceeded the erosion of jobs, although many suburbanites commute to the city to work. And in cases of economic growth, as when New York turned around in the 1980s, the white population has not kept pace with the increase in jobs. Generational change within the white population has further amplified the need for replacement labor. European immigrants and their immediate descendants have cycled out of industries like apparel or retailing in which they long provided the bulk of entrepreneurs and workers alike. Thus, compositional change has given rise to a sustained demand for replacements—supplied by groups that had previously been at the bottom of the queue. This revised queueing model provides an adequate prediction of how changes in the number and characteristics of white workers will affect the gross opportunities for new immigrants and for blacks. What it does not tell us is how the jobs vacated by departing whites will be allocated among the contending successor groups. The queueing metaphor suggests that both jobs and groups are ranked in a stable, orderly way, with top-ranked groups moving into higher-ranked jobs and so on down the line. But this image of orderly succession is far removed from reality. First of all, not every group shares the same ranking system. Second, access is not a matter of qualifications alone. Rather than climbing straight up the totem pole, groups instead branch off into particular fields where they try to close off entry to outsiders and monopolize jobs for members of their club. Thus, as whites have become a diminishing presence in New York's labor market, a new ethnic division of labor emerged, with blacks and new immigrants carving out distinctive niches of their own.

Garments and Hotels: Through the Revolving Door

Though the shift from goods to services in New York has driven the number of easy-entry jobs down, recent immigrants still start where their predecessors began: at the bottom. They inherit the low-status, insecure jobs that native New Yorkers are no longer willing to do. Nowhere is this transition clearer than in the city's quintessential trade: the garment industry.

When the bottom fell out of the market for New York's garment industry in the 1970s, hourly earnings dropped relative to those in the rest of the city's already depressed manufacturing sector; working conditions—never good to begin with—got worse; and seasonality became more pronounced, producing a small weekly paycheck. Consequently, native workers realized, as one employer put it, "that they can get more doing something else" and they dropped out of the industry's labor supply. By 1980, just over a third of the industry's production workers were white—a drop of almost 50 percent since 1970—and most of these workers were on the far side of their careers.

Replacements came from a familiar source: immigration from abroad. In contrast to the natives, to whom a garment shop is far worse than an office or hospital job, the immigrants came "hoping to find any job, it didn't matter … as long as it was a job." The turnover of workers—high even in bad times—meant that employers were always looking to add a new hand. The industry had already adapted to Puerto Rican workers with supervisors who were bilingual or could at least mediate between Spanish-speaking workers and non-Hispanic employers; hence there was an infrastructure ready to absorb new cohorts of Latino immigrants, the largest group of whom came from the Dominican Republic.

Informal networks helped newcomers find jobs where other immigrants were already employed: Three-quarters of a group of Hispanic immigrants interviewed for an earlier study found their first job through connections with relatives or friends. Some arrivals started out by working in a factory owned by a fellow (or sister) immigrant garment capitalist. Thus, by 1980, newcomers from the third world made up almost half of New York's needle trades proletariat. The consensus among garment employers: "If there were no immigrants, the needle trades would be out of New York."[34]

But why did immigrants—and not native blacks—take over these entry-level jobs? The case of the hotel industry—where immigrants and blacks have long labored—suggests that two common explanations, immigrants' supposed predisposition for wages and susceptibility to exploitation, do *not* provide the answers. An immigrant-dominated occupation like housekeeping, for example, is paid above the rate for front-desk occupations, where the immigrant penetration is much lower. Still higher wages are to be found in the kitchen, where the disparity between immigrant and black employment levels is the greatest. Nor can a strong case be made for employers' preference for immigrants on the grounds of the latter's greater vulnerability, as pay rates in the nonunion hotels equal, when not surpassing, union rates and their benefit packages are often better.

Instead there appear to be a complex of interacting sociological and psychological factors that have led blacks to move out of the industry's effective labor supply. Whereas hotels have been a traditional employer of blacks, they have employed them in the traditional service jobs to which African-Americans had long been confined. Today's generation, as employers and union officials perceive, no longer accept these conditions.

Whereas entry-level jobs are of diminishing attractiveness to blacks, movement into better positions is problematic. For example, food service occupations contain a range of opportunities for upward mobility through on-the-job training for workers with manual skills, yet relatively few blacks are to be found in these jobs. The problem is that blacks are poorly represented among the sources from which hotels get their skilled kitchen help: restaurant cooks and culinary graduates. Blacks are particularly disadvantaged in comparison to immigrants, who may come with cooking skills or have opportunities to obtain them in the burgeoning sector of immigrant restaurants.

Finally, the natural starting point for movement into hotel management lies in the front of the house, but it is here where the brunt of discrimination has been felt. To be sure, the blatant discriminatory practices that previously kept blacks out operate with much less force than before, but the basic pattern remains in place. Moreover, other factors—limited skill backgrounds, problems in communicating, lack of facility with computers—impede access to those front-of-the-house positions that are directly linked to managerial tracks. In the words of one personnel official, minority workers who want to move up to front-desk jobs "must be trained explicitly for middle-class norms." And here, blacks suffer from competition with hotels' preferred source of labor: white, largely college-educated workers who come equipped with the "middle-class" norms that management seeks.[35]

Enterprising Immigrants

The changing social structure of New York's traditional ethnic entrepreneurs has opened the door to new immigrant capitalists—who have rushed in to fill the breach. The case of the garment industry can be drawn on to show how the stage has been set for change. For most of the industry's history in New York there was an ample supply of Jewish and Italian sewing-machine operators, cutters, salespeople, and patternmakers eager to move ahead by starting up a business of their own. But both groups are now largely middle class, and though a predilection for self-employment persists, it takes the form of being a professional, not a factory owner. Of course, the high-profit, higher-status worlds of garment designing and manufacturing still draw in plenty of ethnics who have grown up in, or have connections to, the garment trade. But new blood has deserted the business of garment contracting. Although there remain many Jewish and Italian-owned garment factories, they are almost all long lived; their owners are aging, with little hope for the future of the industry ("Going into the industry? I wouldn't wish this business on a dog"). And successors eager to keep the family firm alive are few and far between.

Why do the newcomers gravitate toward business? In some cases, they bring traditions of self-employment of skills that give them an edge in some particular business line: Greeks from the province of Kastoria, where a traditional apprenticeship in fur making is common; Israelis, who go into diamonds, a traditional Jewish business centered in New York, Tel Aviv, and Antwerp; and Indians from Gujarat, renowned for their prowess in trading, arrive to extend the family business. But for many immigrants, it is neither a love affair with business nor a preference for being one's own boss that leads them into the petite bourgeoisie. More compelling is the quest for profit as a compensation for professional frustration: Though highly educated, many immigrants arrive speaking little English and lacking the licenses and certifications needed to enter the fields for which they have trained. "This kind of hardship is for the first generation only," said a Korean fishstore owner who had been a teacher in Seoul.

But the crucial factor is that opportunity beckons: There is considerable demand for the particular services that immigrant owners offer. Immigrants have their own special consumer tastes, not just the old staples like foodstuffs or newspaper, but also foreign language videos and electrical goods with current adapters for use back home. The business of adaptation is also a thriving one: The immigrant travel agent, accountant, and lawyer trades on the offer of confidentiality, trust, and a more personal way of doing business. And finally, the immigrant network serves as a conduit to lower-cost, reliable labor in the broader community.

Working for the State

The mythology of ethnic business is that immigrants do well because they have a special knack for turning a dollar. The reality is that immigrants are more willing to take their chances on what are often bad bets. In the small-business field, where the mortality of new firms is appallingly high, the key is the *rate* at which new businesses start up. And the immigrant self-employment rate is high: In 1980, almost 13 percent of foreign-born male adults were working for themselves, and among groups like Koreans, Chinese, Indians, or Greeks, the proportion was considerably higher. By contrast, just over 3.5 percent of native black males were self-employed in 1980 and among native Hispanics the self-employment rate was almost as low.

Instead of business, native blacks have concentrated in the public sector, where by the late 1980s almost two of every five employed African-Americans were to be found. This, too, is a story of ethnic succession, though one with a more conflictual twist. Although blacks began getting municipal jobs in the 1930s and 1940s, the jobs they found were at the very bottom of the civil service system—and exams and educational requirements made it very hard to move up. In the 1960s, the civil rights explosion pushed local officials to open access to the higher civil service. But the system proved resistant to reform. And efforts to increase access to blacks and other minorities led to explosive conflicts—of which the most notorious was the 1968 teachers' strike.

The crucial change came with the fiscal crisis of the 1970s. Fiscal stringency forced the city to pare down payrolls, but jobs were shed mainly through attrition, not layoffs. Most of those who retired were civil servants high in seniority, who, as it happened, were mainly white. Empty municipal coffers also led to lower wages and reduced fringes, which in turn lowered the public sector's attractiveness to whites.

Black workers thus increased their share of public jobs when the municipal sector was shrinking. They did even better when it later began to replenish its ranks—in burgeoning numbers—as it did when good times returned in the 1980s. In a situation where "the city was hiring a great deal and not turning away anyone who was qualified," as one deputy commissioner explained in an interview, disparities in the availability of minority and white workers led to rapid recruitment of minority workers. And notwithstanding the civil service system, with its emphasis on exams and formal procedures, informal networks steered prospective black workers into the civil service, as a union official representing the heavily black clerical workers' local explained: "My people have an excellent communications system: They know that jobs are available; they refer cousins, sons, daughters. People walk into personnel and drop off resumes like there's no tomorrow." Thus, by 1990, blacks made up 36 percent of the city's total work force, 40 percent of its administrators, and 36 percent of its professionals. Though unevenly represented among the city's many agencies, blacks were often a dominant presence, accounting for more than 40 percent of employment in six of the ten largest agencies, and more than 50 percent of employment in three of the largest ten.

Conclusion: Beyond the Ethnic Niche

And so, the conventional stories of postindustrial New York—whether in mismatch or "tale of two cities" version—can be misleading. What we have witnessed is an extended game of musical chairs, in which positions as well as players have changed and in which differences among minorities stand out almost as sharply as those between whites and nonwhites. Immigrants have settled into small business, especially retailing and manufacturing, whereas native blacks have lost ground there. But the latter are gaining in the public sector, which does not loom large in the immigrant employment picture.

But if the case studies illustrate the making and remaking of the ethnic niche in late twentieth-century New York, the question remains of where these ethnic specializations lead. Broadening the economic base is imperative. Only small groups, or large groups ensconced in a large growing area of specialization, can rest assured that the employment needs of the group can be satisfied within the niche. The best specializations, therefore, are those in which the resources and skills developed within the initial niche can be used to move backward, forward, or sideways into related economic sectors.

Business and government are the strategic platforms for niche-expansion strategies. Though small businesses die off at an appalling rate, they also offer a route for expansion into higher-profit, more dynamic lines. Retailers evolve into wholesalers; construction firms learn how to develop real estate; garment contractors gain the capital, expertise, and contacts to design and merchandise their own clothing. As the ethnic niche expands and diversifies, the opportunities for related ethnic suppliers and customers also grow.

For blacks especially, public-sector employment offered opportunities for stable employment and more. Government was a place where blacks could move ahead when other sectors of the economy were considerably less hospitable. And better opportunities for job mobility also made government the arena where movement into the middle class was particularly likely to occur. Although these factors tell us much about why the public sector has become the black concentration that it is, the problem is that government, though rewarding, is a limited ethnic niche. The historical problem for blacks has been how to extend its advantages to the private sector.

The Irish experience shows just what the consequences of this problem can be. Reformers railed against the corrupt ties between Irish machine politicians and the businesses they supported. But those connections never translated into substantial business opportunities for Irish immigrants and their descendants—who to this day display very low self-employment rates.

If concentration in government produced mixed dividends for the Irish, consider the implications for blacks—against whom the level of prejudice is so much higher. Moreover, blacks are like the Irish in still another respect: They have yet to produce a substantial business class. The black business sector is still a cluster of small and marginal businesses in the personal service and petty retail lines with virtually no employment-expanding potential.

The dismal state of black business means heightened black vulnerability to discrimination on two fronts. First, there is no private-sector industry to which blacks have privileged access. As a result, traditional exclusionary mechanisms that have barred black entry into preferred jobs continue to operate. The impact of those exclusionary mechanisms is particularly great in industries where the prevalence of small firms and informal training practices impedes the task of government regulation.

Second, the growth of immigrant economic enclaves is a source of potential displacement from easy-entry jobs. Ethnic succession in small business has provided new immigrants with a chance to emerge as replacement entrepreneurs. This niche for business owners has led to the deployment of immigrant workers as well. Thus the growth of immigrant business, it is believed by many, has threatened to close off sectors that had previously been open to blacks.

Two caveats need be added to this observation about competition. First, competition is more indirect than direct. It is not so much a matter of existing employers firing their black workers and replacing them with immigrants as of immigrant businesses gradually replacing the white businesses that previously employed blacks. And even if some displacement of natives occurs, the ramifications of the immigrant presence redound, in part, to the benefit of native workers, white and black alike. Were there not so many immigrants in cities like New York or Los Angeles there would be much less demand for many activities that employ natives as well as the foreign-born.[36]

Second, competition is an after-product of the process of niche selection. But niche specialization itself complements a group's own characteristics and the resources it can mobilize to infiltrate and maintain an economic niche. Thus, prior to immigrant-black competition, there must be differences that produce the pattern of specialization that in turn allows displacement. There is also reason to think that the classical immigrant industries would not become black concentrations, even if there were no immigrants with whom to compete.

In the end, our perspective locates the urban fates of African-Americans and new immigrants on two axes: the obstacles, in particular the discriminatory barriers, that impede their progress, and the group and community resources that can be mobilized to surmount these barriers. This diagnosis suggests policies that focus on manipulating these same two axes. To barriers, we propose a strategy of strengthening the economic *protection* of minorities. To enhance group resources, we propose measures directed toward economic *empowerment*. In the economic context, we suggest, empowerment means the creation and development of economic niches. By analyzing the variety of niche-creation and niche-development strategies, we will show how successful strategies could be promoted by public policy.

In making these proposals we diverge from the conventional view that emphasizes strengthening education as the solution to minority employment problems. Better education is indeed crucial. But educational changes must be part of a broader strategy. And any fundamental improvement in urban education will also require a strategy designed to facilitate the mobilization of group resources. Thus more and better education belongs to a comprehensive strategy that seeks to make progress on both the schooling and employment fronts.

Immigration legislation is another potential area of policy innovation. To the extent that immigrants weaken the economic opportunity of native minorities, then immigration restriction should at least be considered. But our argument suggests that, given the differences between immigrants and native blacks, at this time any realistic changes in immigration legislation would have little effect on black employment. But if the type of policies that we advocate were to be effective, then the current differences between the groups might weaken and at that time, immigration reform might become more effective.

Notes

1. Terry K. Adams, Greg J. Duncan, and Willard L. Rodgers, "The Persistence of Urban Poverty," pp. 78–99 in Fred R. Harris and Roger Wilkins, eds., *Quiet Riots: Race and Poverty in the United States* (New York: Pantheon, 1988); Walter Stafford, "Political Dimensions of the Underclass Concept," forthcoming in Herbert Gans, ed., *American Sociological Association Presidential Series*.

2. Sharon Zukin, "Gentrification," *Annual Review of Sociology* 13(1987):129–147; William Frey and Alden Speare, *Regional and Metropolitan Growth and Decline in the United States* (New York: Russell Sage Foundation, 1988).

3. George Sternlieb and James Hughes, "The Uncertain Future of the Central City," *Urban Affairs Quarterly* 18(4)(1983):455–472; John Kasarda, "Jobs, Mismatches, and Emerging Urban Mismatches," pp. 148–198 in M.G.H. Geary and L. Lynn, eds., *Urban Change and Poverty* (Washington, D.C.: National Academy Press, 1988).

4. Saskia Sassen, *The Mobility of Capital and Labor* (New York: Cambridge University Press, 1988); Bennett Harrison and Barry Bluestone, *The Great U-Turn* (New York: Basic Books, 1988).

5. The two perspectives also contradict one another on the issue of the direction of job change: Is the problem the disappearance or the proliferation of low-level jobs? The answer is that neither mismatch nor polarization proponents are sure. Thus, the most recent writings of William Wilson and his collaborators continue to emphasize the decline of manufacturing but then point out the "explosion of low-pay, part-time work" (L. J. Wacquant and W. J. Wilson, "The Cost of Racial and Class Exclusion in the Inner City," *Annals* 501[January 1989]:11), the growth of sweatshops, and the "peripheralization and recomposition of the core," code words for economic polarization (L. J. Wacquant, "The Ghetto, the State, and the New Capitalist Economy," *Dissent* 36[4][1989]:512). As we point out later in this chapter, a further contradiction has to do with the implications of job change for blacks and for new immigrants.

6. For declines in the white central-city population from 1970 to the mid-1980s, see Kasarda, "Jobs, Mismatches, and Emerging Urban Mismatches." The concept of compositional change is borrowed from Stanley Lieberson, *A Piece of the Pie* (Berkeley: University of California Press, 1980), pp. 294–298. Our earlier efforts to apply the argument outlined here to New York include R. Waldinger, "Changing Ladders and Musical Chairs: Ethnicity and Opportunity in Post-Industrial New York," *Politics and Society* 15(4)(1986-1987); and T. Bailey and R. Waldinger, "The Ethnic Division of Labor," paper presented at the "Dual City Workshop," SSRC Committee on New York City, 1988.

7. Although the concept of "replacement labor" has more often been applied to European, rather than American, discussions of labor migration (see, for example, W. R. Bohning, *The Effects of the Employment of Foreign Workers* [Paris: St. Martin's Press, 1974]), the scholarly literature on U.S. immigration has often highlighted the recruitment of new immigration populations as older streams have dwindled or cut off. See, for example, Michael Piore, *Birds of Passage* (New York: Cambridge University Press, 1979), chapter 6. Our earlier work on ethnic business has also emphasized the importance of replacement demand for ethnic entrepreneurs: See Roger Waldinger et al., *Immigrant Entrepreneurs: Minority Business in Europe and the United States* (Newbury Park, Calif.: Sage, 1990).

8. William Wilson and his collaborators, for example, refer to Hispanics and blacks jointly for the purposes of *describing* changes in the size and distribution of the poverty population in Chicago. But when analyzing the impact of economic change, their discussion focuses solely on blacks; that Hispanics suffer lower unemployment and poverty rates is simply noted in passing. Why this should be so, especially since the educational level of Hispanics is so much lower than that of blacks, is an issue that they never raise. See, for example, W. J. Wilson et al., "The Ghetto Underclass and the Changing Structure of Poverty," in Harris and Wilkins, *Quiet Riots*, especially pp. 125–131 and 134–135.

9. These points are emphasized in our earlier work. See Thomas Bailey, *Immigrant and Native Workers: Contrasts and Competition* (Boulder: Westview, 1987); Roger Waldinger, "Race and Ethnicity in New York," chapter 2 in C. Brecher and

R. Horton, eds., *Setting Municipal Priorities 1990* (New York: New York University Press, 1989).

10. See, for example, Lawrence Mead, "Social Responsibility and Minority Poverty: A Response to William Wilson," pp. 253–263 in Gary D. Sandefur and Marta Tienda, eds., *Divided Opportunities: Minorities, Poverty, and Social Policy* (New York: Plenum, 1988).

11. Frank Levy, *Dollars and Dreams: The Changing American Income Distribution* (New York: Russell Sage Foundation, 1987), p. 112.

12. John Kasarda, "Entry-level Jobs, Mobility, and Urban Minority Employment," *Urban Affairs Quarterly* 19(1)(1984):21–40.

13. Levy, *Dollars and Dreams*, p. 113.

14. William J. Wilson, "The Urban Underclass in Advanced Industrial Society," in Paul Peterson, ed., *The New Urban Reality* (Washington, D.C.: Brookings Institution, 1985), p. 150.

15. Gary Orfield, "Separate Societies: Have the Kerner Warnings Come True?" in Harris and Wilkins, *Quiet Riots*, p. 118.

16. Hudson Institute, *Workforce 2000: Work and Workers for the 20th Century* (Indianapolis, Ind.: Hudson Institute, 1987), p. 100.

17. Ibid., p. 100.

18. Edward Fiske, "Impending Jobs 'Disaster': Work Force Unqualified to Work," *New York Times*, September 21, 1989, p. 1.

19. Hudson Institute, *Workforce 2000*, p. 91.

20. National Advisory Commission on Civil Disorders, *Report* (New York: Bantam, 1968), p. 278.

21. Stanley Lieberson, "A Reconsideration of Income Differences Found Between Migrants and Northern-born Blacks," *American Journal of Sociology* 83 (January 1978):940–966; and Larry Long, "Poverty Status and Receipt of Welfare Among Migrants and Nonmigrants in Large Cities," *American Sociological Review* 39(February 1974):44–56.

22. Calculated from the Census of Population, 5 Percent Public Use Microdata Sample.

23. Of course, if one believes that educational levels have risen so high that employers screen solely on the basis of schooling, leaving race aside, then one need not linger on the troubling matter of whether employment discrimination persists. The problem is that this belief, though commonsensical, does not have empirical support. Hence, one can't dismiss discrimination as mismatch proponents do.

24. Thomas Bailey, "Black Employment Opportunities," in Charles Brecher and Raymond Horton, eds., *Setting Municipal Priorities* (New York: New York University Press, 1989).

25. Michael P. Smith, *City, State, and Market* (New York: Basil Blackwell, 1988), p. 200.

26. Saskia Sassen-Koob, *Exporting Capital and Importing Labor: The Role of Caribbean Migration to New York City*, Occasional Papers, Center for Latin American and Caribbean Studies, New York University, 1981.

27. Bennett Harrison and Barry Bluestone, *The Great U-Turn: Corporate Restructuring and the Polarizing of America* (New York: Basic Books, 1988), p. 70.

28. Joe Feagin and Michael P. Smith, "Cities and the New International Division of Labor: An Overview," in Joe Feagin and Michael P. Smith, eds., *The Capitalist City* (New York: Basil Blackwell, 1987), p. 15.

29. For a detailed analysis of the relationship between occupational growth rates and occupational educational levels, see Thomas Bailey, "Changes in the Nature and Structure of Work: Implications for Skills and Skill Formation," technical report (New York: National Center on Education and Employment, Teachers College, Columbia University, 1989), appendix.

30. These data are from the Public Use Samples of the 1970 and 1980 U.S. Censuses of Population.

31. Bailey and Waldinger, "The Ethnic Division of Labor."

32. U.S. Department of Labor, *The Effects of Immigration on the Economy and Labor Market* (Washington, D.C.: Government Printing Office, 1989), p. 158.

33. Roger Waldinger and Michael Lapp, "Back to the Sweatshop or Ahead to the Informal Sector," *International Journal of Urban and Regional Research,* forthcoming.

34. For a fuller exposition, see Roger Waldinger, *Through the Eye of the Needle: Immigrants and Enterprise in New York's Garment Trades* (New York: New York University Press, 1986).

35. For a fuller treatment of the hotel industry, see Roger Waldinger, "Taking Care of the Guests: The Impact of Immigrants on Services—An Industry Case Study," *International Journal of Urban and Regional Research* 16(1)(March 1992).

36. For a review of the theoretical arguments about the impact of immigration on the employment of natives, see Bailey, *Immigrant and Native Workers,* chapter 1.

7

School to Work: The Integration Principle

Thomas Bailey

Anxieties about national productivity growth and international competitiveness have sustained interest in educational reform for over a decade. One purpose of this chapter is to strengthen the reform movement by developing an educational model that draws on knowledge and analyses from three broad areas—current thinking about teaching and schools, research on the educational implications of the changing economy, and analyses of the contemporary efforts to restructure the organization of work. I refer to the approach developed in this chapter as the *integration strategy*. A central component of the strategy involves strengthened links, along several dimensions, between education and work.

The current educational reform movement can be dated from the early 1980s. Over the same period, there has also been an active movement to reform work. Managers, academics, consultants, and various reformers have called for significant changes in the way in which work is organized in the country's offices and factories, arguing that organizational performance will rise and that our economy will be more competitive if work is more decentralized, if lower-level workers have more responsibility, if jobs are more broadly defined, and if organizations break down traditional boundaries and functions.

This chapter draws heavily on the parallels between the current educational reform movement and contemporary efforts to reform work. Indeed, as I shall show, there are many parallels as well as points of contact between the two reform movements. First, many analysts argue that the "transformed" or "high-performance" workplace requires higher levels of education and different types of skills—ends that will be achieved only through significant educational reform. Second, schools are also organizations and their performance may also be improved through the types of reforms being developed in the workplace. Third, there are close parallels in the historical development of the two movements over the past fifteen years. Fourth, the boundaries between working and learning are increasingly blurred.

Thus if the barriers and distinctions between work and learning are being challenged, it does not make sense for their respective reform movements to continue to be discussed, planned, and evaluated separately. At the most simplistic level, educators have much to learn from the reform experience of other employers. But just as important, schools and educators may have a significant influence on the workplace. There is a consensus that increased productivity and a rising standard of living requires both changes and reform in schools and educational programs as well as in the organization of work. If employers adhere to a traditional approach to production, then improved education may have little effect. Indeed, reforming work may itself be a key to improved skills since a great deal of learning takes place on the job. And some of the current educational reform proposals, such as apprenticeship, call for an expansion of the workplace as a learning site even for adolescents.

This chapter therefore develops the integration model as a conceptual framework for analyzing school reform and its relationship to the changing economy and contemporaneous work reform efforts. I first describe the contemporary changes in the economy and in related innovations in the organization of work. The subsequent section centers around past conceptualizations of the relationship between school and work and their relevance to earlier educational reform movements. Next, I describe the integration model in more detail. The final part of the chapter applies that model to a discussion of educational equity, access, and the education of minorities.

Changes in the Nature
and Organization of Work

Since the 1980s, employers in the United States have been confronted with profound economic and labor market changes. These developments have far-reaching effects on skills needed in the workplace and on the educational processes of schools, colleges, universities, and even of the firms themselves. A variety of factors are driving the contemporary transformation of work, including the increase in international trade, a continuing growth in services, the diffusion of computers and sophisticated communications equipment, changes in the nature of markets and consumer demand, and a general increase in the level of change and uncertainty.

These developments have created conditions that represent a break with the earlier post–World War II era. Many industries see profound changes in technology, markets, and industry structure, which in turn are reshaping human resource strategies and educational and training requirements (Bailey, 1989).

On the technology side, the spread of microelectronics is a major influence. Nontechnological factors are equally important: intensified competition, particularly from abroad; increased importance of variety, style, quality, and service; quickening of change in technology, products, and services; and an accompanying rise in the general level of uncertainty.

These changes have led firms both to increase the variety of their output and to try to be more responsive to the market. In pursuit of the latter goal, firms are increasing the extent and depth of their interactions with customers and suppliers and reducing the time that it takes to conceive, design, produce, market, and distribute their products. Modern computer technology has greatly increased the ability of firms to carry out these objectives, but new technology alone is not sufficient. Technological innovation and modernization have been accompanied by efforts to reshape both the organization of firms and the structure of industries.

Some progressive firms are shifting from an emphasis on rationalizing individual steps of the production process, primarily through cost cutting and especially labor cost cutting, to a strategy that seeks to improve the production process as a whole and to align it more closely with the market. This change in strategy can be conceptualized as a shift from a sequential to an integrated process. The sequential approach was best reflected in the assembly line. But the sequential and departmentalized system permeated the entire organization. Production, research and development, finance, training, quality control (if it existed), equipment maintenance or repair, and other functions had separate places in the overall process. One process or function ran its course before others began, or, in the case of repair, one process stopped while the others were carried out. Moreover, there was little ongoing interaction among firms and their suppliers and customers.

This sequential approach was efficient for producing large quantities of standardized goods and services that changed little from year to year. But although producers achieved low unit costs and minimized the skills needed by production and lower-level clerical workers, the system had potentially serious problems. The sequential approach relied on the accumulation of in-process inventory (in the case of manufacturing) and semiprocessed paperwork (in the case of services) between each step. This tied up capital and lengthened the time required to design, produce, and deliver the goods or services. Quality was difficult to maintain not only because quality control was the responsibility of different individuals in the sequence of steps, but because defective parts or errors in processing accumulated between steps before they had a chance to become apparent in the next stage of the process. The communication among individuals carrying out the various tasks that made up the overall process and among the firms and their suppliers and customers was also weak. This slowed the development of ideas for new products and services or for improvements in productive techniques that might have emerged from more holistic views of the collective activities. Engineers, designers, marketers, retailers, production workers, supervisors, repair personnel, quality assurance specialists, and others could have benefited from each others' insights and ideas, but the sequential strategy minimized the opportunities for interaction among them.

Greater international competition and changing market demand created new conditions that weakened the sequential approach. These new conditions favored faster innovation, shorter production cycles, improved quality, closer contact with customers, and the ability to efficiently produce smaller quantities of a larger variety of products and services. In other words, the opportunities to prosper by producing large quantities of low-cost standardized goods, which was the forte of the sequential approach, diminished. A better fit with the new environment could be achieved by more responsive and flexible organizations. Thus in progressive firms the relationships among individuals within firms, among the departments and divisions of firms, and among firms in the overall supply chain are more immediate, integrated, interactive, and complex.

This new model of work and production organization places increased intellectual and skill demands on lower- and middle-level workers. Workers without basic literacy and numeracy skills find fewer opportunities, and firms increasingly demand technical skills to operate, maintain, and repair the new technology. But the new environment also calls for a greater ability to work in a more uncertain and nonroutine environment. Workers need a stronger basic education, knowledge of a wider range of tasks, and a better conceptual understanding of the overall production process in which they are involved, of the products and services that their firms produce, and of the markets that they serve. In more flexible organizations, workers as well as middle management must be better able to act on their own rather than awaiting instruction or permission from superiors.

Thus I have emphasized that the drive for more flexibility and a greater emphasis on continuous innovation and fast response to the market have led to a variety of strategies on the part of firms. Investments in new technology are crucial, but firms have also learned that the flexibility and productivity potential of new technology cannot be attained without other changes. These changes involve a more market- and product-oriented organization of the firm and closer interactions among firms in the supply chain. These trends create a much denser and more integrated production system. Lead times, buffer inventories, and other types of slack and margins for error and relaxation are all, at least in principle, being squeezed out of the production system. Firms and workers are now involved in more integrated and interdependent networks. These patterns yield greater autonomy at lower levels and decentralization of decisionmaking. This juxtaposition of interdependence and autonomy and its attendant technological and organizational developments can have a strong influence on skill needs, human resources, and educational strategies.

Many analysts argue that achieving this vision of a reformed organization is increasingly the key to economic success in the globalized economy (Hayes, Wheelwright, and Clark, 1988; Zuboff, 1988; Dertouzos, Lester, and Solow, 1989). Others are even more alarmist. The Commission on the Skills in the American Workforce (1990) asserted that without a significant shift to this form of "high-performance work organization," the United States is doomed to a future of low productivity, low wages, and increasing inequality. But the effects and diffusion of innovative work reorganization remain complex. Considerable empirical evidence suggests that work reform increases organizational performance; nevertheless, according to the little survey information available, the spread of these innovations has been slow and still only a minority of firms have adopted them (Bailey, 1992). One of the most popular hypotheses about the failure of work reform to spread faster is that the U.S. education system does a poor job in teaching the types of skills and competencies needed in restructured workplaces (Dertouzos, Lester, and Solow, 1989; Commission on the Skills in the American Workforce, 1990). There is some support for this conclusion; nevertheless, better skills alone cannot, over the next few years, dramatically accelerate the adoption of innovative work organization. Firms must also take independent actions, and other public policy measures are also crucial (Bailey, 1992).

Thus the changing economy has created incentives for firms to change their work organization, and a reformed education system would facilitate the adoption of such innovations. But experience with work reform, in addition to creating a demand for educational reform, also contains direct lessons for that reform. These lessons will be discussed in more detail later.

Education and the Workplace

Over the past century, changes in the educational system have often been closely associated with changes in the economy. Historians have argued that the basic structure of schooling today emerged as the basis of work moved away from craft and agricultural skills to a more hierarchical, bureaucratized production process (Kantor and Tyack, 1982). Prior to industrialization, education, of which skills instruction was but one part, was integrated into the process of production and indeed into the overall maturation process. This process was most obvious on the farm, where children learned from their parents on the job. Traditional craft training was similar. Work did not start after education and training ended.

But the development of an industrial division of labor broke down craft skills and moved work out of the home or the farm and workshop closely integrated with the home and into mills and offices. The home and common school were no longer adequate to train and socialize a work force for the factory and bureaucracy.

Bowles and Gintis (1976) in particular have argued that the organization of schools and the power relations within them correspond to the organization and relations of the industrial workplace. They state that

> Specifically, the relationship of authority and control between administrators and teachers, teachers and students, students and students, and students and their work replicate the hierarchical division of labor which dominates the work place. Power is organized along vertical lines of authority from administration to faculty to student body; students have a degree of control over their curriculum comparable to that of the worker over the content of his job. (Bowles and Gintis, 1976, p. 12)

According to this point of view, schools played the role of socializing students to their future subordinate, routine, and undemanding jobs. The actual content that schools taught was less important.

To be sure, this image of an education system serving the needs of a hierarchical capitalist workplace has been widely attacked. Reformers, economists, and structural sociologists have argued that the form and organization taken on by schools during the Progressive Era arose as a result of the skill and technological needs of the emerging industrial economy (Grubb and Lazerson, 1974). Indeed the whole "revisionist" school of education history that linked schooling explicitly to power, stratification, and inequality has been controversial (Ravitch, 1978).

Nevertheless, most participants in the debate agree that school reform was closely related to the decline of an economy based on agriculture and on craft production carried out primarily in small firms and the rise of industrial mass production–based economy.[1] Indeed, there is much in the twentieth-century educational system that reminds us of the sequential, mass production model. Schools were organized like factories and often had similar architecture. The curriculum was segmented and students destined for different levels of the employment hierarchy received differing types of education. Vocational education in particular was often very narrowly conceived. And as Joseph Kett (1989) argues, education at the correspondence schools that proliferated during the early decades of the century "was conducted like a factory, specifically a factory organized along Taylorite lines. Like a Taylorite factory, with its systematic subdivision of job tasks, ICS [a prominent correspondence school] displayed a near mania for subdividing its courses."

Much may have changed since the turn of the century, but analysts continue to conclude that the form of education prepares students for the types of jobs that would characterize a hierarchical, Taylorite workplace. This position is hardly limited to radical analysts or revisionist historians. In the 1988 book *Winning the Brain Race,* David Kearns, the CEO of Xerox Corporation, and Dennis Doyle, a prominent educational analyst from the conservative Hudson Institute, made the following statement, which would hardly seem out of place in Bowles and Gintis's *Schooling in Capitalist America.*

> The contemporary school is an outgrowth of the scientific management movement of the early 20th century. The most important part of that movement was the belief that regimentation fostered efficient productivity. Whether making steel or teaching school, raw materials would be processed in a central place by a mass of unskilled workers in a repetitive fashion that was supervised by a few skilled workers. (Kearns and Doyle, 1988, pp. 35–36)

In a 1988 article, Hermine Marshall (1988, pp. 9–16) argued that the assembly-line workplace metaphor continued to be influential in teaching and curriculum design.[2] And after their massive study of American high schools in the early 1980s, Arthur Powell and his associates concluded that "perhaps high schools teach students what they most need to know: how to endure boredom without protest" (Powell, Farrar, and Cohen, 1985, p. 303).

The debate about whether and why the schools prepare students for their proper places in the hierarchical world of work will undoubtedly continue. Much less noticed, however, is the extent to which the educational system corresponds to the *sequential* strategy that has characterized the twentieth-century production system. Child labor laws kept young workers out of the labor market and the depression in particular drove them into schools for want of anything else to do. This was part of a trend in which schooling began to precede work. The vocational education movement was an explicit movement toward education that was presumably directly related to work but that took place off the worksite and before the working life started.

The incorporation of work-related education into the basic public secondary education system did not come about immediately. Vocational education first became widely available through night and correspondence schools that attracted young adults who were already on the job and wanted to upgrade their skills (Kett, 1989). It was not until the 1930s that public secondary schools came to dominate vocational education.

This sharp distinction between school and society was challenged during the reform movements of the 1960s and 1970s. Lawrence Cremin (1989) has argued that educational reform in the post–World War II era has been motivated by three "grand stories."[3] The first was articulated most clearly by James Conant during the 1950s. According to Cremin, "[Conant] enunciated a Jeffersonian philosophy that embraced universal elementary education, comprehensive secondary education, and highly selective meritocratic higher education—the combination, he believed, would be America's best guarantee of a free and 'classless' society" (Cremin, 1989, p. 22).

It was the second grand story that superseded Conant's views in which the distinction between school and society was challenged. Cremin dates this movement from the 1960 publication of *Summerhill,* but the story was set out in more detail in a series of reports on high school reform published in the early 1970s. These reports

> portrayed the American high school as an institution victimized by its own success: the closer it came to achieving universality, the larger, the less responsive, and the more isolated an institution it became, walling adolescents off from other segments of society, organizing them into rigidly defined age groups, and locking them into tight and inflexible academic programs. As a result, the ordinary processes by which young people became adults had become weak, confused and disjointed. (Cremin, 1989, p. 27)

Adherents to this perspective advocated smaller, more flexible schools with broader curricular options, more active involvement of students and teachers, and much greater contacts with other institutions in the society such as museums, libraries, employers, and government agencies. The popularization of education was admirable and "crucial to the American polity and economy" (Cremin, 1989, p. 27), but the system needed to be reconnected to the life of society.

Ironically, although the type of connection to society advocated by adherents of the second grand story seems more consistent with the increasingly integrated (rather than sequential) nature of the emerging economy, it was concern about the economy that precipitated the era of the third grand story that championed the sequential and separate nature of education. This era was signaled by the publication of *A Nation at Risk.* The corresponding reform agenda can be characterized by a focus on the "new basics" (four years of English, three of mathematics, and three of social studies); an increase in the time spent in school; strengthening the quality and professionalization of the teaching corps; an increased emphasis on standards and accountability; a suspicion of vocational education in secondary school; and a focus on dropout prevention and universal high school completion. According to this perspective, education was a special endeavor emphasizing academic subjects. The best preparation for work did not require bringing education closer to the workplace or the community but rather enhancing its separate character.

There is evidence to support the argument that the emerging economy calls for more education of the traditional type. Research on the effects of education has shown that education promotes a student's ability to deal with change or disequilibrium (Schultz, 1975). More recent research shows that industries and firms experiencing faster technological change employ more highly educated workers (Bartel and Lichtenberg, 1987). If change and uncertainty are increasing, so should the demand for more highly educated workers. In fact, an emerging body of evidence shows that the economic rewards associated with a college degree are rising relative to the returns for high school education, suggesting that the demand for more educated workers is indeed growing (Levy and Murnane, 1992). These studies therefore suggest that changes in the economy call for more education and a larger educational system; they are consistent with data from occupational projections that suggest that the majority of job growth over the next decade will take place among occupations that are currently filled by workers with some postsecondary education (Bailey, 1991). But all of this research simply uses years of education as a measure of skills and of course the education measured in those studies was education of the traditional type—as it was organized in the past.

But what we know about the changing nature of work suggests that "more of the same" is an inadequate theme for contemporary educational reform. Indeed there are indications that the sequential model in which the student learns in school and works on the job is increasingly out of step with current trends. One of the most obvious implications of the increasing pace of change is the growing need for retraining throughout an individual's career. As John Dewey argued almost seventy-five years ago, "Above all it [education] would train power of readaptation to changing conditions so that future workers would not become blindly subject to a fate imposed upon them" (Dewey, 1916, pp. 318–319). Change also implies a need for continued formal learning, so it is hardly surprising that education is increasingly an adult endeavor. Firm-based education is already an immense institution. Estimates suggest that more money is spent by firms in training their work force than is spent on all of postsecondary education.[4] Indeed, there are increases in firm-based training even for basic skills. Moreover, much of the formal firm-based training is actually carried out by the formal educational system. Increasingly, adults are returning to school. The average age of students in postsecondary institutions is rising. In 1985, 41 percent of all students enrolled in community, technical, and junior colleges were 25 years of age and older (El-Khawas, Carter, and Ottinger, 1988, p. 13). Part-time and nondegree enrollments also grew in community colleges. The share of part-time enrollments grew from 50 percent in 1970 to 65 percent in 1984 (Zwerling, 1986). Students in customized programs constitute an important part of nondegree enrollments (Pincus, 1986; Teitel, 1988). And community colleges in general are extensively involved in employer-sponsored training (Carnevale and Goldstein, 1989).

Thus, as I shall argue in more detail later, the boundaries between employing and educating institutions are increasingly difficult to distinguish. Nevertheless, the "sequential and separate" model continues to be influential in thinking about education. Much of the current discussion of educational reform is focused on one-dimensional quantitative outcome measures—test scores, high school completion or dropout rates, annual hours of schooling. Despite the growing realization that work is a collective process in which each participant's effectiveness is inextricably linked to his or her ability to work in a group, schools maintain their overwhelming emphasis on individual learning and isolated achievement. Customized training in community colleges has attracted a good deal of attention, yet it frequently grows up outside the central community college programs, often with different faculty and a separate funding structure. Relationships between the private sector and schools are referred to as "links," suggesting rather tenuous interactions, and many of the relationships are superficial or even primarily associated with public relations. We still refer to the "transition of youth from school to work" as if it is a onetime event. And economists studying the relationship between education and earnings still separate initial "years of schooling" from "experience," or postschool learning on the job.[5]

Although many reformers are skeptical about the reform agenda that emerged from the reports of the early and mid-1980s, the perspective continues to dominate the discussion of educational reform—increased required academic courses and suspicion of a wide selection of courses (the shopping mall high school) remain central components of educational reform in most states. And President Bush's 1991 educational reform strategy outlined in *America 2000: An Education Strategy* also included a list of basic academic courses: English, mathematics, science, history, and geography. Indeed, one could characterize *America 2000* as another *A Nation at Risk* with a greater emphasis on school choice.

But other developments suggest a shift away from the emphasis on the sequential approach. For example, the U.S. Department of Labor has increased its emphasis on learning on the job through a reorganization that created an Office of Workbased Learning. Policymakers have viewed the development of the high school academies model with great enthusiasm, and that model encourages greater interaction between school and workplaces (Stern, Raby, and Dayton, 1992). Perhaps most notable has been the growing interest in youth apprenticeship, which involves a much greater use of the workplace as a site of learning for late adolescents (Bailey and Merritt, 1992).

Nevertheless, although these developments are significant, they remain changes around the edges of the core educational institutions and systems, which continue to be dominated by the sequential approach. Thus our understanding of the opportunities and pitfalls of the current educational reform movement is limited by habits of thought that continue to emphasize the sequential educational model, that downplay the significance of learning in the workplace, and that conceptualize the institutional interactions between schools and workplaces in very narrow terms. Although the intellectual elements of a fourth grand educational story that might move away from the sequential and quantitative approach are present, they remain scattered. This chapter represents an attempt to develop a conceptual framework based on the integration strategy that can help form the basis of a fourth grand story.

The Integration Principle in Education

This analysis is based on a unified conceptual paradigm. It draws from our understanding of the transformation of the work process, especially the shift from a sequential to an integrated approach. The first step is to recognize the weakening of the distinction between schools and work.

Progressive firms have tried to change in three ways: what they do, how they are organized internally to do it, and how they relate to outside constituencies and institutions, especially suppliers and customers. Similarly, new conditions call for similar changes in the educational system. These three factors will be referred to as curricular, organizational, and institutional integration. *Curricular integration* (what they do) refers to increasing similarity between the content of education and learning in school and on the job. *Organizational integration* (how they are organized to do it) refers to the similarity between the organization of schools and of workplaces. *Institutional integration* (how they relate to outside constituencies and institutions) involves institutional relationships between the educational system and employing organizations. Each of these three areas has received a good deal of attention. Furthermore, each of these corresponds to a major strand of the educational reform movement as it existed at the end of the 1980s. But these strands were usually viewed as separate reforms or good pedagogic techniques applicable in all circumstances and have not been brought together and integrated into a broad conception of education and its relationship to changes in the economy. Employers are learning that attempts to integrate the processes through which they produce goods and services often fail if they take a partial approach. Likewise, efforts to integrate school and work may have only limited success if the focus is too narrow.

Curricular Integration

In the past few years, many analysts have called for the integration of vocational and academic education. This issue goes beyond the narrow problem of what to do with traditional high school vocational education programs. In its immediate sense, the underlying idea is that the distinction between traditional academic work and particular skills needed on the job is fading. But this is backed by further pedagogic and cognitive psychological theory that argues that even abstract issues can possibly be learned more effectively through concrete applications (Resnick, 1987). A growing body of research suggests the effectiveness of "functional context learning" that teaches basic skills using job-related material.[6] The strategy of integrating academic and vocational education has gained wide support and is indeed one of the cornerstones of the 1990 amendments to the Perkins Act. And the "cognitive apprenticeship" strategy suggests that traditional academic subjects such as reading and mathematics can be learned through techniques similar to those used by traditional apprenticeship, which involve close interaction between "experts" and "novices" in concrete situations (Collins, Brown, and Newman, 1989; Berryman and Bailey, 1992). Several innovative high schools are organized around job-related themes and appear to do an effective job of providing a broad college preparatory education. This strengthens both job-specific skills as well as more general basic skills. Thus students who will end up at all levels of the occupational hierarchy can benefit from this type of integration. Moreover, educators have long believed that work-related instruction serves to motivate many students who would otherwise have little interest in education.

But at the same time, education that takes place on the job is now becoming much broader. Perhaps one can say that firms are beginning to see a need for workers with much broader skills. Indeed analysts of work argue that the workplace should be turned into a "learning environment." The business press is beginning to pay more attention to learning organizations or learning companies (Kiechel, 1990). One definition of a learning company is "an organization which facilitates the learning of all of its members and continuously transforms itself in order to meet its strategic goals" (Pedler, Boydell, and Burgoyne, 1989, p. 92). Shoshana Zuboff argued that "the behaviors that define learning and the behaviors that define being productive are one and the same. Learning is not something that requires time out from being engaged in productive activity; learning is the heart of productive activity. To put it simply, learning is the new form of labor" (Zuboff, 1988, p. 395). Zuboff's may be an extreme statement of the position, but employer-provided training is moving away from a narrow focus on immediately useful skills.

Finally, recent research in cognitive psychology provides further reasons to be skeptical about a sequential approach to education. Resnick, in her review of studies on the nature of human thinking and of the acquisition of thinking and learning skills, concluded that "the kind of activities traditionally associated with thinking are not limited to advanced levels of development. Instead these activities are an intimate part of even elementary levels of reading, mathematics, and other branches of learning—when learning is proceeding well" (Resnick, 1987, p. 8). Thus according to Resnick, this research challenges educational theories that posit a sequence from lower-level activities not requiring independent thinking or judgment to higher-level thinking.

Organizational Integration

A central component of the shift from sequential to integrated production systems involves changes in the organization of firms. In sequential systems, work was subdivided and the coordination of the process was left to higher-level management; firms moving toward more integrated systems often develop more decentralized systems that emphasize teamwork. This not only allows more flexibility and promotes more continuous innovation, but it also broadens jobs and makes them more interesting. Similarly, many school officials have now become convinced of the need for organizational change in the educational system. Perhaps the most obvious trend in this direction involves so-called school-based management programs in which principals and especially teachers are given more responsibility. Proponents of school-based management argue that if decentralization in firms can make firms more flexible and responsive to constituents and can enrich the jobs of employees, this reform will have the same effects in schools.

But the decentralization movement is extremely complex and there are many competing models. One model that is used in very large urban systems involves the delegation of more authority to teachers and principals while the central bureaucracy maintains overall control. This is the type of plan advocated by Joseph Fernandez, the chancellor of the New York City schools. This is perhaps most analogous to the type of decentralization used in some progressive businesses. A second model gives much stronger political power over the operation of neighborhood schools to local groups that include parents, teachers, and principals. This model, implemented in Chicago, is designed to bring about change by giving power to those with the greatest interest in the operation of each school. A third model involves giving more autonomy to individual schools and allowing parents and students to choose which school they want to attend (the Chicago plan maintains many neighborhood schools, especially in the elementary years). The extreme case of this is the voucher system, which has had advocates among economists for many years and has gained popularity due to a 1990 book by John Chubb and Terry Moe (1990). In this case, parents are given the opportunity to leave poor schools and enroll in better schools, leading to the natural, marketlike elimination of low-quality institutions. If the Chicago case tries to increase the "voice"—in Albert Hirschman's (1971) terms—of parents, the voucher or choice model increases their power to "exit."

It is important to note that a similar variety of decentralization and worker empowerment programs are also flourishing at the workplace. For example, although firms in Japan and in some parts of northern Italy place greater responsibility on lower-level workers than do typical firms in the United States, the Japanese system is based on decentralization within very strong central control whereas the Italian system relies more on cooperation among small entrepreneurial firms (Best, 1990). Both of these models seem to be successful. This could also suggest that there might be a variety of school-based management or decentralization plans that could be successful under different circumstances.

Finally, other organizational changes besides decentralization might also promote flexibility and responsiveness in the education system. Some community colleges have increased their flexibility through the use of noncredit courses and training programs and movement away from rigid adherence to standard academic hours and calendars. Proprietary schools, despite their many problems, have been particularly active in experimentation with alternative schedules and calendars. In effect, I am arguing that, as the correspondence principle would suggest, a major change in the organization of work would lead to a corresponding change in the organization of schools.

Institutional Integration

Institutional integration involves actual relationships between schools and employers. In the sequential model of production, the role of each step in a process was to prepare the inputs for the following step. To be sure, the requirements for the subsequent steps needed to be communicated to those responsible for preparing the inputs, but constant and interactive communication among the steps was often minimized. As I have argued, the sequential approach works well when production is standardized and predictable. However, greater volatility, change, and the need for innovation require more interactive relationships among the steps in the overall process. Similarly, in an era of much faster change, schools must alter their relationships to other institutions.

As an example, consider the ways in which schools decide what skills they need to teach. There are basically two approaches to educational planning. One, which can be referred to as the occupational/job content approach, relies on occupational forecasting and task analysis. The second perspective emphasizes increasing the adaptability of students and of educational institutions. This approach is based on the idea that although improved forecasting is important, it has serious limitations. In effect, the faster that students and schools can adapt, the shorter the required forecasting horizon. Moreover, institutional adaptability does not just involve fast response to information, but rather the ability of local-level institutions to collect and use both local information and broader types of information not available from forecasts about technology and developments in relevant industries.

Although improved forecasting would certainly be helpful, for the purposes of educational planning it has several serious problems. First, even though forecasting might give some sense of trends at an aggregate level, it is less useful for the limited local areas that most educational institutions serve. Second, the task and skill analysis of occupations has always been difficult but more rapid change has now increased the frequency with which those forecasts must be updated. Third, there is no well-defined relationship between occupations and given technologies on the one hand and skill requirements on the other hand. Many other factors intervene, including the industrial relations system, the organization of the firm, and the characteristics of the markets that the firm serves. These intervening factors may be particularly important at the local level. Finally, all of these factors are exacerbated by the increasing pace of change in markets, technology, and production processes.

In contrast, the adaptability perspective emphasizes the ability of the schools, through ongoing relationships to employing and other institutions, to gather and interpret information themselves. Thus schools need a knowledge of conditions, technologies, and organization of the local industries and economy. This information can come from experts, outside research institutions, as well as formal and informal contacts with employers. Educators also need to keep up with broader technological and organizational developments in the appropriate fields. In this case, they can serve an information-diffusion role in their geographical areas—they may have better access to information than many local employers. This type of educational input to firms also extends to programs in which schools or community colleges actually carry out firm-based training. Additionally, initiatives such as Tech Prep have illustrated the increasing need for interinstitutional linkages within the educational structure itself. Students who desire to attain more or a different type of education need to have the proper channels available to them within the educational structure to foster transitions with minimal administrative difficulty and coursework redundancy (Dornsife, 1991). An important point here is that this requires an active participation of the local-level personnel. Indeed, rather than seeing a centralized data center as the primary source of information on new technologies and skill requirements, local-level personnel might actually serve as sources of some types of information for the centralized data collection agencies. Thus organizational integration interacts with institutional integration to create an educational system more in tune with current conditions in the labor and educational market.

There is now an increasing number of these types of relationships, including various partnerships between specific employers and schools, placement services, employer advisory boards, cooperative education programs, customized training programs at community colleges, and employer tuition remission programs. The U.S. Department of Education (1989) counted about 42,000 partnerships between corporations and public schools in the 1983–1984 school year but found over 140,000 in 1987–1988. Customized programs have also increased and according to a 1987 survey by the Census Department, 31 percent of all formal training carried out by employers was conducted by outside providers and over 60 percent of that by schools or the government (U.S. Bureau of the Census, 1987). Indeed, most major companies with large education programs do much of the training through local community colleges. At the secondary level, employers are primarily seen as providing various types of services, advice, or job placements for schools. There is very much a sense that schools have gone to the private sector for help, but the reverse is also true: In many cases the growth of workplace literacy programs has sent employers to secondary schools. At the postsecondary level, it is often the employers who use the programs directly to train their employed work force, or they see the local community college or technical school as a direct source of potential recruits.

International comparisons also suggest an increasing importance of institutional integration. As many commentators have noted, there is much more integration between schools and employing institutions in Germany and Japan, and their economic success has led to calls to try to implement similar systems here. In Germany, about 70 percent of a cohort graduates from three-year apprenticeship programs that they enter at age 15. During the program, the students work four days a week and spend the fifth day in formal public school instruction. Graduates must pass tests based on a national syllabus of vocational training produced by a tripartite institution consisting of representatives of the public sector, employers, and labor (Hamilton, 1990, chapters 3, 4, and 5). Apprenticeship is much less important in Japan, but in other ways the integration between schools and workplaces is just as strong. Many employers have long-term relationships with particular schools. Employers submit job openings to the school staff, who then nominate students for the openings. Students can apply for only one job at a time. In about 80 percent of the cases, the student applicants are selected for the first job for which they are nominated and most of the others are accepted into the second job for which they are nominated (Rosenbaum, 1989).[7] There have been arguments in favor of applying these or similar models in the United States. The U.S. Department of Labor has launched a large reassessment of its apprenticeship system and in the past decade there have been many local-level efforts to improve the job placement counseling in high schools. Although these more integrated educational models from Japan and Germany have received favorable comment, it remains to be seen the extent to which they are appropriate models for this country.

The Effects of School-Work Integration

I have argued that the logic of economic developments implies a greater integration between education and work. To some extent, this is already happening, as we shall see later. To what extent will it improve the country's economic performance? There is little empirical evidence tying educational reform to overall economic performance. Much of the strength of the argument comes from international comparisons in which it is perceived that other countries, especially Japan and West Germany, have stronger economic performance than the United States and, as I have argued, in some ways have stronger work-school integration—especially institutional integration. But these are highly dubious conclusions, not only because the comparative economic performance is not as simple as a direct comparison of trade deficits might suggest, but also because there are obviously many other differences among these countries that account for difference in economic performance.

Analysis of the effectiveness of educational reforms usually relates changes in educational programs to measurable educational outcomes such as test scores. Much of this research is reviewed by Lorraine McDonnell (1988), who concludes that there is suggestive evidence that the types of curricular and organizational innovations discussed here can be effective. But there is very little evidence about the effects of institutional linkages between schools and employing institutions.[8] However, the institutional integration emphasized here is perhaps more concentrated in postsecondary institutions whereas McDonnell focuses primarily on public secondary and elementary schools. Moreover, the school-work integration discussed here is much more than a strategy to improve schools. Rather, it refers to a movement away from the sequential education-then-work model and to a blurring of the distinctions between learning in school and on the job. If nothing else, the greater need for education throughout life and the accelerating need for firms to retrain their employees will push this trend forward.

Furthermore, another factor, also emphasized by McDonnell, is that although many of these strategies may have potential, they probably will have little effect if they are implemented in isolation. Firms have learned that isolated attempts at this or that innovation rarely work, even if they might be crucial components of a necessary overall strategy. Similarly, curriculum reform without organizational or institutional integration, or a school-business partnership that provides a few services to a school that is otherwise unchanged, will probably mean little.[9]

School-Work Integration, Equity, Opportunity, and Race

Thus both the logic of the nature of changes in work, as we understand them, and some empirical evidence suggest that a comprehensive strategy including curricular, organizational, and institutional integration could contribute to strengthening this country's economic performance and competitiveness. Nevertheless, the goal of the school system is not only to prepare the work force. Schools are expected to provide the basic knowledge for participation in a democratic society and to widen economic opportunity for all of the country's citizens. Certainly in addition to the needs of the workplace, the national commitment to popular education extending back to the nineteenth century (at least for whites) and the perceived importance of education for social mobility have shaped the education system during the first two-thirds of the twentieth century.

There is a tradition in education research that argues that the stronger links between schools and the private sector tend to weaken the communitarian and democratic roles that the schools are expected to play. Indeed, in the past, schools have been accused of reproducing inequalities inherent in advanced capitalist economies. Vocational education, according to this argument, was part of a broader trend during the Progressive Era that allowed secondary schooling to be open to all but that also reproduced the stratification within the schools (Labaree, 1987). One purpose served by community colleges, argue Steven Brint and Jerome Karabel (1989, chapter 1), is to "manage the ambition" of students not destined for higher-level jobs. Given that more students will aspire to the more prestigious jobs than can possibly be accommodated, some mechanism is necessary to "cool out" the ambitions and aspirations of many. Many of the measures that characterize what I have called institutional integration—customized training, closer links between community colleges and businesses, increased "lifetime" education, and a greater emphasis on firm-based education—have all been attacked as promoting inequality.[10] Moreover, in this country perpetuating disparities in economic opportunities usually means perpetuating disparities in opportunities among different races. Thus blacks tend to be overrepresented in those types of schools, tracks, and colleges that are associated with lower levels of the employment hierarchy.[11]

International comparisons, in this case, should provide cautionary examples. Greater integration between work and school in Japan and West Germany are suggested as characteristics to emulate in this country, but these countries track students in early adolescence.[12] Most advocates of educational reform in this country are increasingly opposed to secondary-school tracking.

Nevertheless, in anticipating the implications for stratification and inequality, we should not forget that the current system already is highly stratified and that many popular reforms could strengthen that inequality. For example, the quantitative agenda that dominated the reform movement throughout the 1980s has been attacked for overlooking the problems of many students who are not academically oriented. As Cremin has suggested, it is possible that a greater emphasis on traditional academic curricula has increased the dropout rate as well as pushing some students to higher levels of achievement. In many cities, the dropout rate has increased, although the relationship between this increase and educational reform has not been definitively established (Cremin, 1989, p. 36).

Normative conclusions about the trend toward school-work integration also depend on the judgments about the nature of the workplace with which education is to be integrated. From this perspective, in the past the schools prepared a majority of students for routine, boring, and subordinate positions in a hierarchical structure. Today, these traditional organizational and hierarchical characteristics of the economy are being challenged and in some cases transformed. If competitiveness calls for an upgrading of lower-level positions and investing them with greater responsibility and scope of action, then an appropriate response by the education system would be consistent with the goals of most educational reformers. Indeed, what I have referred to as curricular and organizational integration has strong supporters among reformers who might be most skeptical about the wisdom of greater correspondence between schools and work. Although vocational programs in many schools continue to constitute lower tracks, some of the most successful programs for minority students in secondary schools involve occupationally oriented programs (Mitchell, Russell, and Benson, 1989). In some community colleges, occupational tracks that were originally conceived of as terminal programs actually send higher proportions of their participants to further education than liberal arts programs designed explicitly to prepare students for continued schooling.

The social implications of school-work integration also depend on the influence that schools and education in general might have on work. As Carnoy and Levin (1985) argue, although schools may in many ways reproduce the stratification in the workplace, educational services and educational outcomes are much more equally distributed than income, status, or power associated with employment. And they emphasize that schools, as public institutions, are much more subject to the political influence of working-class and other groups than are private businesses. Thus, to the extent that education can affect work, it represents a potential window of public influence over private institutions.

Of course the implication of much historical writing on education is that the influence goes the other way. It is plausible that, as Lindblom (1977) argues, business has vastly disproportionate power in this public arena both through its ability to influence the political process directly (because of its greater resources) and, perhaps more important, because employers eventually hire the graduates of the school system. John Dewey argued that schools could have a strong influence on society, stating that

> a right educational use of [science] would react upon intelligence and interest so as to modify, in connection with legislation and administration, the socially obnoxious features of the present industrial and commercial order. ... It would give those who engage in industrial callings desire and ability to share in social control, and ability to become masters of their industrial fate. (Dewey, 1916, p. 320)

Viewed from the perspective of the 1990s, when the schools have been subject to scathing criticism for being boring, ineffective, hierarchical, rigid, and anti-intellectual, Dewey's views seem naive. That is, rather than the schools instilling a spirit of inquiry, learning, and democracy in the workplace, it seems that the needs of the economy drove that spirit out of the schools.

But the nature of current trends toward school-work integration may be creating a different context for the interactive influence of school and work. For Dewey, the influence would come through the schools' effects on the lives, beliefs, and behavior of students. But now there is much more institutional interaction between schools and work. Once we move away from the sequential role of schooling, the influence of schools need not be exercised simply through the schools' effects on their students. Employers are looking to educators and schools to help them impart skills such as literacy and technical know-how, but this gives schools the opportunity to have broader influence. The more the firm can turn toward community colleges or universities for their training, the stronger will be the potential influence.[13]

Thus, changes in technology and markets provide an opportunity for a major restructuring of work. Although it is by no means certain that employers will move willingly toward significant change and certainly incompetent and conservative management may thwart such trends, reforms in the educational system can help enable work force reforms (by preparing a work force that can be used in a restructured workplace) and have some direct influence on promoting them.

The Integration Principle
and Education for Minorities

Despite the myriad shortcomings of this country's school system, that system did open education to most residents. To be sure, it was highly stratified, and in many educational sectors the quality of the instruction was questionable, at least its cognitive aspects. Nevertheless, schools did supply the growing need for technical skills and from the point of view of the overall economy, the schools did well enough to propel the country to international economic leadership during and after World War II.

But if this system worked more or less for the white working class during the earlier postwar decades, the same could not be said for most blacks, who were either excluded from education or confined to patently inferior schools. Until the 1950s and the onset of the Civil Rights Movement, there was little political pressure to extend decent education to blacks, and the jobs to which most blacks were confined by discrimination had little need for the cognitive offerings of secondary schools and in many cases even primary schools. Blacks made important progress during the 1960s and 1970s, but their progress was stalled by their concentration in major metropolitan centers, where busing and other policies to promote integration weakened the political support for the public schools among whites (Katznelson and Weir, 1985). Thus urban school systems were confronted with the need to respond to fundamental changes even before they could create schools appropriate for the old economic conditions.

Consequently there were many unresolved problems for minority education as the country moved away from a reform movement with a strong

emphasis on equality and access (Cremin's second grand story) to one focused on education for economic competitiveness (the third grand story).
How will the trend away from a sequential system toward more work-
school integration affect the lingering educational problems for blacks
and other minorities?

Changes in technology and the economy have generally increased the
skill requirements in the workplace. Low-skilled jobs remain but their
numbers are falling. In the past, employers have been able to ignore the
educational problems of some percentage of the minority population, but
this will become increasingly difficult. Broad forces to improve urban
schools may become even stronger if labor markets continue to be tight
over the next decade, as many analysts predict. The growing relative minority populations in urban areas and their increasing political influence
may also create an improved environment in which to address these problems.

Community colleges may also represent significant opportunities to
strengthen urban minority education. Although there have been community and junior colleges for many decades, the past twenty years have
witnessed dramatic growth in their enrollments. Many blacks and other
minorities are already enrolled in community colleges, many of which
have strong links to local employers, and the structure of these colleges is
flexible enough to respond to changing circumstances. To be sure, these
institutions have many problems, but potentially they seem well positioned to serve important educational needs of urban minority groups in
the context of the transforming economy.

Curricular Integration

Curricular integration implies a reduction in the differentiation between
what is learned in school and on the job and between learning for work
and learning for broader educational goals. First, if this turns out to be
good pedagogy, and if it is used in schools with large numbers of black or
minority students, then their students will benefit. But the movement toward a more integrated curriculum may also create a better environment
for reducing inequalities in education. For example, curricular integration
implies a reduction in the differentiation between what is learned in
school and on the job and between learning for work and learning for
broader educational goals and this may create a better environment for reducing inequalities in education. Curricular integration at least provides
the basis for reducing tracking and other types of differentiated curriculum in which work-related education is considered a lower and separate
track. One advantage of this is that occupationally oriented programs, in
which blacks have traditionally been overrepresented, will no longer be

identified as inferior tracks for inferior students. Thus students who can benefit from and are better motivated by a more concrete or occupationally oriented curriculum need not be stuck in lower tracks and labeled as inferior students. And a more integrated curriculum may also reduce the differentiation between community colleges and the lower divisions of four-year colleges—graduates of occupationally oriented courses will be prepared both to go on immediately with their education or to start work. Finally, increased and broader education on the job and for adults reduces the long-term penalties for earlier labor market entry, which students from lower-income families disproportionately undergo for economic reasons.

Organizational Integration

If changes in the organization of schools such as decentralization, more parent and teacher involvement in school management, and increased flexibility lead to stronger and more effective schools and if these innovations are implemented in major cities, they will strengthen black and minority education. Moreover, increased community and parental participation is particularly important to school reform efforts in inner cities. This perspective is certainly one of the motivations behind the recent decentralization reform in Chicago. But at the same time, these reforms may need more resources than more traditional forms of organization. Thus once again, the central city schools with weaker financial bases will be at a disadvantage.

Institutional Integration

Like most of the reforms discussed here, institutional integration represents opportunities and problems for improving minority education in major urban centers. Strong relationships between employers, schools, and community colleges certainly have the potential to create opportunities for minority students in large cities. Furthermore, the increase in education and training at the workplace creates possibilities for blacks who are working to strengthen their skills. Yet to the extent that education is more linked to work, job discrimination will exacerbate educational inequality among races. Education linked to work favors those individuals who have access to education-rich employment. Discrimination and racial stereotypes can also make it difficult to transform occupationally oriented programs and schools from lower-level tracks into high-quality educational opportunities. Tracking through vocational programs is still widespread. Given typical attitudes among employers, it may be more difficult to move vocational programs with predominantly minority participants beyond the traditional lower-track role.

Thus the integration strategy appears to create a potential to improve education for minorities, but large questions and uncertainties remain. One reason why hard conclusions are difficult to come by is that much of the discussion of the integration-related reforms has not focussed on problems of minorities. Equity and access have never regained the place in educational reform that they held during the 1960s and 1970s.

Conclusion

In this chapter I have emphasized several parallels between educational and work reform. Innovative approaches in both realms emphasize moving from a sequential to a more integrated strategy. In both cases, the integrated strategy is based on content, organizational, and institutional integration—changes in the content of work or learning, in the organization of firms and schools, and in the relationships to outside institutions. Moreover, in workplaces and in schools, reforms appear to be more effective if they are combined into a broad strategy rather than implemented as separate initiatives or programs.

Other parallels are also salient. Faced by anxieties about international competition and overall productivity growth in the late 1970s and early 1980s, both schools and employers initially returned to past successful strategies. Educators tried to recapture an image of past success by arguing that educational problems could be solved if traditional academic education was strengthened and spread to all students. Employers turned to automation and straightforward technological solutions as they had in the heyday of mass production. Thus both sets of institutions at first tried a strategy based on more, but better, of the same, and they both found these solutions inadequate. Both have now turned in a similar direction, away from a sequential or quantitative approach to a more integrated strategy.

Furthermore, much of the current discussions of reform in both sets of institutions do not focus on the particular problems of minorities and the poor. This is perhaps not surprising given that both movements have been spurred by anxieties about productivity and international competitiveness. Most of the discussion of work reform has emphasized efforts in large firms where workers with significant economic and social problems are not to be found. Little specifically has been said about work reform as a solution to very low incomes or inequality (Bailey, 1992). The considerations of minority issues in many of the reform proposals associated with the integration strategy are perhaps more common. Nevertheless, many current innovative programs have selection criteria or processes that tend to exclude students with serious problems.

Also in both cases, there is suggestive, but by no means definitive, evidence that the integrated strategy will enhance the performance of the organization. The evidence is strong enough to push for wider implementation and experimentation, but many questions remain.

Finally, many of the individual reform proposals that have been widely discussed during the late 1980s and early 1990s are consistent with the integration strategy. These include school-based management, the integration of vocational and academic education, calls to evaluate students on the basis of projects or portfolios rather than paper-and-pencil tests, the questioning of divisions between traditional academic disciplines, and the renewed interest in apprenticeship, customized training, and cooperative education among others. But though each of these reforms may make sense individually, how do they fit together? The integration approach developed in this chapter provides a framework that can help reform move from a plethora of tactics and proposals toward the development of a comprehensive and coherent strategy.

Notes

1. Historians such as those published in the volume edited by Kantor and Tyack (1982) argue that the roots of vocationalism and the general relationship between education and work are much more complex than these two polar positions suggest—see the essay by Rogers and Tyack for an overview. Nevertheless, the essays in the collection place a great deal of importance on the relationship between the changes in the structure of firms and in the nature of skills. See the essay by Grubb and Lazerson for the most explicit statement.

2. Marshall pointed out that metaphors of more open and less bureaucratic workplace management styles had also been applied to schools but that the assembly-line approach had been the most influential.

3. A grand story is a "large loose set of ideas about how society works, why it goes wrong and how it can be set right" (Cremin, 1989, p. 21). Cremin attributes this concept to David Cohen and Michael Garet (1975).

4. Various experts estimate that outlays on firm-based education could approach $200 billion annually. *Training Magazine* estimated that firms with 100 or more employees spent about $40 billion annually on formal training programs (Feuer, 1988). And this is a gross underestimate. The largest part of these expenditures was accounted for by the salaries of trainers, thus little account was taken of the opportunity costs of the time spent by the trainees. Moreover, the numbers included neither an amount for small firms nor for informal training, which some experts believe may be as high as $180 billion (Carnevale, Gainer, and Yillet 1989, p. 15). Mincer (1989) estimates that the level of investment in on-the-job education and skills is between $66 and $210 billion, including employee contributions in foregone earnings. Although the precision of these estimates is open to question, there is little doubt that expenditures on education by employing institutions in 1988 exceeded the $125 billion spent that year on public and private postsecondary education and may be close to the $185 billion spent on primary and secondary schooling (U.S. Department of Education, 1989, table 24).

5. They would, to be sure, make more sophisticated disaggregations if they had the data, but the universal willingness to accept this schooling-experience convention testifies to the hegemony of the sequential model.

6. Research in the military shows that retention of basic skills education is much higher if job-related material is used in the instruction (Sticht, 1975).

7. Some advocates of this type of system argue that it creates very strong incentives for students to work hard in school. That is, their school records very directly determine their jobs. Although this is true for U.S. students bound for elite colleges, school performance appears to have little effect on job finding for the noncollege bound. The recent Commission on Workforce Quality and Labor Market Efficiency (1989) organized jointly by the U.S. Departments of Labor and Education made the issue of incentives a cornerstone of their proposals.

8. McDonnell also emphasizes that there are serious implementation problems that are often ignored in the discussions of educational restructuring.

9. The much-touted Boston Compact is a telling example of the drawbacks of partial reform. The compact was originally designed as a program that would involve both internal organizational reform within the school system and stronger links with the private sector, primarily through job guarantees to all who succeed in graduating. The program was able to find jobs for all of the graduates of the city's high schools. As the Boston economy cools down, it remains to be seen how important the very low unemployment rate was for the success of the placement efforts. But it was never able to make much progress in school-level reform. Indeed, the dropout rate actually rose since the inception of the compact. Now, the private-sector supporters apparently are beginning to lose interest faced with the absence of progress within the schools themselves (Farrar, 1988; Rothman, 1988).

10. Brint and Karabel (1989) argue that customized training might lead to greater stratification. Zwerling (1986) argues that the extent to which education is associated with a job, then access to better jobs, will be the key to acquiring advanced education. Thus initial disadvantages will compound. Data on firm-based education also suggest that those with higher levels of outside education also received more firm-based education (Lilliard and Tan, 1986)—that is, the educationally rich get richer.

11. For example, in postsecondary institutions in 1986, blacks accounted for 8 percent of the students in four-year schools, 9 percent of those in two-year public institutions, 14 percent of those in public vocational schools, and 21 percent in proprietary schools (Goodwin, 1989, p. 22). Wilson (1986) argues that blacks are overrepresented in vocational tracks in community colleges and that whites predominate in the "elite" community college programs such as nursing, electronics, and pre-engineering.

12. Hamilton (1990, chapters 3 and 4) argues that the German system is more open than commonly perceived in the United States. Apprentice graduates can go on to postsecondary training that allows them to rise to supervisory and some managerial positions. It is possible, but rare, for skilled craftspeople to enter the university, which opens higher-level professional positions.

13. Certainly to the extent that firms go to schools for training, those schools have the opportunity to influence those firms. Yet if the schools simply see themselves as providing a more or less technical service according to the firm's specifi-

cations (perhaps with the conviction that the firms know what they want and have a well-developed idea of the best course to pursue), then the schools will forfeit that opportunity to have a broader effect.

References

Bailey, T. (1992). Discretionary effort and the organization of work: Employee participation and work reform since Hawthorne. Unpublished paper prepared for the Sloan Foundation.

————. (1991). Forecasting future educational needs. *Educational Researcher*. Washington, DC: American Educational Research Association.

————. (1989). *Changes in the nature and structure of work: Implications for skill requirements and skill formation*. Berkeley: University of California, National Center for Research in Vocational Education, May.

Bailey, T., and Merritt, D. (1992). *School-to-work transition and youth apprenticeship in the United States*. New York: Manpower Demonstration Research Corporation.

Bartel, A., and Lichtenberg, F. (1987). The comparative advantage of educated workers in implementing new technology. *Review of Economics and Statistics* 69, 1–11.

Berryman, S., and Bailey, T. (1992). *The double helix of education and the economy*. New York: Institute on Education and the Economy, Teachers College, Columbia University.

Best, M. (1990). *The new competition: Institutions of industrial restructuring*. Cambridge: Harvard University Press.

Bowles, S., and Gintis, H. (1976). *Schooling in capitalist America: Educational reform and the contradictions of economic life*. New York: Basic Books.

Brint, S., and Karabel, J. (1989). *The diverted dream: Community colleges and the promise of educational opportunity in America, 1900–1985*. New York: Oxford University Press.

Carnevale, A. P., Gainer, L. J., and Villet, J. (1989). *Best Practices: What Works in Training and Development, Organization and Strategic Role*. Alexandria, VA: American Society for Training and Development, March.

Carnevale, A. P., and Goldstein, H. (1989). *Schooling and training for work in America: An overview*. Alexandria, VA: American Society for Training and Development, March.

Carnoy, M., and Levin, H. (1985). *Schooling and work in the democratic state*. Stanford: Stanford University Press.

Chubb, J., and Moe, T. (1990). *Politics, markets, and schools*. Washington, DC: Brookings Institution.

Cohen, D. K., and Garet, M. S. (1975). Reforming educational policy with applied social research. *Harvard Educational Review* 45 (February 1975):21.

Collins, A., Brown, J. S., and Newman, S. (1989). Cognitive apprenticeship: Teaching the craft of reading, writing, and mathematics. In Lauren Resnick (ed.), *Knowing, learning, and instruction: Essays in honor of Robert Glaser*. Hillsdale, NJ: Lawrence Erlbaum.

Commission on Skills in the American Workforce. (1990). *America's choice: High skills or low wages!* Rochester, NY: National Center on Education and the Economy.

Cremin, L. (1989). *Popular education and its discontents.* New York: Harper and Row.

Dertouzos, M., Lester, R., and Solow, R. (1989). *Made in America: Regaining the productive edge.* Cambridge: MIT Press.

Dewey, J. (1916). *Democracy and education.* New York: Free Press.

Dornsife, Carolyn. (1991). Beyond articulation: The development of tech prep programs. Berkeley: National Center for Research in Vocational Education, University of California at Berkeley, October.

El-Khawas, E., Carter, D., and Ottinger, C. (1988). *Community college fact book.* New York: Macmillan.

Farrar, E. (1988). *The Boston compact: A teaching case.* New Brunswick, NJ: Center for Policy Research in Education, Eagleton Institute of Policy, Rutgers, State University of New Jersey.

Feuer, D. (1988). Training Magazine's Industry Report 1988. *Training* (October):31–39.

Goodwin, D. (1989). *Postsecondary vocational education.* Washington, DC: National Assessment of Vocational Education, U.S. Department of Education.

Grubb, W. N., and Lazerson, M., eds. (1974). *American education and vocationalism.* New York: Teachers College, Columbia University.

Hamilton, S. F. (1990). *Apprenticeship for adulthood: Preparing youth for the future.* New York: Free Press.

Hayes, R., Wheelwright, S., and Clark, K. (1988). *Dynamic manufacturing: Creating the learning organization.* New York: Free Press.

Hirschman, A. (1971). *Exit, voice, and loyalty.* Cambridge: Harvard University Press.

Kantor, H., and Tyack, D. B. (eds.) (1982). *Work, youth and schooling: Historical perspectives on vocationalism in American education.* Stanford: Stanford University Press.

Katznelson, I., and Weir, M. (1985). *Schooling for all: Class, race, and the decline of the democratic ideal.* New York: Basic Books.

Kearns, D., and Doyle, D. (1988). *Winning the brain race: A bold plan to make our schools competitive.* San Francisco: Institute for Contemporary Studies Press.

Kett, J. (1989). From useful knowledge to vocational education. Paper prepared for the Conference on Education and the Economy: Hard Questions, Hard Answers. Sponsored by the Institute on Education and the Economy, Teachers College, Columbia University, New York, September.

Kiechel, W. (1990). The organization that learns. *Fortune,* March 12, 133–136.

Labaree, D. (1987). Politics, markets, and the compromised curriculum. Review essay. *Harvard Educational Review,* 57 (November):483–494.

Levy, F., and Murnane, R. (1992). US earnings levels and earnings inequity: A review of recent trends and proposed explanations. *Journal of Economic Literature* 30 (September 1992):1333–1381.

Lilliard, L., and Hong, T. (1986). *Private sector training: Who gets it and what are its effects?* Santa Monica: Rand Corporation.

Lindblom, C. F. (1977). *Politics and markets: The world's political economic system.* New York: Basic Books.

McDonnell, L. M. (1988). *Coursework in five states and its implications for indicator development.* Santa Monica: Rand Working Paper.

Marshall, H. (1988). Work or learning: Implications of classroom metaphors. *Educational Researcher* 17 (December): 9–16.

Mitchell, V., Russell, E., and Benson, C. (1989). Exemplary urban career-oriented high schools. A report prepared for the National Center for Research on Vocational Education. Berkeley: NCRVE, University of California.

Pedler, M., Boydell, T., and Burgoyne, J. (1989). The learning company. *Studies in Continuing Education* 11(2): 91–101.

Pincus, F. (1986). Vocational education: More false promises. In L. S. Zwerling (ed.), *The community college and its critics,* pp. 31–39. San Francisco: Jossey-Bass.

Powell, A., Farrar, E., and Cohen, D. (1985). *The shopping mall high school: Winners and losers in the educational marketplace.* Boston: Houghton Mifflin.

Ravitch, D. (1978). *The revisionists revised: A critique of the radical attack on the schools.* New York: Basic Books.

Resnick, L. (1987). *Education and learning to think.* Washington, DC: National Academy Press.

Rosenbaum, J. (1989). Linkages between high schools and work: Lessons from Japan. Paper prepared for the National Assessment of Vocational Education, U.S. Department of Education, Washington, DC, March.

Rothman, R. (1988). Businesses refuse to sign "Boston Compact II." *Education Week,* November 9, 5.

Schultz, T. (1975). The value of the ability to deal with disequilibria. *Journal of Economic Literature,* 13 (September), 827–846.

Stern, D., Raby, M., and Dayton, C. (1992). *Career academies: Partnerships for reconstructing American high schools.* San Francisco: Jossey-Bass.

Sticht, T. G. (1975). *Reading for work: A functional literacy anthology.* Alexandria, Va.: Human Resources Research Organization.

Teitel, L. (1988). The impact of business and industry oriented programs on community colleges. Unpublished dissertation. Cambridge: Graduate School of Education, Harvard University.

United States Bureau of the Census. (1987). *Survey of participation in adult education.* Washington, DC: U.S. Government Printing Office.

U.S. Department of Education. (1991). *America 2000: An educational strategy.* Washington, DC: U.S. Department of Education.

———. (1989). *Educational partnerships in public elementary and secondary schools.* Washington, DC: National Center for Education Statistics, Office of Education Research and Improvement, February.

Wilson, R. (1986). Minority students and the community college. In L. S. Zwerling (ed.), *The community college and its critics,* pp. 61–70. San Francisco: Jossey-Bass.

Zuboff, S. (1988). *In the age of the smart machine: The future of work and power.* New York: Basic Books.

Zwerling, L. S. (1986). Lifelong learning: A new form of tracking. In L. S. Zwerling (ed.), *The community college and its critics,* pp. 52–60. San Francisco: Jossey-Bass.

8

The Health Sector:
Employment Frontier

Eli Ginzberg

In 1965 the total expenditures for U.S. health care amounted to $41.6 billion, about 6 percent of the GNP. For 1992 the level of expenditures is estimated to be over $830 billion, about 14 percent of GNP. With corrections for the declining value of the dollar and the increase in the population, health care expenditures per capita rose more than fourfold in these twenty-seven years.

The explanations for such a large and rapid rise in health care outlays are many and diverse. Among the most important are the much enlarged therapeutic and diagnostic capabilities of modern medicine; the rapid growth of the U.S. economy, which made it easier for both the private and public sectors to spend more on health care; the radical changes that occurred in the financing of health care with primary reliance on private health insurance and governmental entitlement programs (Medicare and Medicaid); and the strong efforts of the hospital leadership—trustees, administrators, and physician staffs—to provide quality in-patient care as close to home as possible for most, if not all, Americans.

The aim of this chapter is to focus specifically on the human resource and labor market dimensions of the sustained expansion that occurred between 1966 and 1992. Although money and technology played critical roles in the delivery of more and better health care, the successful exploitation of these resources depends on more and better-trained health care personnel, from medical and surgical specialists to the different supporting groups required for the effective functioning of a complex hospital center with a wide array of sophisticated high-tech services for a diversified patient population.

Table 8.1 summarizes the number and principal occupational categories of persons employed in the health care sector in 1966 and 1991.

The principal questions that this chapter will explore are the following:

- What were the major decision paths and institutional adaptations that enabled the United States to almost double its ratio of physicians per 100,000 population over these four decades?
- How does one explain the paradox that in the face of such a substantial increase in the number of physicians, their absolute and relative earnings increased rather than declined?
- What forces were responsible for the transformation in the education and training of physicians that has led to the predominance of specialists and subspecialists among new entrants into the profession?
- What labor market developments led to the rapid expansion of the nursing profession and the shift in nursing education from hospital-based apprenticeship training to formal preparation in institutions of higher learning?
- What were the principal factors that enabled the health care educational system to respond to the expanding requirements for a larger, more diverse group of allied health personnel?
- How was the health care sector able to attract a vastly increased number of support personnel, from administrators and financial officers to hospital and nursing home housekeeping staff?

The answers to such questions must be viewed in a historical context. In 1950 the American Medical Association was by far the nation's most influential health policy group. Its primary concern was to prevent the federal government from influencing in any way the education of physicians, their modes of practice, or how they were recompensed. Despite strong support from President Truman, the 1948 congressional effort to introduce national health insurance was derailed by the AMA, a repeat of its successful opposition to the inclusion of health insurance in the New Deal reform agenda of 1935.

In the American health care system, the states, rather than the federal government, play the leading role. The majority of medical schools are state schools, and the states have primary responsibility for providing care to the indigent as well as access to emergency care. The states are also empowered to license and regulate health facilities, physicians, other health professionals, and a wide variety of subprofessional personnel.

On a final note, most acute care hospitals are in the voluntary sector, formally under the control of their respective lay boards of directors, which historically have had primary responsibility for covering the operating deficits and providing the capital funding for new plant and equipment. Much of the decisionmaking, however, rests with the physician staff who admit the paying patients, who are the source of most of the revenue needed to keep the hospital operating. The changes in the health care sector can be assessed only within this institutional framework.

Physicians

The Physician Supply

Although there was increasing pressure on Congress from 1948 on to make federal funding available for medical education in order to expand the number of physicians available to care for the American people, the AMA blocked such action until 1963 when it shifted all of its political efforts to defeating Medicare. From 1963 until 1976, when Congress concluded that the physician shortage was at an end, a sizable and continuing flow of federal moneys became available to the medical education sector—to expand existing schools, start new ones, recruit minority students, provide funds for residency training (through Medicare reimbursement), and still other related educational purposes. Although the post-1963 years marked a new relationship between the federal government and the medical educational establishment, it needs to be emphasized that prior to this direct intervention, large-scale federal funding for biomedical research, which was initiated after the conclusion of World War II and accelerated steadily thereafter, had a major impact on medical education. The decision to award these funds for the conduct of research primarily to the universities profoundly altered the orientation and mission of the nation's research-oriented medical schools. Most of their attention was shifted from instructing undergraduate medical students in favor of laboratory research and the training of subspecialists.

Note must also be taken of the 1965 revision of the immigration statutes that resulted in a much enlarged, continuing inflow of physicians from foreign lands. In 1992 foreign medical graduates (FMGs) accounted for almost one of every four physicians in active practice. Many of these FMGs were willing, at least initially and often permanently, to practice among groups that U.S. graduates avoided, thus helping to ease, if not solve, the access problem for many recent immigrants, low-income rural populations, and the inner-city poor, who have serious difficulties in finding physicians who are willing to treat them.

It should be noted that the availability of federal funding for medical education encouraged a large number of states with low physician-population ratios to establish new medical schools, often in outlying areas, in the hope that their graduates would be more amenable to entering practice in these areas, a hope that was fulfilled only in part. The federal financing did lead, however, to an increase of about 50 percent in the number of medical schools—from 80 to 126—and a doubling in the number of graduates from around 8,000 to 16,000 annually.

There was some fear that the medical schools would be unable to expand their physical plant and double the size of their student body without lowering academic standards. This fear turned out to be unfounded; medicine continued to be an attractive career choice for many college graduates, particularly for qualified women who today account for two out of every five admissions, up from one in ten in 1960.

Physician Earnings

Many economists favored a substantial increase in the physician supply on the ground that only such a trend would brake physicians' rising fees and earnings; in fact, they argued, with an expanding supply, incomes would actually decline. But this was no traditional market where an increase in supply, absent an offsetting increase in demand, leads to a decline in price. In 1992 the AMA reported that the average physician's earnings, net of expenses but before taxes, amounted to $165,000 annually, with net earnings of selected surgical and other specialists about $300,000.

The determinants of physicians' earnings are a subject of great analytic complexity,[1] but within the present context two points, one major and one minor, may be identified that explain why mainline economists erred in assuming that an increased supply would lead to lower physicians' earnings. The first is that they failed to recognize that it was not the public's disposable income that determined the demand of consumers for physician services, but rather employer or government-provided insurance, which covered about 80 percent of their expenditures for physician services. In short, the demand constraints of the competitive market did not apply to the market for physician services. Moreover, the dominant fee-for-service mode of physician payment encouraged many physicians to provide services without thought of economizing, because they would be reimbursed without question by third-party payers. The second major departure from traditional market pricing was the fact that in the health care industry supply creates its own demand. Since physicians determine about 75 percent of all medical services provided, the increase in the supply of physicians resulted in an increase in service utilization and in the level of costs.

Generalist-Specialist Distribution

For many reasons, from the growing complexity of medical knowledge and technique to life-style preferences of physicians for greater control over their time as well as higher income to compensate for their elongated period of training, an increasing proportion of medical school graduates entered residency training in a specialty and subsequently in a subspecialty. Instead of starting to practice after one or two years of internship, as most physicians had previously done, a significant proportion of graduates now take eight years of postmedical school training before entering independent professional practice. Clearly, talented young men and women who submit themselves to such a long preparatory period are desirous of recapturing both lost time and lost earnings.

Another economic consideration: As medical schools confronted a relative decline in the 1970s and 1980s in the revenues they received from both the federal and state governments, they resorted to successive increases in tuition. At the present time, four out of every five students complete medical school with an average debt of $50,000, with repayment scheduled to begin after two years of residency training. The accrual of a sizable educational debt together with the prospect of limited earnings from generalist practice offer a reasonable explanation for the pursuit of specialist and subspecialist training by a steadily increasing proportion of young physicians.

Money, however, is not the sole reason for their choice of specialty training. The medical leadership by actions, honors, and rewards has underscored its belief that what is important in modern medicine is work at the frontiers—in the laboratory or in the operating suite. They do not deny that many patients can profit from the care of a well-trained generalist, but many implicitly or explicitly are skeptical that a primary care physician can remain informed and abreast of the rapid advances in diagnostic and therapeutic medicine. And if they cannot keep pace, it is less likely they can provide quality care to their patients.

There is a further difficulty. Since four out of every five Americans live in a metropolitan area and are thus within reasonable proximity to a specialist, it is obvious that the better educated turn to specialists for treatment of all but minor disorders. The entire educational financing delivery system has thus become geared to specialist, rather than generalist, care. This situation may change, but until major reforms are in place, the odds favor the continuing dominance of specialist care.

Nurses

The Supply of Nurses

In 1966 there were 584,100 registered nurses and 254,500 physicians (Table 8.1), a ratio of 2.3 to 1. The corresponding figures for 1991 are 1,612,000 nurses, 650,000 physicians, and a ratio of 2.48 to 1. Although the major efforts of the federal and state governments after the early 1960s succeeded in doubling the physician supply, the absolute and relative increases in the supply of nurses were even more impressive.

TABLE 8.1   Number Employed in Health Care, 1966 and 1991

	1966	1991
Physicians	254,500	650,000
Dentists	94,900	170,000
Nurses (RN)	584,100	1,612,000
Allied health personnel	556,000	3,922,000
Support personnel	2,082,100	2,755,000
Total	3,571,600	9,109,000

Source: U.S. Department of Commerce, *Statistical Abstract of the United States, 1992* (Washington, DC: GPO).

On the demand side, about three out of every five nurses are employed by hospitals. This suggests that the key to the marked increase in the demand for nurses was the vast post–World War II expansion of the nation's hospital plant, reinforced by the increasing intensity of the medical and surgical services that hospitals provide to their in-patients and, more recently, to their rapidly growing number of ambulatory care patients. The proliferation of intensive care units, in particular, has heightened the demand for registered nurses and also for practical nurses and nurse assistants.

The substantial increase in the number of physicians in private practice, solo, group, or other arrangements also generated additional demand for nurses, as did federal funding in the second half of the 1960s for the establishment and operation of rural and urban clinics that provide primary care for low-income populations in their vicinity. Clinic expansion was not limited to programs financed with federal funds; states, local governments, the private sector, and the voluntary sector also engaged in initiating and operating various types of ambulatory care facilities, from community mental health centers to ambulatory surgical centers.

Reference should also be made to the substantial expansion in the volume and types of health care services provided to persons living at home, which currently represent an annual outlay of $12 billion, up from $3 billion as recently as 1983. Registered nurses play a key role as supervisors of the rapidly expanding home care services and are engaged to a lesser extent in the direct provision of more sophisticated therapies and rehabilitative services to patients in their homes. In short, an increasing demand for nurses has paralleled the expansion of hospitals, physician practice sites, clinics, nursing homes, and home care organizations.

Changes in Nurse Recruitment and Education

Until 1950 the hospital-based nursing school was the principal site for the training of registered nurses. Most nursing students were young white women from farms, small communities, and to a lesser degree from selected immigrant groups in urban centers to whom nursing offered the opportunity for independence and self-support before marriage. However, achievement of these goals required a three-year period of arduous apprenticeship training under a quasimilitary regimen. Hospital nursing schools were run under strict discipline with the young women working, eating, and sleeping under the constant supervision of the director of the school and her senior staff. Their living expenses were met by the uncompensated hospital duties they performed during the three years spent in preparation for the state licensing examination. A study of nursing education in 1948 estimated that didactic instruction, primarily by the hospital staff, accounted for no more than one-quarter of the total training period.[2] The other three-quarters reflected on-the-job training.

The early post–World War II decades witnessed a revolutionary change in the site and nature of nurse training. For fiscal and other reasons most hospitals closed their schools of nursing so that today only about one in ten of all newly licensed nurses is a graduate of a diploma (hospital-based) program; over half pursue their education at community colleges for a minimum of two years and one-third graduate from a four-year baccalaureate program. The shift from the hospital nursing school to the community college created the preconditions for the rapid expansion in the number of students graduating from a nursing program and qualifying for R.N. licensure.

Nurse educational leaders, physicians, hospital administrators, and directors of nursing have been engaged in a continuing debate about the appropriate educational preparation for tomorrow's nurses. With few exceptions, the leading nurse educators advocate a four-year baccalaureate degree as the minimum requirement for a licensed nurse, although many physicians, hospital administrators, and the public at large do not agree. The contentious issue of the baccalaureate degree became moot, however, once better-paying professional and business career opportunities became increasingly available to college-trained women, although many of the leading nurse educators were among the last to recognize the implications of this fact. The growing demand for nursing personnel could never have been met except for the explosive growth of postsecondary education at the community college level, which enabled a large number of young women from low-income families to live at home while they prepared for a career in nursing. But once they have started their nursing careers, many community college graduates soon recognize that education is the route to advancement in professional responsibility and pay and they return to school to acquire further degrees.

Nursing Wages and Labor Market Adjustments

Since the cadre of baby boomers entering the labor market was relatively small at the time that the needs of the health and hospital sector for trained workers spurted, the fact that the community colleges were able to expand their nursing programs without great difficulty was a fortuitous coincidence. Hospitals were particularly dependent on an enlarged nursing student enrollment because the vast majority of newly graduated nurses—over 90 percent—start their careers as bedside nurses.

In fact, this dependence of hospitals on recent graduates convinced hospital administrators in many locales to refrain from bidding up starting salaries, arguing that to do so would be counterproductive, since if all employers competed for the same scarce resources the only thing that salary increases would accomplish would be to raise their expenditures without increasing the supply.

As more desirable fields of work opened up for educated women, however, this wage strategy was short-lived. Furthermore, the characteristic compression in nursing wage scales, which failed to recognize the need for increases in pay commensurate with increases in experience, had to be scrapped if the profession was to attract the additional numbers that the market required. Wages were not, however, the only issue that created distortions in supply. Hospital administrators were slow to recognize that an ever larger number of nurses were married, with young children at home, and required more flexible work schedules. Most hospitals were also slow to recognize that their recruitment area was limited, with most nurses commuting no more than a half-hour between home and work. The directors of nursing education programs, in turn, did not readily recognize changes in their applicant pool, which had become older and more ethnically mixed. In the early post–World War II years the overwhelming majority of nursing students were white women in their early twenties. More recently a growing proportion—almost a third—consist of married women, over 30, looking for a second career (or a first career) since they no longer have young children to care for at home, with a fair number nonwhite. There have also been marginal increases in the number of males.

In the late 1980s the demand for registered nurses increased substantially in such metropolitan centers as Boston, New York, Houston, and Los Angeles and to a lesser extent in other urban areas at a time when the number of available applicants to nursing programs had dropped because of competing opportunities for young women in better-paying, less demanding occupations. As a consequence, substantial advances were made in starting salaries for newly licensed graduates (of about $30,000) as well as in the salaries of experienced nurse specialists. In New York and on the West Coast clinical nurse specialists with twenty years of experience could earn between $60,000 and $70,000 per year. These salary adjustments of the late 1980s went far to return most nursing markets to equilibrium, in tandem with an increase in the number of new graduates from nursing programs, the recession of 1990, and a decreasing in-patient hospital census.

The Scope of Nursing Practice

There have been ongoing tensions between physicians who dominate the health care sector and nurses who have been seeking to broaden the scope of nursing practice and enhance the status of their profession. Over the past several decades there has been a modest expansion in a variety of nursing specialties requiring advanced training and degrees, including nurse anesthetists, nurse practitioners, and psychiatric nurses, as well as in some older, well-established specialized areas such as public health nurses and operating room nurses.

Much of the tension between the organized medical profession and the nursing profession has centered on such issues as proposed changes in state practice codes to enable all nurses or subgroups of nurses with specialized training to write prescriptions and to perform various procedures formerly restricted to physicians. Another critical issue is the right of nurses to bill payers independently for their services. A growing number of states have amended their nurse practice acts to permit nurses under specified conditions (rural settings, for example) to write prescriptions, and the federal government has authorized nurses in federally subsidized rural health centers to bill for their services. These and a few other exceptions aside, however, the dominance of the physician continues. Although the scope of the nursing function has expanded from the assessment of well babies to highly technical procedures and services for patients in intensive care units, for the most part nurses still work under the supervision and control of licensed physicians. If at some future time, the organization, financing, and delivery of health care in the United States should undergo major changes, the new conditions may involve a realignment of the duties, responsibilities, and rewards of physicians and nurses. For the present, however, the wide gap between physicians and nurses is not likely to be significantly narrowed.

Allied Health and Support Personnel

In the twenty years between 1970 and 1990, total employment in the health care sector doubled from about 4.5 million to 9.1 million, about equally divided between hospital and nonhospital settings. A large part of this growth stemmed from the substantial increase in the number of allied health and support personnel.

Although there has been only one serious study of the allied health segment of the health care labor force, which dealt in depth with only ten principal categories,[3] federal data sources permit a reasonable estimate of the overall numbers employed in these occupations.

Deducting 2.4 million physicians, dentists, and registered nurses from the total of 9.1 million health care employees leaves a residual of 6.7 million allied health and support personnel. The number of allied health workers and their distribution by occupation are presented in Table 8.2.

Exclusive of the 3.9 million employees in the allied health fields, the remainder of the nonprofessional segment of health care workers consists of about 2.8 million hospital support personnel employed in housekeeping jobs, food preparation, transport, security, clerical services, and other areas as well as a sizable number of non–health-specific professionals and technicians performing managerial and support functions in both hospitals and other health care settings.

Several aspects of this sizable growth in health personnel warrant special attention. Although women accounted for 45 percent of the employees in all industries in 1989, in the health services sector they accounted for over 75 percent. The past two decades have seen an increasing number of women seeking regular employment, and the explosive growth in the health care sector absorbed many of these job seekers.

Similarly, although blacks accounted for only 10 percent of all employed workers in 1989, they represented 16 percent of all hospital workers. Clearly, this is another case where workers in search of job opportunities were able to find openings in the rapidly expanding hospital sector. It should be noted that blacks were less successful in obtaining nonhospital jobs in the health sector, although these too expanded rapidly.

Between the beginning of the 1970s and the end of the 1980s the number of hospital personnel per 100 patients rose from slightly over 220 to about 440, a reflection of the upgrading of hospitals and the intensification of their services. This trend was encouraged by the third-party payers, which, after the passage of Medicare and Medicaid, covered more than 90 percent of hospital expenditures on a cost-reimbursement basis until the mid-1980s. The other contributory factor to this expansion in personnel was advancing technology that steadily increased the sophistication and range of services that hospitals performed.

Although hospitals have long hired large complements of unskilled workers for housekeeping, food preparation and serving, patient transportation, and similar activities, the majority of hospital employees have had postsecondary school training, varying in length from one to four years, and in some cases even more. In the early years after World War II most hospitals had little alternative but to train most of their own allied health personnel, since external training programs were few and far between. However, once the community college movement gained momentum in the 1950s and 1960s, hospitals found that just as they no longer had

TABLE 8.2   Number Employed in Allied Health Care, 1990

Health assessment and treatment occupations (other than RN)	
Therapists	324,000
Pharmacists	174,000
Dieticians	83,000
Physician assistants	62,000
Subtotal	643,000
Health technologists/technicians	
Licensed practical nurses	414,000
Clinical lab technicians	308,000
Radiologic clinicians	124,000
Dental hygienists	80,000
Health records	72,000
All other	278,000
Subtotal	1,276,000
Health services occupations	
Nursing aides and orderlies	1,400,000
Non-nursing aides	416,000
Dental assistants	187,000
Subtotal	2,003,000
Total	3,922,000

Source: U.S. Department of Commerce, *Statistical Abstract of the United States, 1991* (Washington, DC: GPO).

to train their own nurses, they could depend on the community colleges for the growing numbers of technologists and technicians required to cope with the complexities of advancing medical technology and the intensive care required by their patient population.

The expanding community colleges were in general eager to respond to the needs of the hospitals for trained workers since their prospects for enrollment growth depended heavily on their ability to assure students that jobs would be available for them on completion of their training.

Problems, however, surfaced. Many of the new, rapidly proliferating organizations involved in the education and employment of medical technologists and technicians faced formidable obstacles at different levels. These included negotiating with the states for certification and licensing of the graduates of accredited programs. Many states sought to avoid the extension of licensing, having learned from experience that once an occupation was licensed it would attempt to limit the numbers of individuals authorized to perform specific types of work, thus making it more difficult and more costly for hospitals and health care providers to meet their needs for additional trained personnel.

Over the years the AMA has accredited educational programs in twenty-eight allied health professions. For the academic year of 1990–

1991, an overall enrollment of 92,500 was reported in over 1,500 educational institutions in twenty-six of these programs, over 36,500 graduates and attrition of 15,759. The largest field by far is radiography, with over 7,500 graduates. Following in descending order are medical assistant and respiratory therapy technician, 4,600 and 4,000 graduates respectively; respiratory therapist, over 3,000; emergency medical technician-paramedic, medical technologist, and occupational therapist, over 2,000 graduates each. In eight of the twenty-six fields, the number of graduates reported was under 100, reflecting the relatively small number of training programs.[4]

Additional Perspectives

Several important correlates of the vast expansion in the health sector work force warrant at least brief comment. First and foremost is the fact that a supply expansion policy, even one targeted at the entire spectrum of health personnel—from physicians to hospital service workers—does not necessarily translate into broadened access to health services for all persons in need of care. In the absence of physicians willing to practice in depressed, unattractive environments, and without supporting hospitals and other health provider organizations in reasonable proximity to their place of residence, many of the underserved will remain underserved regardless of their ability to pay and the adequacy of the aggregate supply of personnel. In other words, unless significant private-sector and/or government efforts are focused on reducing the gaps that exist between providers and patients, some proportion of the population will be deprived of adequate medical care.

Relatively little attention has been paid, either by health policy or labor market analysts, to the roles that the nation's 5,500 acute care hospitals, whose revenues now approach $300 billion annually, play in their local economies. In many low-income neighborhoods in the inner city and in rural areas, the local hospital is the single most important source of income and employment for the local population. At the same time, hospital occupancy has declined nationally to slightly over 60 percent and a modest number of hospitals, mostly small facilities, close every year, with many more likely to be at risk in the remaining years of this decade as medical care is shifted increasingly to outpatient settings. This trend poses a dilemma for policy decisions re hospital mergers and closures: the need to balance criteria of access and quality of care against net economic and employment costs and benefits.

During the 1980s the nurse labor market underwent several novel developments, all related to the periodic tightness in the supply of nurses and the need to utilize nursing staffs more efficiently. In response to the traditional rigidities of many hospital nursing services, which hesitated to deviate from their long-established practice of regularly rotating full-time nurses among the three shifts and consequently lost many staff nurses, private for-profit nurse agencies proliferated in many tight labor markets. These agencies catered both to hospital employers willing to pay the higher costs of per diem nurses in return for flexibility in personnel deployment and to the many nurses who were unable or unwilling to comply with the conventional requirement of shift rotation. Ultimately, the increased cost of contract nurses to the employing hospital and the perceived losses in the quality of service caused many directors of nursing to review and adjust their rigid scheduling practices.

Baylor Hospital in Dallas, for example, offered a full week's salary for nurses who were willing to work two twelve-hour shifts on Saturdays and Sundays. In the northeast, hospitals in metropolitan Boston provided bus transportation as far away as Maine to accommodate weekend nurses hired to cover weekend shifts.

Fluctuations in demand and supply for health personnel were probably most extreme in the nurse labor market. However, quasi-heroic measures were also undertaken by hospitals hard pressed by shortages of physicians and allied health personnel. During the severe recession of the early 1980s, many hospitals decided to alter their nurse staffing patterns by replacing many practical nurses and nurse assistants with RNs because the modest wage differentials promised to improve patient care at little or no additional cost. By the end of the decade most institutions had to reverse track.

With some inner-city and rural teaching hospitals in a weak position to compete for graduates of U.S. medical schools to fill their residency positions, a number of these institutions have established linkages with universities abroad to attract physicians, known as FMGs (foreign medical graduates), for their house staffs. To recruit and retain adequately trained medical personnel for a variety of therapeutic, diagnostic, and laboratory services, many smaller and medium-sized hospitals developed a wide range of contracting arrangements with physicians. In a recent article in *Hospitals* (August 20, 1992), 495 responding hospitals listed nineteen services for which they had entered into contractual relationships, the most important being physical therapy, emergency care, pharmacy, anesthesiology, and respiratory therapy. Satisfaction with these contractual arrangements was rated high by 56 percent of respondents, medium by 41 percent, and low by 4 percent. Although contracting for clinical services has grown rapidly in recent years, most hospitals prefer to utilize members of their own staff for the provision of all basic medical care services.

The important generalizations that can be drawn from this review and analysis of the interactions between the growth of the health care sector and the responsiveness of the labor market during the past four decades are as follows.

- In face of the rapid growth of the health sector, the vastly increased number of professionals and midlevel personnel needed to staff the system became available, with only periodic and short-lived shortages.
- Large-scale federal and state support to expand the capacity of U.S. medical schools, and the rapid expansion of community colleges, were major enabling factors that assured the availability of the much larger cadres of trained personnel required to operate the expanded health delivery system.
- Except for the inner-city and the rural poor, the expansion of the labor market together with continuing inflows of additional money from third-party payers enabled most Americans to enjoy improved access to an upgraded system of health care delivery.
- The open-sluice funding of the U.S. health care system, in particular during the period from 1966 to the mid-1980s, permitted gains in the absolute and relative earnings and benefits of the entire spectrum of health care personnel, from subspecialists to the unskilled, sufficient to attract and retain the 9 million-plus persons who are currently employed in the health care sector.
- At the same time, uncontrolled financing virtually eliminated the incentives for physicians and hospitals to put in place mechanisms aimed at utilizing health care personnel with optimal efficiency and effectiveness. Since personnel costs are the dominant component in the costs of hospital services, representing about two-thirds of hospital outlays, this remains a major challenge.

Notes

1. See Uwe Reinhardt's excellent chapter in Eli Ginzberg, ed., *Health Services Research* (Cambridge: Harvard University Press, 1991).

2. Eli Ginzberg, ed., *A Program for the Nursing Profession* (New York: Macmillan, 1948).

3. *Allied Health Services: Avoiding Crises.* Committee to Study the Role of Allied Health Personnel, Institute of Medicine (Washington, D.C.: National Academy Press, 1989).

4. *Journal of the American Medical Association*, annual education issue, 1991–1992, Vol. 268, no. 9 (September 2, 1992), p. 1124.

9

The Future of
Employment Policy

Eli Ginzberg

The chapters that constitute the present volume provide important insights into the operations of the U.S. labor market in recent decades. These insights are informed by research into selected changes in the U.S. economy, with a strong focus on the urban scene as well as special emphasis on the transformations under way in New York, the nation's leading city. In this summary chapter selected findings from these research investigations will be analyzed to determine their implications for future employment policy.

The United States has resorted only twice in the present century to using the resources of the federal government to expand the number of jobs directly, once during the Great Depression of the 1930s and second during the presidency of Jimmy Carter (1977–1980), when appropriations for the Comprehensive Employment and Training Act (CETA) reached an annual expenditure level of over $11 billion. This sum was used to fund 750,000 public service jobs as well as a much larger number of training slots aimed at improving the employability skills of many of the unemployed with the expectation that through such training they could be assisted to obtain a regular job.

For most of the post–World War II period the federal government's principal contributions to a high and sustained level of employment depended on the use of fiscal and monetary policies to assure that the general demand for labor would remain at or close to full employment. With the election of Ronald Reagan in 1980, far more emphasis was placed on "supply-side economics," that is, on the establishment of incentives, primarily in the form of lower tax rates, to stimulate private investment and thus an increased demand for labor. But with the advantage of a decade's perspective, it is clear that, language aside, the prosperity of the Reagan era was fueled by a continuing, strong fiscal stimulus that was reflected in ever-increasing annual federal deficits.

When the retrospective view is lengthened by three decades to 1960, the number of employed persons in the United States labor force doubled from 60 million to just under 120 million by 1990, a rate of job growth that was impressive in both absolute and relative terms even when account is taken of the fact that a somewhat larger number of persons worked less than full time at the end of the period than at the beginning. Despite this remarkable rate of job expansion, it is noteworthy that only at the end of the 1960s, at the height of the nation's involvement in Vietnam, did the national unemployment rate drop below 4 percent for a relatively short period.

In the period between the mid-1970s and the present, the U.S. economy experienced several recessions and high levels of unemployment: in 1974–1975, in 1981–1982 when Paul Volker, the chair of the Federal Reserve Board, was determined to check the inflationary cycle, and the recession of the early 1990s.

The fact that the labor market softened substantially on three occasions in eighteen years is important but must be juxtaposed with the fact that in this same period the total number of Americans in the labor force increased from 87 to 120 million, or by just under 40 percent, clearly a strikingly rapid rate of growth.

Two additional developments require attention. In the past two decades, for reasons that have not yet been satisfactorily explained by economists, U.S. productivity has declined sharply, leading to a stagnation in average weekly earnings, in contrast to the substantial gains registered in the decades of the 1950s and the 1960s. To compound the situation, with the disappearance of good blue-collar jobs, the spread between earnings of those at the top and those in the middle and at the lower end of the distribution widened substantially.

If the focus is shifted from the demand side of the labor market to the supply side, it is clear that there were two principal sources of new entrants into the labor force, the "baby boomers," the first of whom reached age 18 in 1964 and whose numbers increased thereafter, and the large increase in the number of women who entered the labor market in search of full-time or part-time jobs. These two sources, combined with the steady increase in the number of immigrants (the majority of working age) stimulated by the 1965 reform of the immigration statutes, led to a net increase in the size of the labor force in spite of the fact that the young were staying in school longer whereas the old were leaving earlier.

The influx of a large number of women into the labor market reflected the continuing shift of the economy from goods to service production, which made it much easier for women to obtain jobs. The fact that many of them had at least a high school diploma made them suitable for clerical and sales work. Many older women whose children no longer required their full-time attention also entered the labor market in large numbers. Those who had been divorced had little option but to seek a paying job, and others, noting the stagnation of their husbands' earnings, decided that the only prospect for a rising standard of living depended on their contribution to the family income. Although there are still a few families that conform to the earlier pattern of the man going to work and the woman staying home to run the household and rear the children, this seems to be a fast-fading model. We have reached a point where the majority of black children are born to single mothers, a pattern that by now also accounts for almost one out of every four births to white women. Clearly, the long-established family-labor market relationships are in great flux, but the outcome is increasingly clear. Most adults, male and female, will be expected to work during all of their productive years, with the possible exception of some mothers with preschool children.

In addition to these substantial changes in the labor force supply during the post–World War II decades (particularly since 1960), there has been a profound transformation in the structure of the U.S. economy that has had a major impact on the demand side of the labor market. The shift from goods to services, more particularly the absolute, and even more important, the relative decline in manufacturing, has resulted in a drastic reduction in the number of well-paying blue-collar jobs.

The decline in manufacturing employment was so substantial that in the 1980s the nation came to label the major industrial states in the Midwest that had been home to steel, rubber, autos, trucks, and heavy machinery production as the "rust belt," with shuttered plants and idled workers. The continuing difficulties facing the big three automotive concerns in 1992 are a potent reminder that although much of the "shakeout" has been completed and many of the surviving firms are now able to compete successfully in the international marketplace, not all American manufacturing has been modernized or made more efficient.

The recent stagnation of the U.S. economy and employment (1990–1992) has seriously affected the service sector, which had once been considered immune to recession, leading to a substantial restructuring of a large number of service companies of all sizes. This new development has resulted in the unemployment of large numbers of middle managers and technicians, a high proportion of whom had considered their jobs permanent until they chose to retire. The pessimistic mood of the American public was accentuated by this unaccustomed joining of the fates of large numbers of middle managers in well-established service companies with skilled blue-collar workers who had earlier encountered unemployment and large-scale declines in their earning power.

But too much should not be read into this recent weakening in employment in some service companies, just as the earlier decline in manufacturing employment had been incorrectly assessed as foreshadowing a permanent erosion of the American economic base. In both instances the more valid assessment would be that during the long post–World War II expansion with its sustained profitability, a great many leading manufacturing and service companies had become accustomed to swollen staffing patterns that weakened their ability to cope with intensified international competition.

Faced with such forces, vulnerable American companies had no option but to resort to a wide-scale reassessment of the competitive forces they were facing in markets, technology, organization, and human resources and to take cost-reducing actions that would leave them better positioned to compete in the future. Although most companies under siege followed this course, the laggards were unable to reposition themselves.

In sum, the U.S. economy has been characterized during the past three decades by nothing less than spectacular increases in the number of jobs in each of three successive decades of the 1960s, 1970s, and 1980s. But despite this success, it did far worse on the productivity front. Except in the late 1970s when President Carter resorted to a much enlarged public service employment program to bring the U.S. economy closer to full employment, the federal government—and for that matter, state and local governments—made only marginal use of employment policy to improve the job prospects of groups that were encountering difficulties.

The potentials and limitations of employment policy in responding to substantial difficulties in the urban and metropolitan labor markets discussed in the earlier chapters will be analyzed in the balance of this chapter. The primary focus will be on the labor market consequences, particularly for inner-city populations, of the steady relocation of persons and firms to the suburbs and outlying metropolitan areas; the extent to which our traditional educational system fails to reflect changes in technology, markets, and the organization and operation of business enterprises; the conflicting and competing roles of minorities and immigrants as successors to many whites who have relocated their residences and relinquished their jobs in the inner city; and, finally, some of the labor market consequences of the explosive growth of the health care sector, including some of the consequences of employment-based health care insurance on the functioning of the U.S. labor market.

The dislocations resulting from the relocation of people and businesses from the inner city to the suburbs and outlying areas have been lessened in those central business districts that have remained vibrant because they have concentrated on providing sophisticated business services (FIRE, legal, consulting, and others) to the local, regional, national and even international economies—services that require at a minimum a large number of professional, college, and, at a minimum, community college graduates. Although these jobs pay considerably above the average, a disproportionate number of them are available only to the better-educated and trained suburbanites who live outside the city limits, commute to work, and have annual earnings often double or more than the earnings of the resident population.

The competition between commuters and residents for the better-paying city jobs, however, explains only part of the urban-suburban job tensions. Many of the better-paying manufacturing and construction jobs that the less-educated city residents might have coped with successfully have also migrated out of the cities to the suburbs. Even many of the less well paying retailing jobs that provide initial opportunities for work for high school graduates or even dropouts have also migrated out of the city.

Even in the absence of job discrimination against racial and other minorities, the transportation networks between the suburbs and the city are dysfunctional for reverse commuting, a lesson that was learned after the Watts riots of the mid-1960s. Sizable federal subsidies to improve commuting for the Watts population to the expanding job markets in the outlying areas proved to be impractical given the dispersal of the industrial sites and the travel time involved. Both the cost of suburban housing and discrimination against racial and ethnic minorities have contributed to preventing the urban groups in need of jobs from relocating to the booming outlying areas.

The economic outlook both for many of the less-educated urban population as well as for the future of the central business districts in our major metropolitan areas thus becomes ominous. The population-job disjunction that we have just identified points to a high level of unemployment and underemployment among poorly educated urban residents, some of whom will be recruited for illicit and illegal work and others of whom will require public support. In both instances the urban environment will face dysfunctional costs growing out of a less congenial environment and heavier taxes, further stimulating the vicious circle of further out-migration of many business enterprises and further weakening the city's economy.

There are, however, several corrective factors at work, as the earlier chapters have sought to make clear. The first, reflective of the growing globalization of the world's economy, has resulted in 1,800 foreign companies from sixty-three countries establishing a business presence in New York City as well as a smaller number in other key business centers such as Dallas, Atlanta, Miami, and still others.

Second, the FIRE sector of New York City's economy underwent a serious loss of jobs after the stock market decline of 1987 but by 1991 a substantial part of New York's financial activities had made a sizable recovery, with correspondingly high personal and firm earnings. The existence of many high earners is not without a favorable effect on the continuing demand for a wide range of lower- as well as higher-level service jobs.

Another point, frequently overlooked, is the fact that advanced services are an important source of exports and contribute significantly to the nation's and the city's economy. There are also opportunities for New Yorkers without higher degrees to get additional jobs if domestic and foreign airlines take a more aggressive role in expanding activities at both the Kennedy and Newark airports and improve the telecommunications infrastructure in the New York City area, which is an important factor in broadening the international ties between the local and the national and foreign economies.

Moving from location to people as a dynamic dimension of labor market changes, we find that the role of the two major streams of newcomers—native blacks and immigrants—as well as the sizable subgroups of Puerto Ricans and Caribbean blacks should be taken into account. But since the earlier focus was on blacks and immigrants, the analysis will be restricted to these two groups alone in exploring some leads for employment policy.

The authors of the chapter on immigrants make a number of salient observations to emphasize serious imbalances in the analytical approaches that have guided most recent discussions on the growing imbalances that have characterized so many of the nation's largest metropolitan areas. Their principal point of attack is the various "mismatch" explanations that stress the explosive growth in demand for better-educated workers who can respond to new technology as well as new market demands for better employee interactions with suppliers and customers and the assumed inability of native blacks to fill these more demanding jobs because of a lack of educational qualifications.

The further assumption of the mismatch theory that is challenged is that many blacks have difficulty in obtaining a regular job in the new labor market because of the rapid shift of the urban economy from manufacturing to services. But the important point is made that blacks, at least in New York, were never an important part of the manufacturing labor force. The authors go on to emphasize that in the early 1980s about half of all employed New Yorkers had less than a high school diploma, presumptive evidence that the skill-education mismatch as the sole or principal explanation for recent urban labor market imbalances is exaggerated.

The authors also point out that as more whites move to the suburbs, even taking account of the fact that many continue to commute to the city, that the movers over time create important vacancies in the middle and even higher ranks of the city's public and private sector, which open opportunities for blacks and immigrants, who are further back in the queue. These two major groups are, however, seen to have major differences, which are reflected in their labor market experiences. A steady and large flow of immigrants keeps coming from third world countries, a high proportion of whom have no knowledge of English and less formal schooling than the local black population; many, unlike the native blacks, become self-supporting. The reasons for this disparate experience are the presence of ethnic networks and entrepreneurial skills among many of the immigrant groups as well as the continuing discrimination against blacks in the labor market. Even casual acquaintance with the experience of different immigrant groups such as the Chinese, the Koreans, the Indians and Pakistanis, and the Russian Jews reinforces the importance that the authors place on ethnic networks, which provide clues to job openings and frequently provide capital to start modest enterprises.

Although blacks also have networks and alert friends and relatives about job openings, there is a strikingly low participation rate among blacks in self-employment, 3.5 percent, about a quarter of the participation rate among immigrant groups. Racial discrimination against blacks, however, remains strong, as witnessed by their low rate of penetration in construction jobs where educational qualifications are largely irrelevant. Yet there has been significant penetration by blacks of the public sectors, not only in lower- or middle-level jobs, but also in the managerial ranks.

It would be a misreading of these revisionist views to assume that limitations in the educational preparation of many young black men and women do not create considerable difficulties in finding jobs, particularly jobs with a future. Rather, the analysis calls attention to the queuing characteristics of most labor markets, with blacks most often at the end of the queue. The combination of job discrimination, limited entrepreneurial experience, and networks, together with inadequate educational preparation of blacks, go a long way to explain many, if not all, of the labor market difficulties that they face in New York City and other metropolitan areas.

Many of the employment problems confronting the nation's urban centers are associated with the shortcomings in the educational experience of many inner-city children and young people who fail to master the basics of language, mathematics, and critical thought and a high proportion of whom fall behind their age group during the years that they are in school and drop out. A favorite explanation for the lessened competitiveness of the U.S. economy has been widely ascribed since the early 1980s to this substantial educational deficiency among the successive groups of young people as they reach working age and find that employers are loath to hire them because of their lack of educational preparation.

The author of the chapter "School to Work: The Integration Principle" submits this conventional wisdom to in-depth study and concludes that the changing relations between school and work are far more complicated than the mismatch hypothesis would suggest.

Although the author acknowledges that the limited intellectual knowledge base as well as other significant deficiencies that characterize so many dropouts, as well as high school graduates, are by no means unjustified criticisms of a significant minority of the new generation of young adults who cannot meet the new requirements of American employers for a better-trained and more flexible group of young people when they need to add to their work forces, the analysis probes more deeply into a wider range of considerations, from the point of view of both the school and the firm.

The author calls attention to the major adjustments that at least a minority of forward-looking firms have made to restructure their basic work processes, one dimension of which is to move away from the previous hierarchical structure of decisionmaking in which the majority of the work force was told what to do—and had to do it. The new pattern is one where those directly responsible for carrying through critical elements of the total process including interacting with suppliers, customers, and fellow workers in other parts of the organization are encouraged to take responsibility for all or most of the planning and execution of the work.

To the extent that firms are engaged in such radical restructuring of their work processes as well as their authority structures, they need a more flexible, responsive, imaginative, energized group of employees who are able and wiling to assume more control over their work and, equally important, are able and willing to undergo repeated training and retraining as changes in technology and the market leave their employing organization little option but to modify their earlier production processes. It is becoming increasingly clear, at least to the most alert and farsighted business leaders, that the future profitability of their enterprises will depend in the first instance on their ability to innovate and to respond quickly to the needs and demands of the marketplace. And flexible organizations need a work force that in turn is flexible and that can cope with frequent and large-scale changes in how work is planned and carried out.

The gaps between the educational system and this new world of work are, however, widening. The current widespread view that the quality of the high school curriculum should be raised by requiring students to master mathematics, a foreign language, science, and communication skills, both written and oral, will, as the late Lawrence Cremin pointed out, most probably raise the dropout rate. This type of curriculum reform ignores the fact that many young people need *less* not more focus on book learning. They need to participate in an environment where learning and work are closely integrated; where they can receive reinforcement from exposure to a learning environment in which the contextual elements loom large; and where they are able to interact with adults who perform real tasks for real customers who are willing to pay for the products that these workers produce.

Admittedly, there is nothing easy about the establishment of such contextual learning-working environments. The conventional high school vocational programs for the most part do not meet the test, although the best of such programs have demonstrated a greater capacity to engage the interest of their nonbookish students. The community college, with its closer links to the employer community, including direct employer financial support for tailored training courses, and more mature and better-focused students, has moved much further to close the wide gap that has long existed between school and work.

There is much more that community colleges, other postsecondary institutions, employers, and the self-learning efforts of adults can do to alter the sharp break that has existed for so many years between education, which was considered an activity for the young, and work, which was the center of adult life. The evidence is overwhelming that this dichotomy no longer fits the current environment and is likely to become increasingly anachronistic as the work environment increasingly requires employees to train and retrain.

It may not be immediately self-evident how the improved integration of school and work relates to the schooling experience of many young people from low-income and minority homes. Many young people are oblivious to the fact that their performance on the educational track will have a great deal to do with opening or closing out future work and earning opportunities for them as they move from school to work. But if the schools that they attend and the curricula that they confront provide them with no direct exposure to the adult world of work, their interests cannot be aroused and their skill acquisition will fall short of what they need for a successful transition into the world of work.

But it is also true that except for the largest employers, most business enterprises will not be able on their own to provide the constant training and retraining of their employees that the new competitive international markets require. They need to be linked much more closely to the educational infrastructure, particularly to the community colleges in their area. The inadequate integration that currently exists between urban school systems and local employers exacts a substantial toll in reduced productivity, but the principal victims are the young people in the inner city who have only limited knowledge of how their performance in school can affect their later lives. The sooner schools and the world of work become more closely integrated, the lower the probability that inner-city youngsters will lack the skills needed to make a successful transition into the adult world of work.

The chapter that examined current concerns about literacy and skills in the face of changing organizational, managerial, and marketing trends supplements and supports earlier findings of the urgent need for the increased integration between school and work. Once again, the analysis stressed the critical importance of a contextual learning environment. It raised serious questions about defining essential skills in terms of specific abstract knowledge rather than in terms of the capacity to learn what is required to handle the tasks that need to be performed by a group of workers engaged in a joint process of producing goods or services. Moreover, the stress was placed on broader considerations that also play large roles in giving definition and quality to the environments in which training and work are carried out and the relationships between these two spheres, which require close integration if optimal results are to be achieved.

The role of the health care sector in creating employment opportunities for inner-city groups, both minorities and immigrants, is considered next. Hospitals have played a significant role in providing job opportunities to minorities and immigrants in many of the nation's major cities. It is well recognized that hospital employment—and for that matter employment in nursing homes and home care agencies—has been expanding steadily and rapidly during the past several decades and that a significant proportion of all hospital and other health care institutions have employed a large number of persons with limited education and skills, particularly large numbers of women workers for housekeeping, laundry, food service, and other basic service functions, as well as a considerable, if lesser, number of such jobs for men.

In cities where the hospital work force is unionized, the wage and benefit structures even for positions at the bottom of the job hierarchy pay reasonably well, surely above the minimum wage. A slower growth in the health care sector during the past several decades would probably have led to a significant increase in the number of women forced to go on welfare. This observation does not imply that the long-overdue efforts to moderate the constant increase in national outlays for health care—up from $250 billion in 1980 to over $800 billion in 1992—should not be aggressively pursued but only to point out the critical role that hospital employment and income generation have played to keep many inner-city areas from total economic collapse.

Important implications for labor market relations flow from the fact that private health insurance (PHI) is tied directly to employment. The evidence has been accumulating that the long-established role of PHI is being eroded by virtue of the risk management tactics of insurers aimed at denying or not renewing coverage for high-risk persons, a practice that "locks in" many insured workers who cannot shift jobs without risking the loss of their insurance coverage. Since the number of persons covered by private health insurance has begun to decline, the odds suggest that the present ties between health care insurance and the job market are likely to be significantly altered in the years immediately ahead.

The other confrontation between the health care sector and the employment area that is already evident relates to the balancing of gains and losses that politicians must confront in the face of growing financial difficulties to keep a number of inner-city hospitals open. In the face of excess beds and a continuing shift to ambulatory care, such closures may be clearly indicated, but when the jobs and income generation for the local population are factored into the equation, the policy evaluation might lead to a decision to keep the institution functioning, at least for some years to come. In many inner-city neighborhoods existing federal and state support for hospital care may account for as much as half to two-thirds of their current operating budgets, which will also play a significant role in political decisions about the fate of underutilized hospitals.

There are several lessons for "employment policy" to be derived from these in-depth research efforts about high-priority problems affecting the U.S. labor market, more particularly the labor markets of our largest metropolitan centers.

The first finding has an equivocal quality: The past three decades have seen a remarkably strong performance of the labor market, with total jobs doubling from 60 to 120 million. At the same time, the level of employment, as reflected in the unemployment rate, fell seriously short of a societal optimum, not once but several times since 1973. Moreover, in the face of a rapid escalation in both the national debt and annual federal budget deficits, the federal government has been seriously constrained in resorting to fiscal and monetary policy in an effort to stimulate employment, even when the proportion of the unemployed has risen to between 7 and 10 percent, a figure that understates the overall dimensions of the problem.

The chapters that make up this volume have called attention to some of the special structural difficulties that confront inner-city residents as they seek to meet the American social norms of becoming economically self-supporting. A number of structural developments have been analyzed that have made it increasingly difficult for sizable numbers of inner-city persons to conform to this norm. Among the more important barriers have been the upgrading of job skills required incident to the shift of urban economies to advanced services; the outmigration from the city of many attractive manufacturing jobs as well as many relatively low-level retailing jobs; the persistence of discrimination against black workers, best revealed by their difficulties in gaining employment in construction; the lack of success of many secondary schools in educating young people from low-income single-parent homes for adulthood and work; and the intensified competition that many native-born low-skilled Americans face from the sizable and continuing inflow of immigrants from the third world.

This list calls attention neither to the considerable number of young women who, because of pregnancy, drop out of school and frequently go on welfare for an extended period of years nor to the sizable number of young men, largely from minority single-parent homes, who drop out of school and become involved in illicit and illegal activities, many subsequently imprisoned and many others killed or injured. Finally, the listing does not include the millions who, despite working full time or part time, are mired in poverty.

In general, employment policy has not addressed the problems of those in serious risk of becoming permanent members of what Marx called the "reserve army of the unemployed." The principal efforts have taken the form of the operation of quite restricted training programs, most of them of relatively short duration; the work-welfare reform measure of 1988, which by sanctions and incentives is seeking to persuade mothers on welfare with young children to return to school and/or work; the continuing operation of the Job Corps, which provides a more comprehensive effort of rehabilitation for the most disadvantaged youth; and a large number of local educational reform efforts, some of which are specifically aimed at establishing and improving the linkages between school and the world of work.

In a free society in which people can decide to change their residence or the location of their business, there is no easy or ready mechanism to improve the linkage between the unskilled and semiskilled urban population left behind and the jobs that have migrated to the outlying areas. In the case of the intensifying competition for work within the metropolitan centers between unskilled natives and immigrants, the obvious answer of revising the immigration statutes to reduce the inflow of immigrants may not be all that obvious once the full impact of the immigrants on the economic vitality of different cities receives in-depth analysis. It is not a foregone conclusion that reducing the number of immigrants would be a boon to the native-born blacks who continue to face serious job difficulties.

The fact that 25 percent of *all* children and two-thirds of all black children are born out of wedlock creates a challenge that transcends the present work-welfare reform. Providing jobs for unmarried mothers represents a challenge that goes far beyond helping them to be trained and find a job. They need to be able to earn an income that will not hold them trapped in poverty, that will enable them to have access to child care facilities, and that will not deprive them of Medicaid (or its equivalent) if they go to work. Similarly, it may be necessary to send many young men to prison, but it makes little or no sense to release them some years later as ill equipped to cope with the world of work as they were before they were committed. They need every encouragement and opportunity to improve their skills prior to their release.

The work reform with the greatest potential would be one that would put in place as quickly as possible and on as large a scale as possible high school–employer integration programs that would enable the sizable minority of young people who cannot profit from exclusive focus on book learning to participate in an integrated school-work program in which their skill acquisition would take place within a real work setting. Admittedly, so radical an effort, especially on a substantial scale, will not be easy to launch. But once launched, it should be easier to maintain since its value would become self-evident.

Is there any other possible contribution that employment policy might make to the current non-fit between the large numbers of persons seeking jobs and the insufficiency of job offers? I believe there is. The time has come when the federal government working through the states and localities—and involving employers in the not-for-profit sector—should experiment with becoming the "employer of last resort." There is much useful work to be done that, if performed, would add to the well-being of the community. The offer of public sector–financed jobs at the minimum wage, or, as Arthur F. Burns, the former chairman of the Federal Reserve Board, recommended, at 10 percent below the minimum wage, is one way to help reconcile the American ethos that every adult is responsible for his or her own support and providing every adult with the opportunity to get a job in the public domain if private-sector jobs are not available. Cash relief will be needed as well to assure that the children of a working parent do not grow up in poverty. Although the cost will not be small, it will be considerably less than the potential losses that will result from a growing number of adults who are reaching a point of explosion by their inability to work and support themselves and their children.

About the Contributors

Thomas Bailey is Adjunct Research Scholar of The Eisenhower Center for the Conservation of Human Resources and Associate Professor of Economics and Education and Director of The Institute for Education and the Economy, Teachers College, Columbia University.

Lauren Benton is Associate Professor of History at Rutgers University and New Jersey Institute of Technology; she is a former member of The Eisenhower Center staff.

Anna B. Dutka is Adjunct Research Scholar at The Eisenhower Center, Columbia University.

Eli Ginzberg has been Director of The Eisenhower Center from its inception and is the A. Barton Hepburn Professor Emeritus of Economics at Columbia University.

Thierry Noyelle is former Deputy Director and Senior Research Scholar of The Eisenhower Center; and Chief Technical Advisor of the Transnational Corporations and Management Division of the United Nations.

Thomas M. Stanback, Jr. is Adjunct Research Scholar at The Eisenhower Center, Columbia University, and Professor of Economics Emeritus, New York University.

Roger Waldinger is Professor of Sociology at the University of California, Los Angeles, and is a former member of The Eisenhower Center staff.

Index